Diary of Mary Henry
The Civil War Out My Window

Jeremy T.K. Farley

To my mother, a woman who has dedicated
her entire life to the service of others.

Special thanks to the Smithsonian Institution for the level of assistance they provided in making this publication a reality.

Americans owe a debt of gratitude to the countless volunteers who work tirelessly in preserving our nation's rich history.

May the Smithsonian Institution ever serve as the clearinghouse "for the increase and diffusion of knowledge."

Contact the Author:

Send an email: jeremy@jeremyfarley.com

Twitter: @JeremyTKFarley

Facebook: Facebook.com/JeremyTKFarley

Introduction to the Diary:

In 1846, Joseph Henry, a native of Albany, New York, was appointed to serve as the first secretary of a new institution devoted "for the increase and diffusion of knowledge," which was to be housed inside the nation's capital city.

Moving his family from New Jersey, the Henry's arrived in Washington to find a city "over ran with harlots, drunkards and thieves."

In the days ahead, Joseph and his family were joined by scores of other influential figures who were determined to change the image of the federal government's seat of power. Thanks to their work, churches were established, children's homes built, and Congressional funds appropriated to finance a more majestic and fitting dome for the nation's Capitol Building.

Soon, a dusty village, once the scorn of Europe, had been transfigured into a charming southern community.

Sadly, the progress made in transforming the tiny village into a capital was halted by a bloody civil war, which in the process of tearing apart a nation, divided an entire city against itself.

A silent witness to all of these events was a young woman named Mary Henry.

The daughter of Joseph Henry, Mary was 21-years-old when her family moved into the only castle in Washington, D.C., the Smithsonian Institution Building – simply referred to as "the castle."

A prolific writer and astute observer, Mary began recording a diary in 1858, including a daily log of her personal reflections, events at the Smithsonian and conversations she had shared with many of the most influential leaders in America.

It would have been impossible for the youthful lady, filled with juvenile yearnings and wanderlust, to have imagined the unspeakable horrors that would soon fill the pages of her blank diary, as she penned her first entry in November 1858.

Mary's entries include personal conversations with Abraham Lincoln, General Ulysses S. Grant, common citizens and captured southern troops.

A staunch unionist and American patriot, the young woman's diary reveals the incredible dilemma held by millions of Americans throughout the war between the states – as she often sympathized with the southern plight, mourned Confederate causalities and criticized the Lincoln administration's every move.

Though her writings provide one of the greatest insights into the Civil War in the past quarter-century, Mary's diary is far more than a collection of random thoughts on matters of science and politics. Her diary is a story of both a young woman and a struggling nation coming to age in the latter half of the nineteenth century.

The Story of this diary:

For nearly a century and a half, Mary's diary sat upon the dusty shelves of her sacred home, the Smithsonian Institution, waiting to be read and shared by a nation in need of the lessons of her life.

In the summer of 2014, a team of volunteers, carefully handling the stiff and cracking pages of her life's most enduring work, set out to transcribe her every word.

Their work was long, difficult and uneasy, as years of aging had rendered many of the diary's pages nearly unreadable, but by July, their work was complete.

With the painstaking job of transcribing her entries now complete, it was then time to share her entries with a generation of Americans desperately in want of direction in a world tormented by uncertainty.

Upon reading the transcripts of her diary, Jeremy T.K. Farley set out to present her words to the American public.

A student of the Civil War, Farley devoted countless hours to formatting, diligently translating and clarifying the entries of her diary, so that they could be presented to readers in a hardcopy format that was both easy to read and accurate to her original text.

Great pain was taken to ensure much of the original spellings, punctuation and words which filled the pages of her aged diary were not lost, while at the same time, recognizing that readers required some level of clarifying, in rare instances in order to ensure the work was readable.

In addition to reformatting her words, Farley also adds footnotes in order to explain important individuals mentioned in Mary's texts.

"After I got done reading this book, I felt like I had lived through the Civil War and found an intimate friend in Mary Henry," said Farley, adding, "It is my hope that everyone who reads her diary will feel the same way."

The Diary of Mary Henry

November 23, 1858

Father has been looking over one of his old books tonight in which are recorded some of the experiments he made while at Princeton. The review has made him somewhat sad. He spoke of one experiment upon the effect of electricity encircling a ray of polarized light. It failed for want of sufficiently strong galvanic battery.

Five years later, Faraday[1] made the same experiment, succeeded & gained the plaudits of the scientific world.

I do not exactly understand this experiment shall ask for an explanation.

November 23, 1858

Had a visit from young Lieutenant Warren this evening. He has been employed lately as an engineer in the West.

He was formerly engaged under Gen. Harvey in punishing the aggression of the Indians.

He gave us an interesting acct. of a conflict with the Indians in which he had had been engaged with under Gen. Harvey.

He is now busy preparing a partial report of his last engineering expedition to Reed Research.

We have had a pleasant evening. Will's[2] presence adding to our enjoyment.

---

[1] Michael Faraday (1791-1867), British scientist whom Albert Einstein kept a picture of on his study wall.

December 18, 1858

How long it is since I have written anything in my journal. I must be more regular now that we are once more in order. Chaos has come out of confusion once more & home seems like home again, since last writing we have had a visit from Prof. Hall the geologist: Dr. Lowrey and my Uncle.

Dr. Lowrey is greatly troubled with his affairs at the mintute.

Uncle left us this morning, he has been lecturing at Richmond, Norfolk & Petersburg. Flattering notice was taken of his lecture.

One repeated a remark of Prof. Pierce of Cambridge that if Kepler had never lived, Alexander would have been the K of our day.

Yesterday, we enjoyed having uncle with us greatly. Dr. Gurley[3] preached for us in the morning upon the pursuit of happiness, choosing for his text "a rest for the people of God."

His evening discourse was an exposition upon the first six verses of the second chapter of Matthew. His words, plainly spoken in sincerity from the fullness of a good man's heart. How powerful are they. Simple wisdom they may be, but how often do they sink down deep in our heart to remain there when the effects of soul stirring changes in life may have faded away.

Plain every day words to help us on with our everyday duty.

It has been raining hard all day. I have not felt very well & have been very idle.

Learned of the death of Mr. Cox. I feel deeply for his daughter.

Undated Entry

Mother & myself went this morning to Mr. Cox's funeral, poor old man, there were few there who cared. For his daughter's tears were the only one that fell for his loss. The only one to weep for him.

Money was his god, but it could not buy him friends & he was carried to the grave with none to weep for him, but his lonely daughter.

He was buried in the Rock Creek Church grave yard.

The last time I had been there was in the Spring when the grass was green & the trees bright with foliage to day there were bare branches on the ground and a mist underneath the shadow of his grave.

---

[2] William Alexander Henry (1832–1862), Mary's older brother.

[3] The Rev. Phineas D. Gurley, D.D., a graduate of Princeton Theological Seminary, assumed the pastorate of the F Street Church in 1854 and served the congregation until his death in 1868. Dr. Gurley was an "Old School Presbyterian," holding traditional Calvinistic beliefs. Gurley, who served as the U.S. Senate Chaplain, was loyal to the Union cause and provided pastoral care following the death of Lincoln's son and ministered at President Lincoln's funeral service.

December 21, 1858

Called on Mr. Saxe & his wife.

The poet, on closer acquaintance, we found very agreeable. He is tall with florid complexion has a slight impediment in his speech. His manners are frank & genial. He said he was always perfectly contented if he pleased the very young & the very old people of his audience – He knew the sentiments must be delicate & pure that could win the admiration of young fresh hearts. While on his other hand, ideas could not be extravagant or absurd if approved by the old & experienced.

In speaking of death, one gloomy thought considered with the subject, he could not bear to think he might be separated from those he loved forever.

"I trust," said he, to "put my own safety in one greater."

He could trust in the Lord for his own individual salvation, but it was terrible to think that those he loved so dearly might never meet him in heaven or even if they did meet him their relations might be changed – it was a very disagreeable thought, he said.

His wife is a charming modest little woman & answers well to his description of a model wife

"So full of women's duties & delights, she has no time to think of woman's rights"

December 22, 1858

Went out with Dr. E. & wife in the morning.

Dr. Roby dined with us. Everything went off nicely. Mother looked well & did the harmony gracefully. Father was pleased.

Dr. Robby was full of life & spirits. We young people, teasing him about his old aged condition, he returning our jokes with interest.

His lecture was almost a repetition of his former, with an additional account of the history of the Hudsons' Bay Company. He appeared in an Artic dress after the lecture which became him exceedingly.

Mr. Melling was in the park when we returned from the lecture with Mr. & Mrs. He.

December 23, 1858

Made calls in the morning, it passed very quietly. Looked over some of Rol. & Niles' drawings with Mrs. Easter.

Miss Dix came unexpectedly.

Spent the evening reading some experiments of Dr. H.'s father.

Miss Dix was in conversation with Dr. Antisel at the other end of the room discussing some of Fuller's experiments, as far as I could hear – for I could only catch a word here and there.

13

I heard father say that the happiest hours of his life were found in making his experiments and sharing their results every other meeting of the Philosophical Society at Philadelphia.

December 24, 1858
Will read Dicken's *Christmas Carol* to us in the evening we could not have spent our Christmas eve more profitably.

December 25, 1858
Christmas day passed finely. We went with our Mission School of 16 years to the Young Men's Christian Association[4].

Going room to room to make the presentation of candies.

How our hearts warm to see so many happy faces. I could have cried with the little fellows when they threw off their caps & shouted for me.

Passed the evening at Miss Bradley's.

December 26, 1858
As usual, Miss Cox in the afternoon.

December 27, 1858
In the evening, had a lecture by Prof. Grimes. It was carefully prepared & full of interesting subject… The lecturer's description was interesting. Just what I should imagine… genial, gentle & earnest, he moved among his pupils.

December 28, 1858
A French letter from Father.

Went with Ca. to Madam to speak about French lessons.

December 29, 1858
Went on with translations all day.

December 30, 1858
He and Father with us all this evening.

Moddeled his profile in clay while he read to us.

---

[4] Known to be a city brimming with saloons, gambling dens and crime, Thomas Duncan, a Treasury Department employee, with the help of 60 other young men, set out in 1852 to establish the city's first YMCA.

Their mission was to elevate the "spiritual and moral condition" of their fellows in a "crude, raw and highly transient city of 40,000…where vice, alcoholism, delinquency and crime defied imagination."

January 4, 1859

Had more calls than are expected on New Year's day. Was sorry I did not see Dr. Craig.

Enjoyed Baron Osten Sacken's call.

Nell was sick since morning, so I staid with her, but went to church in the evening. Stopped at Mrs. Bell's on our way home to wait for Laliner who had gone to the Chief Justice.

Yesterday, Prof. Dana came to us – he is a small slender man with a sober countenance, light hair and eyes. He has a very pleasant smile.

In the morning had a visit from Mr. Tyler. Father enjoys his conversation.

November 6, 1860

Election day. It seemed strange to see the streets so quiet when the rest of the country was so excited.

November 7, 1860

Lincoln elected.

Mr. _____ came in for a few moments after tea. He had just returned from a Western survey. Told us about the Digger Indians[5]. He said they are the dregs of the neighboring tribes. They live chiefly upon rats. The country they inhabit is exceedingly barren. Rabbits are their largest game. Their children are frequently stolen by the neighboring Indians & sold as slaves to the Mexicans.

Mr. Williams, a missionary from China, gave us some very interesting information. He said the population of China was 360,000,000.

On the seaside many of the inhabitants found it more economical to live on the water than on the land & the shore was sometimes entirely concealed by the quantity of small boats, each containing it's respective family. He said it was quite amusing to see the little children, with life preservers in the shape of large gourds tied about them to prevent their sinking should they fall overboard.

Heaven, Earth & the Emperor form the Trinity with the Chinese. The latter is worshiped as the vicegerent of the two former & as such renders them homage twice a year, at the vernal & autumnal Equanox, his place of worship being two large mounds in the vicinity of Peking.

He is held responsible for good weather, good crops, & the general prosperity of the Empire. He is supposed to delegate his power over the elements to his officers & it not infrequently the latter petition for a suspension of their salaries after a heavy drought -- as a proof of penitence for their maladministration.

---

[5] The Paiute Indians.

Woe to the unfortunate who has incurred the hatred of the populace, the first unfavorable rain may deprive him of his office if not of his head.

Any person may rise from the lowest grade of society to the highest office in China. Every year, in each province an examination is held of competitors for a degree, conferred upon 70 or more persons, according to the size of the province. The successful candidate finds his social position much altered for the better. He may now try for the second degree. Should he again succeed he is eligible to an office under government. A third & fourth degree offer further inducements to energy & good conduct. The examinations for these four degrees are conducted with great care – the dress of the competitor is searched so that no book or paper may be concealed about them. They are then placed in separate stalls & questions in writing given them.

There are 4 classes of society in China:

1st the literary aristocracy, 2nd farmers, 3rd mechanics, 4th merchants.

Mr. Williams then proceeded to give us a brief account of the insurrection. He said _____ is the name of the most powerful god of the Chinese. The Emperor alone worships him, to address prayers to him is to raise the standard of revolt. This name is used by the missionaries to represent the true God.

The leader of the rebellion[6] was an enthusiastic young man, a disappointed competitor for one of the degrees. As he was leaving from the examination, a translation of a portion of the scriptures was handed to him by one of the emissarys of Christianity. Attracted by the name _____ he read it with avidity. He soon formed a party of adherents.

The number of his followers increased daily, & finally obtained possession of a fort in the province of Hwangsi, where they were ineffectually beseigded.

This, I think, was in 1851.

They afterwards proceeded up the country, as far as Peking, but were driven back to Nankin, which is now in their possession where ever they went they destroyed the idols instituted the observance of the Sabbath.

Taught that Jehovah was the true God -- that he had sent his son into the world to die for man & other Bible doctrine, but possessed very little of the spirit of Christianity. Brutally murdering all who opposed them, sparing neither woman, nor children.

---

[6] The Taiping Rebellion: A massive civil war in southern China, lasting from 1850 to 1864, against the ruling Manchu Qing dynasty. Led by Hong Xiuquan, who announced that he had received visions, in which he learned that he was the younger brother of Jesus. At least 20 million people died, mainly civilians, in one of the deadliest military conflicts in human history.

Bread, he said, was never made in China; wheat, although made into flour, was eaten in the form of pastry.

He said he had seen the Great Wall. It was commenced about 400 years before Christ; by an Emperor, who destroyed all records of his predecessors, in order that he might be considered the first reigning monarch. The wall near the sea side is as much as 40 feet in height.

January 1, 1861

The sun is shining clear & bright.

We could not have had a more beautiful New Year's Day. Would that our political horizon was as free from clouds as the blue sky that bends above us, but the storm which has been gathering darkly for months, seems nearly now to break upon us: Even the stoutest hearts are beginning to tremble. God alone knows what is before us, may He preserve us from the horrors of civil war.

The speech of Mr. Benjamin[7] on Monday was very impressive; The papers give a very poor idea of its merit. The excitement in the galleries was very great, particularly at its close when shouts of applause resounded from one side to the other.

In clear musical tones, he addressed his brother Senators, telling them they must leave those halls, e'er many weeks had passed, to meet no more under one common government.

It was too late now to settle the difficulties between the North & South. Too late – too late – that time must come for all things it had come for the preservation of the tie which had so long united us. Our only hope now was in parting peaceably, but if that were impossible he was ready to defend his fireside with his life's blood – appealing to the All-powerful God for Assistance or aid.

10 A.M.

We had more calls than we expected Miss Dix came in about noon & spent the remainder of the day with us. Gentle as she is strong, she seems

---

[7] Judah Benjamin's farewell speech in the U.S. Senate. Speaking before a packed gallery, Benjamin foresaw that the South's departure would lead to civil war: *"What may be the fate of this horrible contest none can foretell; but this much I will say: the fortunes of war may be adverse to our arms; you may carry desolation into our peaceful land, and with torch and firebrand may set our cities in flames ... you may do all this, and more, but you never can subjugate us; you never can convert the free sons of the soil into vassals, paying tribute to your power; you never can degrade them to a servile and inferior race. Never! Never!"*

indeed, a noble woman. Nobly planned to cheer, to comfort or command, and yet a spirit still as bright, with something of an angle's light.

January 2, 1861
Judge Campbell's[8] daughters spent the evening with us.

January 3, 1861
Mr. Baker spoke in the Senate.

January 4, 1861
A day of fasting and prayer[9].

All the churches were open at 11 O'clock or at 2 h. a very impressive address was delivered in the House of Representatives by the chaplain Mr. Stockton. The room upstairs or down, was thronged with eager listeners & many a strong man's eyes were filled with tears at the simple earnestness of the old man. It was grand to hear so many voices united in one common hymn of praise.

A telegram tonight announced that an armed vessel had sailed for Fort Sumter from Norfolk.

Father has just returned from a visit to Senators Douglas & Hunter[10]. The former seemed to think the pride of seniors in the Republican party would prevent their making concessions to the South.

Mr. Hunter thought our prospects very dark. His state of Virginia would adhere to the Union as long as possible.

January 5, 1861
Went to Miss Craig's reception. It was well attended. Gen. Cass was there, Scientific club in the evening. Spanish with Jack.

January 10, 1861

---

[8] John Archibald Campbell was appointed by Franklin Pierce to the United States Supreme Court in 1853, he served until the outbreak of the American Civil War, when he became an official of the Confederacy.

[9] On December 14, 1860, President James Buchanan designated Friday, January 4, 1861, as a day to be "set apart for fasting, humiliation, and prayer throughout the nation." Throughout the nation, special services were held in churches and public buildings were closed, along with many places of business.

[10] Both Democrats, Senators Stephen A. Douglas of Illinois and Robert M.T. Hunter of Virginia. Douglas would die in office in June of 1861, while Hunter would serve as the Secretary of State for the C.S.A. and be pictured on the nation's $10 bill.

On Monday & Wednesday, lectures by Prof Fairman Rodgers on roads & bridges.

The Inteligencer announces today the resignation of Hon. Jacob Thompson, Secretary of the Interior. He did not agree with the President as regard to the abstract right of secession, but had consented to remain in the Cabinet "on the faith" that the practical policy of the Government would not be hostile to the South.

Mr. Secretary Holt having, however, sent reinforcement to Major Anderson in Fort Sumter, in spite of Mr. Thompson's remonstrances, he immediately gave us his commission.

Went to the Capitol this morning, heard Mr. Davis[11] spoke. He discussed the old question of the right of a state to secede. He there addressed the Republican party, telling them that now as the last moment, it was in their power to avoid civil war. He was willing for the few days he remained with them, to aid in the restoration of peace. He would leave the question in their hands.

Mr. Trumbull[12] said that it had been very hard for himself, & he had no doubt for his Republican friends, to hear the constant misrepresentations of his Party. "If civil war came it was from the other side of the chamber. It was the Democratic party who were pullng down the pillars of the Union. It was they who were making war & calling upon the Republicans to submit."

After a warm debate the senate adjourned.

January 11, 1861

Mr. Shaud & Germain occupied the morning.

Prof. Rodgers drives with us.

Measures have been adopted to prevent all vessels of an offensive character from entering the harbor of Charleston.

Yesterday, the *Star of the West*, a government-vessel was fired upon by sloops stationed on Morris Island, about three quarters of a mile from the Battery.

Major Anderson addressed a letter to the Governor of S.C., asking whether the hostile act was committed in obedeince to his instructions & having received an affirmative reply from Gov. Pickens, Lieutenant Talbot was sent with dispatches to the General Government.

Lecture in the evening by Prof Rodgers.

---

[11] Jefferson Davis, U.S. Senator and future president of the Confederate States of America was a close family friend of the Henry's, prior to the Civil War.

[12] Lyman Trumbull, Republican, U.S. Senator from Illinois and co-author of the 13th Amendment to the U.S. Constitution, which eliminated slavery.

January 14, 1861

Rain all day.

In the evening, Father brought in the works of Calhoun[13].

I've read his disquisition on Government. Father was greatly delighted with it. He said Mr. Cahoun had always greatly interested him. He was a true mans as well as a clear logical thinker.

When Father first knew him the great man did not-quite understand the objects of the Smithsonian and was opposed to it. One day he came to Father & told him there was a position in a Southern college he was very anxious he should accept. He thought he never could make anything of the Institution and wished him to leave it.

Father told him it might be greatly to his own personal advantage to give up the Smithsonian, but his honour now was pledged and he must carry out his plans.

Calhoun took him warmly by the hand, as he said "Prof. you are a man after my own heart. I might have been President of the United States if I had chosen to give up my principals."

Father saw him only a few days before his death. He was perfectly aware of his condition. He said he was approaching the great-change which awaits all mankind. He has gone to stand in the presence of the Deity. He trusted in the mercy of God.

January 15, 1861

Read Seward's speech[14], delivered on Saturday last. It seems very concilatory in it's tones but pleases neither the North or South.

Spent the evening with Judge Scarborough. He is a warm admirer & supporter of Calhoun.

January 16, 1861

---

[13] John C. Calhoun (1782-1850), American statesman from South Carolina.

[14] William H. Seward, Republican Senator from New York, later to serve as the Secretary of State. Responsible for the Alaska Purchase. At the time of this speech, Seward was known to be Lincoln's choice to serve as Secretary of State, and in the absence of any statement from the president-elect, Seward served as the first member of the incoming Lincoln Administration to speak publicly. He urged the preservation of the Union, and called for a constitutional convention, once passions had cooled, hinting that New Mexico Territory might be a slave state. Seward urged the construction of two transcontinental railroads, one northern, one southern. Attending his speech was Senator Jefferson Davis.

The ordinance of secession was signed at Tallahassee, Florida, Jan. 12th. There are three states out of the Union now, Florida Mississippi & South Carolina.

January 17, 1861

We heard today Judge Campbell has resigned.

January 18, 1861

President Barnard[15] with his wife are with us. He lectured tonight upon polarized light.

Father told us when he was in London, Edinburough, he was one day in a Lapidary shop. A feeble old man came in, to whom Father was introduced, as a gentleman from America. "What?" exclaimed Father, on hearing his name, Nichol, "Is this Nichol who invented the polerizing eye piece glass?" The old man was so pleased to think anyone from such a distance should know about his polerizing glass instrument, that he treated him with the greatest kindness, invited him to his house & presented him with a very valuable chrystal of Iceland sperm.

January 21, 1861[16]

Lecture by Mr. Barnard.

Mr. Welling called in the evening. He did not seem to fear civil war. It was delightful to meet with at least one hopeful person.

January 22, 1861

Yesterday, the Senators & members of the returning states gave their valedictory addresses. Everyone is particularly gloomy today in consequence, realizing more fully that we are no longer the United States.

January 23, 1861

Father saw a number of his friends at the Senate this morning, all very desponding.

Mr. Pierce thought Virginia would join the cesessionists not that such would be the wish of her people but she is so sparsely inhabited, that - were the politicians to bring matters quickly to a crisis, only those in the neighborhood of the poles would have probably an opportunity of voting

---

[15] John G. Barnard, President of Columbia University & namesake of Barnard College.

[16] January 21, 1861, a date Jefferson Davis called, "The saddest day of my life." Mississippi adopted an ordinace of secession on January 9 and upon receiving official word, Davis delivered a farewell address to the U.S. Senate, resigned and returned to his home state.

& the cesession movement might thus be easily carried over the heads of her peace loving citizens.

The Mississippi river has been blockaded & all vessel are required to stop & give an account of themselves.

Went to the reception at the Navy Yard.

February 4, 1861

Monday, Mr. Benjamin made his farewell speech His audience was affected to tears. He was one of the clearest thinkers in the Senate & a most agreeable speaker. The echo of his dear silvery tones soon died away in these halls, but they must linger long in the memory of those who heard him.

February 12, 1861

We had a very pleasant dinner. Mr. Lord, the historian who is lecturing before the Institution, The Rev. Dr. Bullock, Mr. Williams, a retired merchant from New York, Mr. Varnon & Mr. Alexander were present.

Mr. Alexander was my neighbor & entertained me so pleasantly I heard but little of the conversation of the other members of the party.

He told several very amusing stories one of which is worthy of repetition:

In the times of James the Sixth of Scotland first of England, there lived a certain Dean whos congregation greatly annoyed him by sleeping while he was delivering his sermons. The annoyance, having become insupportable, he preached a violent sermon discourse under the text, "Awake thou that Sleepeth."

His people were most effectually aroused & complained of him to the King, who commanded him to appear in his presence.

His Majesty was so much pleased with the Dean's ready wit that he was greatly puzzled what to do with him.

In the meanwhile, the King made him his chaplain & sent him back to take leave of his people.

"Breathern," he said, "Some time ago, I preached to you from the text, 'Awake thou that sleepeth.' The King has since removed me to a more influencial position. Today, I preach, as taking leave of you, the words, 'Sleep on now & take thy rest.'"

February 13, 1861

Today, the Electors' votes were counted.

Some trouble had been anticipated, armed forces were stationed at the various entrances of the Capitol & between the Houses of Congress to prevent ingress to the Hall of Representatives during the ceremony.

The galleries were crowded but there was not the slightest demonstration of hostile feeling.

February 14, 1861

Mr. Hunter spoke upon the tarif question[17].

February 15, 1861

Mr. Lord lectured to night upon Bacon & his times. His manner is very peculiar he has a queer way of contorting his body as if the delivery of his words was excessively painful.

The Southern Congress in now fairly organized. The name of the new Government is the "Confederate States of America."

Jefferson Davis had been appointed President. Alexander H. Stephens of Georgia, Vice President.

Mr. Alexander seems quite confident that the convention will settle matters peacably.

The North, however, seems still unwilling to make any concessions.[18]

February 23, 1861

Yesterday, Washington-Birthday was observed with more than usual interest. The display of military was fine, besides the volunteer companies of the District, the Government forces amounted to 600 men.

In the evening, Senator Foster called with his wife. Also other friends.

Later, father brought in from the Institution Mr. Douglas, Mr. Pierce of Maryland & Gen Totten. The latter was very melancholy in regard to the political troubles, he seemed to think civil war inevitable.

We dined with Mrs. Merrick.

The President-elect reached here this morning.[19]

---

[17] The Morrill Tariff of 1861, adopted on March 2, 1861, was a key element of the platform of the new Republican Party, appealing to industrialists and factory workers in the Northeast, the tariff's purpose was to limit competition from lower-wage industries in Europe.

[18] Though an employee of the federal government, resident of the nation's capital city and native child of Albany, New York, it is interesting to hear Mary Joseph's southern sympathies.

[19] In late-Frebruary, government officials began suspecting that an alleged conspiracy was being brewed, dubbed "The Baltimore Plan." As a precaution, Lincoln's train traveled through Balitmore, throughout the night, without stopping. For the remainder of his presidency, Lincoln's critics would hound him for the seemingly cowardly act of sneaking through Baltimore at night, in disguise, sacrificing his honor for his personal safety.

PHOTO: 1861 Presidential Inauguration.

March 4, 1861

The day[20] has passed off quietly in spite of the predictions of the people. The display of military was fine.

Mr. & Mrs. Bell are with us, hopes are entertained that the President may put him in his cabinet.

"A majority held in restraint by constitutional checks and limitations, and always changing easily with deliberate changes of popular opinions and sentiments, is the only true sovereign of a free people... I am loath to close.

---

[20] Inauguration Day.

We are not enemies, but friends. We must not be enemies. Though passion may have strained it must not break our bonds of affection. The mystic chords of memory, stretching from every battlefield and patriot grave to every living heart and hearthstone all over this broad land, will yet swell the chorus of the Union, when again touched, as surely they will be, by the better angels of our nature." – **Abraham Lincoln, March 4, 1861**

April 13, 1861

It is a long time since I have written in my journal. Nothing of any great importance occurred.

For so long we began to hope the threatened war might be averted, it was a false hope, a lull before the storm.

On Friday, armed troops were sent, with sealed orders to Fort Sumter, or rather the vessels of war reached that fort on Friday.

The accounts to night are very gloomy. When the last telegram was received, Fort Sumter was in flames, the flag at half mast, the number of killed & wounded uncertain.

April 15, 1861

The papers to day give a full account of the bombardment of Fort Sumter. The demand to surrender was sent to Major Anderson on the Eleventh.

He replied that his duty to his Government prevented his compliance, adding "I will await the first shot & if you do not batter us to pieces we will be starved out in a few days."

Gen. Beauregard then proposed to Major Anderson to state the length of time the provisions of the fort would last & promise not to use his guns against the batteries unless he was attacked, under which conditions the bombardment would be postponed.

Major A., of course, declined this offer, as it would have obliged him to remain silent should any attempt be made to aid him so long as Fort Sumter itself was not fired upon.

On Friday morning at 4 o'clock, the firing commenced from Fort Moultrie & was answered at long intervals from Major Anderson's guns.

Hostilities were discontinued during the night, but recommenced early the next morning. Fort Sumter was soon in flames & Major Anderson was obliged to run up the white flag, withdrawing the Stars & Stripes.

On Sunday, Major A. embarked on board the Isabella for New York.

Before leaving the Fort, he was allowed to fire a salute to his flag when four of his men were killed by the bursting of two of his guns; Most strange to relate these were the only lives lost, during the engagement.

The nation is yet guiltless of the horrible sin of fratricide. There has been considerable excitement in the streets to day.

The President has issued a proclamation, calling forth the seventy five thousand militia for the preservation of the Union, or rather for the vain attempt to restore to its pristine glory the temple whose columns lie prostrate.

Miss Dix was with us yesterday, she was very sad indeed about the state of affairs. Said the South was determined to fight. Said she had never shed so many tears in one year before, with the earliest lessons of her childhood, her prayers to God, was instilled the love of her country. That country she feared was soon to be desolated by a war too fearful to imagine.

War preparations are rapidly proceeding in New York. Gov. Sprague of Providence R. I. has offered 1,000 men for the protection of the Capitol.

Penn. supports the president.

N.J. may join the cecessionsionists, Gov. Andrews (Boston) is said to have left for W. on Sunday.

The course of events has been so exceedingly rapid it is almost impossible to realize the war we now occupy in regard to the South.

Virginia, the home of Washington, is no longer in the Union. It was hoped she might maintain an armed neutrality & perhaps act the part of peace maker between her sisters states. We went up on the high tower of the Smithsonian on Thursday morning & saw the secession flags waving in Alexandria, while every public building in Washington was surmounted by the Stars & Stripes.

Undated: April 1861

Thursday, the arsenal at Harper's Ferry was burned by order of the Government to prevent the Virginian troops from seizing the arms. They were within three miles of it & as the force was in the building was not sufficient to protect it, it was thought best to set it on fire.

On Friday, Miss Dix arrived, she came to offer her services to Mr. Lincoln in forming a hospital for wounded soldiers. She was an eye witness of the terrible assault made in Baltimore upon the Massachusetts troops on their way to the Capitol[21].

As she drove rapidly through the streets one of the windows of her carriage was shattered by a paving stone, but she received no personal injury. The excitement in Baltimore was very great on Saturday since troops were expected from the North.

---

[21] Now known as the "Baltimore Riot of 1861," as the Massachusetts militia marched through Maryland, they were confronted on April 19, 1861, in Baltimore, Maryland, by anti-War Democrats (the largest political party in Maryland), as well as Confederate sympathizers. In total, 4 militiamen were killed, 36 wounded, while 12 Confederate sympathizers were killed.

The evening was a gloomy one for us all – it was supposed an attack in the city might be made at any moment.

Sunday evening we were alarmed as we were going to church by the report of ten heavy guns. As we heard nothing more, we proceeded on our way, but during the service the rumbling of what we supposed to be artillery further increased our disquietude.

Our alarm was increased, later, by heavy wagons carrying flour to the capitol & other flour for the use of the troops. A small vessel had been seized at Georgetown & robbed of its contents.

On Monday the excitement in the city was considerably allayed, the Seventh regiment from New York was hourly expected & then all fear of an attack from the upon the city was at an end for the present.

This regiment has not yet made its appearance, however, it is now supposed to be at Annapolis.

Mayor Brown & Gov. Hicks have refused to allow the passage of troops through Baltimore, so their route must necessarily be circuitous.

The Marylanders seem determined to oppose their passage through any part of the State. It is supposed that they may be awaiting the arrival of other troops so as to fight their way if necessary.

The President has declared his sole object in bringing them further is to defend the Capitol.

We are now entirely cut off from all intercourse with the North. The bridges have been burned the rails taken up & telegraph wires destroyed between Baltimore & Philadelphia.

The New York papers, of Saturday, were received yesterday by pony express. Our friends are of course very anxious about us, but we have no means of letting them know of our safety. We cannot now leave the city & must face the danger, whatever it may be.

The rise in provisions was very great, on Monday the price of flour from $6 per barrel rose to $15. It proved to be a panic, however, they have now gone down again.

To night we went to see Mrs. Captain Rodgers, whose husband is at Richmond held as a hostage with another captain.

The Southerners charge is an attempt to destroy one of the Government vessels. He was detailed of the unpleasant duty of destroying the Government property in Norfolk Harbor & was then taken prisoner.

Mrs. Rodgers said she had heard indirectly from him; he was well treated.

April 26, 1861

The Seventh Regiment arrived yesterday. They were greeted with enthusiastic applause as they marched up the avenue.

Their conduct on their march through Maryland was characterized by energy & good will. Wherever they were obliged to break down fences or otherwise injure property, they paid for damage immediately.

They are a fine looking set of men & seem mostly to be gentlemen.

A part of Gov. Sprague's forces are also here, the rest are still at Annapolis.

We are well guarded, now all fear of an attack on the city at present is at an end. We received our first communication from the North this morning, a letter from Uncle written last Saturday, 6 days ago.

Our friends have of course been very anxious about us.

Miss Dix dined with us, she is industrious in her preparation for the care of those who may be sick or wounded.

LETTER: Joseph Henry to Stephen Alexander
April 26, 1861

Dear Sir,

I perhaps ought not to say anything in the present condition of affairs, considering the position I hold in regarding to the country.

We are all well and in as good spirits as the dark prospect before us will permit. The girls are quite cheerful and have not exhibited the least fear, they have however as yet been merely surrounded with the pomp and circumstance of the war, and have experienced only a few of its horrors.

"He laughs at scars who never felt a wound" is an aphorism which may be applied to many who are panting for battle, as well as to those who are fanning the war spirit, or enjoying the excitement of the eventful times. There is an immense amount of madness in a latent condition in the public mind, which only requires an exciting occasion to break forth into actual mania. The paroxysm may be excited by an apparently trifling incident, the result of design or ignorance, but when once induced it is impossible to check its fury, unless with the effusion of blood.

What is the cause of the present state of the country? Is there any proper grounds for a civil war, are great and important principles to be settled by it? Is the progress of humanity to be accelerated by conquering the slave states? Is slavery to be abolished and the slave not destroyed? After the southern states are conquered will they then be obedient loving members of a brotherhood of free men?

See my views in the accompanying slip from the National Intelligencer

JH

May 3, 1861

Father saw the President for the first time officially. He went to inform him that as President of the United States, he was head of the

28

Smithsonian Institution & was expected to see the Regents & Secretary on the first Tuesday in May.

Father had to wait more than an hour before he was admitted. While in the ante room Capt. Meigs came in, he had just returned from his secret expedition & was about to report himself to the President.

He said he thought it was not betraying confidence to inform Father where he had been; Fort Pickens was the destination of the fleet, sailing with sealed orders. This had reinforced & could not possibly be taken now at least for the next few months.

Colonel Ellsworth, the commander the of the N.Y. Zouaves, & colonel Butler also arrived while Father was waiting. He was admitted finally.

Mr. Lincoln was harassed – seemed care worn,. He was withdrawn & ill at ease. Mr. Seward was with him.

May 7, 1861

Tuesday.

Mr. Strong of Albany called last evening. He said one of the finest sights he had ever witnessed was the swearing in of the Seventh Regiment.

Both Father & himself seemed to think a bloody battle inevitable.

May 8, 1861

Yesterday, we visited the camp of the Seventh Regiment. It is in a beautiful spot opposite Columbia College. The tents were arranged back to back in rows with wide streets between them, they seemed small & comfortless when we approached them, but very picturesque in the distance.

Some of the men seemed quite unfitted for the hard life of a soldier, with their slender forms & delicate complexions. One of the engineer corps, who was our chaperone, seemed to think they would not be called into active service, at least for some time.

About 5 o clock the drill commenced the band playing delightfully about a half an hour before. The military volunteers were very fine & performed with great exactness. The salutes of the officers to the commander was beautiful in the extreme.

A grey headed officer reviewed the troops.

Major Anderson was there & after the drill was presented to the Regiment – each company saluting him in turn with three hearty cheers. I was surprised to find him so small a man, his manner dignified & courteous, his face both noble & gentle – made a very pleasant imppression upon us.

On our return home we brought Mr. Smith of the N.J. Regiment. He found a soldier's life very tiresome. He occupies a room with 130 other men & was delighted to have one comfortable nights rest in a civilized bed room.

Gov. Sprague's men are decided to be the finest here, not excepting the proud N.Y. Seventh. He has clothed most of them himself. They are stationed in the Capitol[22].

The streets are filled with soldiers & the sound of the drum is heard unceasingly from morning until night.

A squad of men in very pretty grey suits with red trimming have just left the Institution.

The N.Y. Zouaves have a very undesirable reputation. They have been quite disorderly since their arrival.

June 1, 1861

We have visited the Seventh Camp since I last wrote. The regiment left us this yesterday. They were sent into Virginia last Saturday – expected some hard fighting, but were engaged in digging trenches in Arlington picnic grounds.

Most of the regiments are now encamped beyond the limits of the city. The Capitol is still occupied by troops.

The fortification on the Virginia shore are said to be very fine we have not yet visited them. Continuous firing in that direction startled us this evening, particularly as we had heard of the encounter at Fairfax Court House.

Twenty of the southerners are said to have been killed there & only two or three of the Northerners.

Jef. Davis is said to be at Richmond. It is rumored that Judge Douglass[23] is dead, he was not expected to live yesterday.

---

[22] The U.S. Capitol Building served as a makeshift bunkhouse for soldiers guarding Washington, D.C. Massachusetts' soldiers, housed in the Senate Chamber, were the most destructive. Isaac Bassett, the Senate's assistant doorkeeper, entered the chamber just in time to hear the sound of splitting wood. Rushing to investigate, he found a group of Union soldiers bayonetting the desk recently vacated by Jefferson Davis, who had resigned his Senate seat and become president of the Confederacy. "Stop! What are you doing?" Bassett shouted. "We are cutting that damned traitor's desk to pieces!" They replied. Bassett stopped them, explaining that the desk belonged to the government, not Jeff Davis. "You were sent here to protect, not destroy," he said. To this day, two small squares of wood, inlaid in the side of the desk, show where the soldiers' damage was repaired. In 1995, a Senate resolution linked Jefferson Davis to his modern successors, permanently assigning his desk to the senior senator from Mississippi.

[23] Senator Stephen A. Douglas, Democrat from Illinois.

Father went to the President's this morning with Prof Felton. Mr. Lincoln had already improved in manner & appearance. His son, the "Prince of Rails," Father said was really a fine young man.

The Seward, the French Minister, Mrs. Montgomery Blair have given pleasant entertainments for the officers.

The Garabaldi guards, who arrived yesterday, are said to be very fine men – I do not like their dress.

A German regiment has been drilling in front of our windows this morning.

The 'Garibaldi Guard' was the nickname given to the 39th New York Volunteer Infantry Regiment. Many of the regiment's members were Italian Americans who had served under Giuseppe Garibaldi in Italy.

A week from last Thursday the bells were tolling for the decease of Colonel Ellsworth & on Saturday we witnessed his funeral procession. The muffled drums, the forced guns, the slow sad step of the soldiers was very impressive. He was only twenty-three years of age. Alexandria now lies under the Stars & Stripes.

June 3, 1861

Monday.

We had Drs. Hannday & Wines to preach for us yesterday. They have just returned from the meeting of the general assembly & took a warm part in the discussions relative to the State of the country.

It cannot be too much regretted that the political questions of the day were agitated in that body.

Judge Bates, the attorney general, telegraphed to the clergymen in answer to a question of one of them, that he hoped all such subjects might be excluded from their deliberations, saying that the Old School's Presbyterian General Assembly was the last collecting link between the North & the South and he hoped earnestly it might not be broken.

Dr. Hogdes' resolutions were defeated however.

We have just returned from a visit to the fortifications on the other side of the river. We were stopped at the foot of the Long Bridge & obliged to show our pass to a very good natured looking officer.

We first visit the N.J. camp the men were busy at their embankments.

PHOTO: Long Bridge, spanning the Potomac River, linking the federal capital to Virginia. Repository: Library of Congress Prints and Photographs Division Washington, D.C. 20540 USA

After again showing our pass twice we entered Arlington grounds

These are very beautiful carefully cultivated man has so skillfully concealed his share in the work it seems as if nature & God the whole. The soldiers gray dress was wholly picturesque. Each turn in the road added new charms to the picture.

In one spot a number of men were lying upon the ground, bundles in hand ready to start at a moment's warning.

An attack is expected to night from a body of secession troops said about 14,000 strong, said to be stationed near Fairfax county court House.

The old House, the home of the descendants of Wash., we found filled with soldiers, a sentinel was maintained with measured step in the wide portico. The view from the grassy slope in front seemed never more beautiful, the city lay before us in the rays of the setting sun each public building already & distinctly defined.

We saw how readily this latter might have been demolished & the Southern succeeded in securing the post & placed their batteries there.

Farther on, opposite Georgetown, are found the 49 N.Y. regiment camp. Here every preparation had been made for a speedy attack. numbers of trees & been felled & placed in front of the encampments across the road between some of the fields to intercept the expected cavalry.

We crossed the river at this point in a ferry boat. It was very sad to think how many of the fine young men we had seen might be cut down before they deserved to die.

Prof. Felton, who has been with us since Thursday, saw Gen Scot this morning. The old man seemed to think a bloody battle might be avoided.

He was moving his forces slowly but surely southward & he thought the people would yield without much loss of life. Mr. Cary, a young friend of Prof. Felton, was wounded at the slight affray at Fairfax. It is said quite a number of secessionists were killed in that engagement.

The death of Judge Douglass, "the little giant" is no longer to be doubted. I pity his poor young wife. It is said that Gen. Baldwin has been taken prisoner.

June 4, 1861

Went to Alexandria with Prof. Felton & Judge Loring's family. The old town seemed deserted by all peace loving citizens, the soldiers alone were to be seen.

We visited the house where Col. Ellsworth was shot. The bannisters, two of the stairs pieces of the windows & doors have already been carried off as relics. We brought away a small piece of the flag staff.

We were greatly interested in the fortifications. They are still incompleted. They command the three roads from Manassas Gap Richmond & Fairfax Court House the scene of a slight engagement with the secessionists.

The Zouaves, the pet lambs as they are called are immediately in the rear of the fortifications, two other regiments are not far off. On our return we met in the omnibus the President of Columbia College who had just come from the South. He said Gen. Beauregard was at Manassas Gap & expected an attack from the Northern troops.

Prof. Felton informed Gen. Scot of this in the evening.

June 7, 1861

F.G. came to tell us she was intended to be married on Sunday next.

Visited the Twelfeth Regiment (N.Y.) Their parade was very fine. We went to the officers' quarters after it was over. Saw Col. Butterfield & Col. Ward[24] & others. The former is very handsome with regular features & dark eyes.

The little shanties occupied by the men are not as picturesque as tents but are said to be more comfortable.

---

[24] Col. William G. Ward

June 8, 1861

Started to go to the Rhode Island Camp but were prevented by the rain.

June 9, 1861

The wedding[25] passed off well. Mr. Elderkin returns tomorrow to Alexandria. He expects to be ordered next week to Harper's Ferry.

June 11, 1861

The papers are filled with accounts of the engagement at Bethel in Virginia. For more than an hour the United States troops were exposed to the fire of a body of their own men. It is not known exactly how many were killed.

June 12, 1861

Went to Mr. Calvert's. His daughter is engaged to Judge Campbell's son. He has joined the Union army & she can hear from him but very rarely- Poor child I pitied her; she looked pale & sad.

June 19, 1861

Harpers Ferry has been evacuated. It was an easy place to hold & the Government anticipated hard fighting there. Father saw Gen. Scot in the evening, he said the place was not of much importance to the Southerners. He did not wonder it was abandoned.

The Gen. was amusing himself with Shakespeare after the cares of the day. Mr. Townsand was with him who had been on the battle field in the engagement at Bethel.

---

[25] Wedding of Mary Frances Gurley (daughter of Dr. Gurley) & William Anthony Elderkin. According to reports, "As soon as the news of the fall of Fort Sumter reached Lincoln, he sent for Dr. Gurley to come to the White House, that they might pray together. After a few hours spent in seeking comfort and advice from God, Dr. Gurley started to leave the White House when the President detained him... ''What of your daughter?' he asked. 'She is engaged to young Elderkin, is she not? And he is a member of the graduating class at West Point, and must be called to the front at once. It will be hard for the little girl.' He talked for some time with the father, and asked him to send his daughter to the White House. 'I must talk with her', he said. 'If there is a war, Elderkin must take part in it.'"

On the couple's wedding day, President & Mrs. Lincoln were in attendance, with the president assisting in the receiving line.

Gen. Scott expressed his disapprobation of the blunder which had been made. He did not like the appointment of Civilians to post of such important command. "The art of War," he said, is certainly as difficult as "the art of shoemaking & who even thought of practicing the latter without serving an apprenticeship?"

The Gen. thinks he might end the war in a year if permitted to carry out his own plans, but great complaints are made of his slow movements.

Most of the troops have left the city now. We have had a visit from the Rev. Mr. Green this week who has just returned from the South.

He says the Southern troops are much inferior to those of the North. They are comprised in part of boys of 14 & 15 years of age. Pres. Davis is in very delicate health, should he die the prospect of the South will be dark.

Gen. Peirce has been very much blamed for the disasterous affairs at Great & Little Bethel. But Gen. Butler, his superior in command, planned the attack & he alone if anyone should be censured. Bethel is not far from Fortress Monroe where Gen. Butler is stationed.

June 15, 1861

Went to visit the camps of the 1st 2nd & 3rd Maine Regiments, they are near together in the vacinity of Columbia College.

A German regiment is not far off. We saw three parades at once from our carriage while the music of two seperate bands blended very sweetly together.

June 17, 1861

Another regiment arrived from Mass. yesterday, we saw them as they marched up the avenue – dusty & travel stained.

PHOTO: Thaddeus Lowe

June 18, 1861

Prof. Lowe[26] made some experiments with his baloon. He wishes to be of service to the Government in reconnoitering the forces & position of the

---

[26] Professor Thaddeus Lowe, a renowned scientist and doctoral advisor for the Smithsonian Institution was an early ballooning pioneer.

Obsessed with the idea of making a trans-Atlantic balloon flight, Lowe left Cincinnati in the early morning of April 19, 1861, for a trial flight to Washington, D.C, two days after Virginia had seceded from the Union.

Changing wind systems misdirected his craft to Unionville, South Carolina, where he was arrested and charged as a Yankee spy.

enemy. He arose to the height of 200 feet caring with him light telegraph wires by means of which he found he could readily communicate with individuals on terra ferma.

About sundown he moved majestically along through the air to the Presidents grounds – the balloon drawn by a crowd of men & boys.

We started for the same place by a shorter road but were soon taken by the Prof. He seemed to be enjoying his ride greatly.

June 19, 1861

The affray at Viena has exited us greatly. It seems that on Sunday, a number of troops were sent from Alexandria to take possession of the Alexandria & Loudon railroad.

They were transported in a train of cars & dropped by companies at different places along the road until only three remained in the cars.

These were stopped by a man in the vicinity of Viena who entreated them for God's sake not to proceed, but the officer in command did not heed the warning & as they turned a corner, a concealed battery opened its fire upon them.

The soldiers were obliged to leave the cars & take shelter in the woods at the sides of the road. They retreated with a loss of seven men. I do not know how many were wounded. The men behaved galently, but could do little under the fire of their concealed foe.

June 19, 1861

The Attorney Gen., Mr. Bates, his wife & daughters took tea with us.

They are pleasant inteligent people, but very simple & plain in dress & manner.

A telegram announces an engagement at Boonville Missouri.

June 20, 1861

Father dined at Judge W. Com. & other distinguished guests were present. Colonel Butterfield (N.Y.: 12th) was there for a short time but was suddenly called away. His regiment have been ordered to leave for Vir. to night.

It is generally supposed that we are on the eve of a great battle Gen. Beauregarde is said to be advancing with a large force. Signal fires have been burning on the Vir. Shores.

After some time, Lowe successfully established his identity as scientist and was permitted to return home. Upon reaching the United States, he summoned by the Secretary of the Treasury, Salmon P. Chase, to come to Washington with his balloon. The American Civil War permanently ended Lowe's attempt at a transatlantic crossing.

We retire with a dread of the news the morning may bring.

July 3, 1861

There have been several small engagements with the secessionists since last I wrote, but the great anticipated conflict between the contending parties is still deferred.

The two armies must soon meet. For Beauregard has been concentrating his forces in Vir. & Gen Scot has forwarded regiment after regiment so that now the Northerners & Southerners are almost within speaking distance.

PHOTO: General Beauregard

We obtained a photograph of Gen. B. a few days ago. He has a dark stern face determined & bold, but little expressive of generosity or sensibility.

Tomorrow, the entire session of Congress opens.

July 4, 1861

It is Independence Day, hallowed & dear to the hearts of the American people, but the Birth Festival of our republic awakens sad thoughts as well as patriotic feelings.

There was a grand parade of the NY regiments early in the morning. That state has already sent 50,000 men to the aid of the Government & is ready to provide more if they are needed.

At twelve o'clock, Congress opened. We went up some time before in order to procure seats, but found very few people in the Senate galleries, the House was crowded.

As we went into the Capitol, we met Mr. Breckenridge. He looked as if the troubles of the country weighed lightly upon him. He seemed pleased with Father's cordial invitation to visit the Smithsonian.

The situation of the few Dems here now is very disagreeable. It was very sad as the Senators took their seats -- to miss the old familiar faces, the tones that had only a few weeks before made those walls ring with heart stirring eloquence.

Mr. Breckenridge introduces us to the Senator who takes the place of Douglass. He is very different in appearance from the Little Giant. Tall with heavy iron grey eyebrows dark, piercing eyes, his head is partly bald.

Last evening, a eulogy was delivered upon Douglass by his friend Col. Forney, clerk of the Senate and for years editor of the *Philadelphia Inquirer.*

Mr. Forney spoke of the Senator's great generosity magnamimosity of disposition. He said it was important for him to ban malice. Father gave us one instance of this; He said that at a meeting of the Agricultural Society, Judge D. attacked the Institution, Father was vexed & said some severe remarks in reply. At the next meeting, S.D. came to Father & said very politely, "Prof., we had some hard words yesterday. I am going to make another speech to day & you must follow me."

Father shook his proffered hand and they were the best of friends until the death of the noble senator. He was one of the Regents of the Institution & always took a warm interest in the affairs of the Inst. especially in Father's reports & addresses.

July 5, 1861

We are almost tired of camp visiting but concluded to pay one more visit to the Twelfth Regiment (N.Y.).

We saw Col. Butterfield Col. Ward & other officers. One of the engineer corps invited us to take tea with them. The regiment is finely drilled, but complain greatly because they are obliged to perform so many evolutions in the double quick.

In the morning we had a visit from one the 71st regiment N.Y. They are at the Navy Yard, but expect to be ordered off to day.

In the evening, we had a visit from Senator Pearce, He looked thin & pale.

July 6, 1861

We have at last succeeded in accomplishing our visit to the Rhode Island regiment. It is encamped in one of the most beautiful places near Washington.

A light mist drapes the distant hills. An approaching thunder cloud some what obscured the setting sun but added new beauties to a landscape almost too exquisite to be real.

The parade was very fine as there were two regiments, at its close the troops formed into a solid square while the chaplain read a chapter in the Bible & stood with uncovered heads while he offered a prayer to the God of battles. It was a beautiful & touching scene.

We did not see the Gov.

Col. Burnside presided. He has a fine voice his clear tones were distinctly heard across the wide parade ground.

July 15, 1861

Monday.

An extra of *The Star* announced the defeat of a body of eight thousand secessionists under Gen Garnett's command in the western part of Virginia at Laurel Hill.

It is said 2,000 of the Southerners were taken prisoners. Gen. Garnett, himself, fell dead upon the field. We at first thought it was Muscoe Garnett, the member of Congress, but subsequently learned it was his cousin.

Went in the evening to Major Hunter's to see Dr. & Mrs. Hodge. The city was obstructed by camp equipment, canteens powder flasks ec. The Major was reclining upon the sofa as we entered the brightly lighted parlor.

He was ready with his young aid, Sam Shelton, to start early tomorrow morning. The eyes of the latter were dancing with excitement & enthusiasm while his mother's rested fondly & tearfully upon him.

At the head of the Major's sofa sat his adopted daughter, fair & gentle with a look of patient sadness upon her face.

Her husband is in the rebel army. She seemed too young to be the mother of the babe nestling in the Majors' arms & pulling his mustache in infantile glee. It's little laughing face a contrast to the older careworn ones.

July 16, 1861

Tuesday.

We went up into the high tower to see the troops pass over into Virginia. 4 regiments crossed the long bridge while we were up there, every now & then they rent the air with their enthusiastic shouts, but it was sad very sad to see them go. I could not feel patriotic. I thought of the sad patient form we saw last night, of the many brothers who were pressing thus eagerly forward to shed the blood of brothers.

Saw Fanny this evening, she came from Alexandria this morning Edward left her at 11 o'clock. He is under Gen Franklin's command.

She said that army 50,000 strong was to be stationed eight miles from Alexandria on the road to Fairfax Court House, as an attack was to be made upon the latter place at 6 o'clock tomorrow. It was expected that the Southerners would retreat to Richmond or rather to Manassas Junction.

Father went to see Mr. Harten, who said he was very, very, sorry to hear Mr. Bell's decision not to remain a unionist.

Father also saw the editor of the principal paper in Nashville. He said he was very sorry he was not in Nashville when Mr B. made the speech, declaring his sentiments.

July 17, 1861

Dr. & Mrs. Hodge came home this morning.

Major H. & Sam left yesterday, I suppose they were among the troops we saw pass over the bridge.

Prof & Mr. Alexander of Balt. were also here. The former looks somewhat like Col. Butterfield.

Met Judge & Mrs. Merrick on the avenue this afternoon. The Judge said it was very probable the armies were fighting then.

Mr. Wechlife had heard from Mr. Seward at the war department, that morning, that Fairfax Court house was to be attacked between 8 & 9 A.M.

Father has just come in from the observatory where he went with Dr. Hodge. Coming home he met Mr. _____ who had just returned from Fairfax Courthouse.

The secessionists had been warned early in the morning of the meditated attack upon the village, a milkman having conveyed a letter from someone in Washington & the place was deserted, women & children as well as the male population had fled. Some depridations had been committed by soldiery, but the officers soon put an end to anything of that kind.

July 18, 1861

The papers to day contain the account we received last night

July 19, 1861

Friday.

Another extra of *The Star* to day, account of an engagement at Bull Run. Half way between Fairfax Court House & Manassas Junction. The Federal army, in its march towards the latter station, were stopped by the fire from a concealed battery, shortly another also concealed commenced cannonading & then a third. The troops braved the storm of balls remarkably well, with the exception of a regiment from Mass & also one from N.Y.

It is very difficult to obtain authentic information in regard to the military movements. Gen. Scott is in constant communication with the army by telegraph, but he keeps his own council.

July 20, 1861

It is reported to night that the Batteries at Bull Run have been taken but Mr. Welling who has just left us says that is a mistake.

July 21, 1861

Sunday, 4 P.M.

This morning, as I went into church, Mr.----- told me that our troops were still fighting at Bull Run.

Gen. Scott was in church, he said he pitied our ladies who sat in front of him, as their husbands were engaged in battle probably at that very time.

I have come home with Fanny, as she is troubled about Mr. Elderkin who is at Bull Run.

Nelly has just come in to tell us our troops have been fighting since early in the morning.

10 P.M.

Mrs. Gurley drew me aside just before we came up stairs to tell me Col. Heintzelman was wounded & the battery in which Mr. Elderkin is was supposed to be cut to pieces. Fanny has fallen asleep tired of worrying – poor little one, she little knows what cause she has for anxiety.

July 22, 1861

Still at Dr. Gurleys.

This has been a very weary day. I am glad night has come at last so that I can forget its sad realities in sleep. Asleep.

Would I might awake from what seems like a hideous dream.

All last night, ambulances were passing the house & we expected every moment one would stop at our door. As we were seated at the breakfast table this morning, a violent pull at the door bell made us all start to our feet.

Two soldiers entered, blood stained & dusty.

Poor little Fanny threw herself on the floor, at my feet, covering her ears, fearing to hear the terrible news they might bring.

They were messengers of good tidings for her, however, E. was safe, but a sad, sad, tale they had to tell.

The Northern Army was ingloriously defeated – driven back before the rebel forces. 100,000 were said to have been engaged on one side & 80,000 on the other.

The loss of life on both sides was very great, but they could, of course, not tell us exactly how many were killed & wounded.

Three times our narrator, a strong man, burst into tears & cried like a child.

About 12 o'clock, Mr. E. arrived. He had not tasted food for twenty four hours. He said the batteries of the confederate forces were arranged in the form of a triangle. One of them had been taken early in the day & seemed to be in the hands of federate army until the confederates were reinforced by a body of troops from Manassas.

I should think this battery had been yielded in order to entrap the federal army, then by cutting off retreat. It was evedently the plan, an attack of calvary in the rear prevented a retreat.

The plan did not quite succeed, however, the calvary "The black Horsemen," were repulsed by Ellsworth.

A panic seized the troops about 4'o they fled precipitately.

A number of Congressmen, who had been exceedingly eager for the battle, had gone down to witness what they were pleasured to call "the Southern Races."

The Rhode Island Regiment was the only one that retreated in good order. We saw them come into the city about 10 A.M. It was a pitiable sight. Many of the men were without shoes in stocking & unduly dirty. Some had succumbed to exhaustion & men come upon the shoelessness of others who seemed less weary than themselves.

They formed sad contrast to the enthusiastic, well dressed military looking men who left us.

All day long, bodies of struggling troops have been coming into the city to the streets lined with men, seated upon the side walks in the pelting rain, their officers, many of them killed, their company broken up, they did not seem to know where to go.

Our army had been completely routed.

Could the Southern army be in the city on Tuesday night? It might readily be possible.

We learned of the deaths of several of our friends, but I am happy to learn Col. Hunter & his young aid are safe. The former is gentle, severely wounded, but is in no danger

It is terrible to think of the hearts bleeding to night of the thousands weeping for some husbands & brothers falling unknown & unnoted, except to swell the number enforcement of the country's loss.

July 23, 1861

This is a beautiful day after yesterday's rain. It is a relief to see sunshine again, but it does not bring happiness with it. A member of the N.J. 71st Regiment has just been here. He fought well & bravely, but says he hopes he may never again see a battlefield. He shuddered & put his hand over his eyes when he told us the horror of that terrible Sunday.

He said the cowardice & inefficiency of the volunteer officers was almost too great to be believed.

One of their captains was about to leave when his men told him if he Should, they would shoot him down. The streets are still crowed with soldiers, every few steps, almost, we encounter crowds collected around some of the Bull's Run adventeres, listening with warmth & eyes wide open.

July 27, 1861

The excitement after the battle is intense. Gen. McDowell is very much blamed. Gen. Scott declares he washes his hands of the affair & before soon, he may be allowed to carry out his plans without molestation.

He is said to have declared to the President that he must be commander in chief, in reality as well as in name or he must resign.

The members of congress who were so eager for the battle and went to see what they were pleased to call the Southern races are said to have caused the panic by their precipitous flight.

Reports are so contradicted it is impossible to know the number of the killed & wounded.

July 29, 1861

Yesterday, a poor man came to Father to know if he could obtain permission to visit the battle field. He wished to look for the body of his son. He heard of him through a companion by whose side he was shot down & who procured him medical assistance, but the bullets were falling thick & fast. The soldier left the poor wounded boy & his friend was obliged to flee for his life.

The unhappy father was overcome with grief, we could hear his groans from one end of the house to the other.

Father saw a son of Gen Meigs who gave him the best description of the battle he had yet received. He is a West Point Cadet at home for the holidays.

He came to his Father on the Saturday before the battle & told him that he could not remain quiet while so many brave men were fighting for their country. Perhaps he might not be of any use, but he wished to do what little good was in his power & requested permission to join the army in Virginia. He told his Mother of his intentions only an hour before he started, saying he thought it was his duty to go & she must not forbid him.

Ruins following the Battle of Bull Run

He distinguished himself most nobly, displaying the coolness intrepidity & skill of an experienced general.

Once he rode forward, alone, to find out whether an advancing body of men belonged to the Federal or confederate forces, with only a pistol in his belt.

Once as an experienced officer was leading his men into the

middle of a force in order to get them to spread, before them he waved his sword & called out at the top of his voice "Men will have you or your lives" &

ordering a retreat, saved a gallant company.

Gen. Scott is justly proud of his young country man.

Much is said of the ferocity of the Southerners at the battle, but the feeling of animosity seems to be equally deep on both sides. One of our friends who had been upon the field, told us he saw two wounded men, a federal & a unionist, lying side by side, attempt to bayonet each other. Too weak for such an effort they sank back exhausted & dying.

August 17, 1861

The city has been very quiet for the last two weeks. Most of the soldiers are encamped beyond the limits of the city and are not allowed to leave their quarters. Even the officers are arrested if they appear in the streets without a pass.

Gen McClellan, the successor of McDowell, seems determined to maintain the strictest discipline in his armies. The utmost secrecy is now preserved by the Government in regard to war movement, a necessary precaution since the Southerners have been kept constantly informed of every important measure of the Northern Army.

When our forces reached Fairfax Court House, they found in the quarters deserted by the rebel officers, maps of fortifications & other photographs made at the Coast Survey[27]. Copies of which had not yet been issued for the use of the Federal officers.

Since I last wrote, we have had a visit from Prince Napoleon. He was the guest of the French minister.

Sec. Seward gave a ball in his honour, the day before he went to Mount Vernon, & as he did not return at the time appointed, great fears were entertained that he had been taken prisoner.

The Secretary was not with his royal guest, however.

It seems that the Prince & the distinguished gentleman with him had made in an evening, & exhausted, the party was obliged to remain at a farm house until others could be obtained.

The Prince is very fine looking & strongly resembles his illustrious ancestor. He thinks the war will not last long since Government will not be able to support the expense. $1,000,000 per day was the lowest estimate.

---

[27] The United States Coast Survey, a forerunner of NOAA, served as a leading scientific agency, charting coastlines and determining land elevations for the nation. In 1861, the agency adjusted quickly to meet the needs of a country at war; however, unlike all other branches, it was not immune to espionage.

He thought France would take no part in the war. She had too much to attend to at home. It is generally supposed that the Prince has other motives than those of men pleasure, seeking in coming to this country at this important era.

The Northern troops have met with reverses in Missouri the death of Gen. Lyon has caused great excitement. We expect to leave home next Tuesday.

September 16, 1861

The important events of the month have been the capture of the forts at Cape Hatteras a severe blow to the Southern confederacy, as it must divide their armies. The proclamation of Fremont, the moderation of the President & another battle in Missouri, in which the Southerners are said to have sustained a great loss.

There is no truth in the report of the death of Jefferson Davis.

We were very much startled last evening by a report that all the regiments of the city has been ordered immediately to Washington, as the southerners had possession of Arlington Height & were shelling the city.

The excitement was very great, both in Phil & Ger. Our capitol is still safe however.

Father started to go there this morning. It was not prudent to venture back so soon after his illness, but he felt uneasy about the affairs of the Institution. Public affairs weigh very heavily upon his mind. He thinks Gen. Fremont's proclamation will only serve to unite the South more strongly.

He thinks too, that if the war continues long, the country must be flooded with treasury notes & another of those terrible financial crises ensue, which have more than once reduced our country to the verge of ruin.

September 18, 1861

Went yesterday to see a parade in Philadelphia, in honour of the day. Mr. Holt & Mr. Dallas were both to preach, but the former did not make his appearance.

September 20, 1861

Have heard from Father. Mrs. Harris was his companion de voyage. She has since been arrested. Her husband was sent to negotiate for the body of Gen. Cameron & was detained by the South. It is suspected that he was not true to the Government. Their youngest daughter is still in Germantown.

The event of the week has been the arrest of the Maryland legislature.

Papers were discovered proving beyond a doubt that the Marylanders were to have acted in concert with the forces around Washington. An attack was to have been made upon the Capitol last Sunday, so that the excitement in the city was not entirely groundless.

Gen. McC. has won the enthusiastic affection of his officers & men. They have given him the appellation of George. His speeches to them are very concise here is one of them:

"We have suffered our last defeat, we have made our last retreat you stand by me & I'll stand by you."

Mesdames Rodgers, Mc Combe, & Meigs are in Germantown.

Cap Meigs has returned from the West. He is said to have gone to Missouri to settle the difficulties between Fremont & the Floyds.

Another naval expedition is said to have left N.Y., it's destination unknown.

The times of this morning gives an account of a skirmish at Mariatown; the confederates were routed, but the Federal officer Col. Johnson was pierced by nine bullets & instantly killed while riding at the head of his column.

September 24, 1861

Saturday.

Our meditated departure has been deferred by the illness of Dr. Hase, one of Father's assistants.

An attack is expected every day upon the city, but there are so many troops here now, we do not feel any anxiety. Regiment after regiment have been come in quietly, almost every night. We have visited the new encampments twice with Mr.____. The street is strongly fortified & a little church that interfered with the range of the guns has been pulled down.

It is supposed that Maryland will rise simultaneously with the attack on the city & perhaps again cut off our communication with the North.

September 25, 1861

Came to Princeton yesterday, at Trenton met a long train of cars filled with soldiers en route for Washington. The air rang with their shouts as they passed us.

Another battle in Missouri. Col. Mulligan has been obliged to surrender Lexington. He fought bravely, but was without water & overpowered by superior numbers.

Col. Fremont is becoming very unpopular – he is charged with mismanagement & extravagance in expenditure. It is said that he has placed Col. F P Blair under arrest for attempting his removal by correspondence with the Government officials at Wash.

Kentucky has been invaded by the Confederate forces at several points. The legislature & the people have declared most emphatically for the Union & have given the command of the state forces to Major Anderson.

The report that the American Minister at Brussels has offered a command in the Union army to Garibaldi is confirmed, but whether the offer will be accepted is not known.

The Prince is now in Boston.

Gen. M.J. Thompson, chief of the confederates forces in Missouri, has issued proclamation, declaring that for every southern soldier put to death in accordance with the proclamation of Gen. Fremont, he will hang, draw, & quarter a minion of Abraham Lincoln.

September 27, 1861
Yesterday the national fast was observed with great solemnity.

September 28, 1861
Had a pleasant journey from Washington, found troops stationed at intervals all along the road & the bridges well guarded. At every station, officers passed through the cars to see whether they contained any run away soldiers.

Mrs. Gen. McCooke & her little daughter were with us. The winning sweetness & merry laugh of the latter greatly relieved the bothersomeness of our journey. We met Sam Stockton in the cars – he said his uncle, Col. Hunter, was to start for Missouri the next day.

Mrs. Gwen, Mrs. Greenhow & Mrs. ___ have been arrested as spys.

September 31, 1861
The body of Gen Lyon passed through the city to day.

October 3, 1861
The Great Eastern has been much injured by a violent storm. She was very nearly wrecked.

October 7, 1861
News have been received of the disloyalty of the Cherokee Indians. They have held a council & appointed Commissioners to make a treaty of alliance with the Southern Government.

October 11, 1861
The paper to day announces the return of Dr. Hays, the Artic Explorer.

October 14, 1861

Gen. Anderson has been relieved of his command in Kentucky and is commanded to report himself at Washington as soon as his health will permit.

Zollicoffer is said to be at Cumberland Ford with a large force.

Advances from Missouri state Gen. Price is moving Southward.

A grand naval expedition is preparing, destiny unknown.

October 19, 1861

Another slight skirmish at Harper's Ferry.

Gen Price has crossed the Osage river.

October 22, 1861

A battle of some importance took place yesterday at Leesburg. Col. Baker, the Senator from Cal., was killed.

November 9, 1861

News from fleet: two vessels driven ashore by gale NY, rest of fleet badly shelled by batteries of Port Royal. Another battle in Missouri, rebels defeated.

November 11, 1861

Rumors from the fleet: Beaufort said to be taken, nothing certainly known. A victory of the rebels in western Virginia

November 12, 1861

Reports concerning the fleet confirmed Gen Fremont removed.

November 14, 1861

The paper today contains the official dispatch of Com Dupont.

Port Royal & Beaufort both taken.

I have been in New York for several weeks, the feeling against the South is exceedingly bitter here & I am afraid will only be satisfied with the immediate emancipation of the negros[28].

December 28, 1861

Reached home last Saturday. Find the city in a frightful condition. The streets dirty & torn up by the heavy army wagons.

Almost every other house on Penn. Avenue displays a sutler's sign or garibaldi neck ties & McClellan's books adorn the dry good stores.

---

[28] An insight to the mindset of many northerners who were in favor of emancipation, not on moral grounds, but as an opportunity to punish the south.

The great subject of interest now, not only before the American public but before the world, is the arrest of Mason & Slidel, by Capt. Wilks. They were seized on board of the English vessel *The Trent* & will be certainly demanded by England. Should we not surrender them, our war of 1812 is for nought. England in demanding.

January 1, 1862

The sun has risen brightly on the new year.

I wish we could think it a good omen, but the sky was as free from clouds the day twelve months ago & sad have been the calamities that have visited the Nation since then.

10 p.m.

We have had a pleasant day, but greatly missed the old familiar faces now separated from, not so much by distance, but by the insurmountable barrier raised by the cries of War.

February 6, 1862

I have commenced the year badly. I have allowed more than a month to go by without writing in my journal.

The question concerning Mason & Slidel has been decided. They have reached England & we have remained true to the principal which cost so much bloodshed in 1812. It is feared, however, that England is not as well disposed toward us as she wishes to appear. Much as she has condemned slavery, her interests are too deeply concerned in the bondage of the negro to allow her to dwell with complacency upon the prospect of their emancipation.

No white man can labor under the scorching sun of the South & the underscored free negro is perfectly worthless.

Sec. Cameron has been removed & given a foreign embasy. Rumours are afloat of other changes to be made in the Cabinet. Financial affairs look dark, the Treasury notes issued in such abundance are already at a discount of 5 percent.

In Congress, much excitement has been created by the trial of Sen. Bright. He wrote to Jef. Davis some time ago, recommending a certain person who had a peculiar sort of firearm to sell.

He was dismissed from his seat.

Yesterday, the two thirds vote decided by two. I was in the Senate on Tuesday & heard Mr. Sumner & Willis of Virginia both discuss the subject.

Bright seemed unabashed & confident that he should be able to retain his seat.

There have been a series of abolition lectures in the Smithsonian building, but unconnected with the Institution They have troubled Father greatly, for by a law of the constitution, all political topics, sectarian religious views or subjects connected with bills before congress are prohibited in the Smithsonian lectures.

A committee of 100 of the most respectable gentleman in the city came to Father early in the season & requested the use of the room for a series of lectures for a charitable purpose & showed him a list of persons whom they expected to invite, among others, Prof. Felton of Harvard. The list was afterward changed, however, & others substituted in their place.

Father was troubled by the direct violation of the rules of the Institution & wished to put a stop to the lectures, but was advised by his friends to allow them to proceed as the course was nearly completed & then exclude all lectures for the future except those immediately imployed by the Institution.

We have been daily expecting a forward movement of the troops, but the state of the roads prevents.

Another naval expedition under command of Gen Burnside has sailed for Cape Hatteras & a third for the Gulf. The latter who deeply interested in Capt Farragut is an old friend of ours & Lieuts. Heisler & Harris the one on the *Hartford* the other on the *Pensacola* left our circle of friends two or three weeks ago.

We heard twice from Mr. Harris while his ship was at Fortress Monroe, awaiting the other vessels of the fleet. She was fitted up in the Washington navy yard & great fears were entertained that she would be destroyed by the batteries on the Patomac. She passed them, however, uninjured with the exception of a splinter knawed from her prow by one of the rebel guns. The dense fog favored her escape.

Col. Alexander is with us. He has been sick for more than two weeks & is greatly reduced in strength. He was in the battle of Mannassas & one of the bravest officers there.

There was a brilliant party at the President Mansion last evening. The Heads of the diplomatic corps, the judges of the Supreme Court, some of the Senate & other distinguished guests were there. It was a very brilliant affair.

The most important military news of the month is the death of Zollicoffer He was strongly entrenched in the _____ part of Kentucky, but left his mountain fortress to attack our troops & was killed & his army routed.

February 7, 1862
News of the capture of Fort Henry by the Federal troops, only one man killed, a rebel general, one colonel, two captains & sixty privates taken prisoner.

February 15, 1862

Saturday.

The young men of the building have all gone into the city to hear the particulars of the great victory of the Burnside Expedition

The papers are full of excitement this evening The Burnside Expedition left Cape Hatteras on the 5th. & headed by Com. Goldsborough proceeded up Croton Sound, lying between Roanoke Island & the main land. The confederates were driven from their batteries in the centre to the upper part of the island & there, forced to surrender.

Over two thousand prisoners were said to have been taken. The whole Island is now in the possession of the Federal army, also Elizabeth City & Edenton. The former was set fire to by the Southerners & partly consumed.

Edenton is a small, but flourishing port town & is the key to the road around the Dismal swamp.

The Generals most conspicuous in the contest besides Goldsborough & Burnside were Foster, Parke, & Reno.

The news from Missouri & Tennessee is of equal interest. Gen Price has been driven from Springfield & virtually from the state. Fort Donelson on the Cumberland river is surrounded by Generals Grant, Smith, & McClernand with 40,000 men. The confederates have about eleven thousand & Generals Johnson Pillow Floyd & Buckner are said to be in the fort: also Beauregard & John Bell.

The news from Great Britain announce the arrival of Mason & Slidell at Southampton. No demonstration was made on their arrival. The former went to London & the latter to Paris.

The French papers conclude from the attitude of the English press that the Trent affair was only a pretext for war & that Eng. wants to force the blockade of the Southern ports.

The speech of the French Emperor at the opening of the legislature is characteristically cautious – it is impossible to discover from it what are his intentions in regard to America.

A bill has passed both Houses of Congress making the Treasury notes a legal tender.

February 17, 1862

Success seems to crown the Federal armies in every quarter just now. Gen Lander has routed a confederate camp at Blooming gap in Maryland & thus opened the Baltimore & Ohio railroad to Bowling Green.

Missouri is in possession of Gen Mitchel & Gen Buel is in pursuit of the enemy.

Gen Curtis has overtaken the retreating army of Gen Price, & taken a number of prisoners.

Fort Donelson is still in the hands of the Southerners, but two of the outer batteries have been taken. Fort Henry has been called Fort Pierce in compliment to the Gen. for his gallant conduct in the capture of Fort Henry.

Nashville, it is supposed will be the next point of attack.

The guns have been fired all day in honor of US victories.

The greatest excitement every where has been received of the of the surrender of Fort Donelson.

The streets have reacted with the rejoicing cries of the populace.

Gen McClellan himself, carried the official dispatch of Gen. Cullum, commandant at Cairo, to the war Department. The Sec. read it aloud & three times there rose cheering from the crowd collected in the hall.

In the Senate & House, the enthusiasm was unbounded. Cheers resounding from gallery to gallery as well as from the floors.

In the house, all attempts to preserve order were in vain – the members left their seats & surrounded Mr. Colfax, who was the bearer of the dispatch.

Mr. Conkling was the object of their attention & received the warm congratulations of Mr. House that Kentucky was at last free from confederate control.

February 18, 1862

The papers are filled with accounts of the reception of the news of victory in the different northern cities. General rejoicing is the order of the day.

The Burnside expedition has taken two more towns.

Our loss in the destruction of Fort Donelson is great many fine officers have fallen.

Generals Pillow, Buckner & Johnston have been made prisoners – the latter should have been mentioned first. He is said to be one of best generals in the confederate army.

Gen Grant (Fed) has been promoted for his gallant conduct. Com. Foote (Fed) is said to be advancing with his fleet on the Cumberland river, about fifty miles from Nashville.

February 20, 1862

Great preparations are making for the illumination of the city on the 22nd. Washington's birth-day. Jefferson Davis is be inaugurated on the same day as President of the Confederate States for six years.

This morning, we attended a wedding of the daughter of Mr. King, the former Post Master Gen.

Father came in from the building about seven with a gentle look upon his face to ask whether we had not something to send to Mrs. Reese's little girl. He was obliged to detain her Father so that she could not attend the wedding as she had been promised.

Overwhelmed, as he was just then with business – few would have been mindful of the disappointment of a baby.

February 21, 1862

Our reception day.

Went in the evening to Willards to call upon Mrs. Erastus Corning, Mrs. Horton & Mrs. Foster & others.

Mr. E. Corning is a noble specimen of man, the mild radius of his dark full eye denotes a nature as gentle as strong.

Saw Dr. Hays for a few moments, he delivered his closing lecture at the Institution last evening.

The President's family is in deep affliction. Willie Lincoln is dead. He was an intelligent child of eleven years of age & a great favorite of the visitors at the White House.

It is reported to night that Nashville has surrendered.

Clarksville has been taken.

The rolling Mills owned by John Bell, near Fort Donelson, have been destroyed.

It is further reported that the southern troops are returning from Manassas.

February 22, 1862

We have been at the Capitol all day & are completely tired out.

We left home at 10 o'clock as we feared we should not otherwise be able to obtain good seats. We were very fortunate in that respect. The House of Rep. had been provided with a number of additional seats for the invited guests.

At 12 o'clock, just as all the bells of the city rang out a merry peal, the members assembled on one side of the Hall & after some discussion as to propriety of presenting the flags taken at the recent battles, which was to have formed part of the order of the day & which was strenuously opposed by the Ven. Mr. Crittenden, on the ground that in accepting these trophies the Government would acknowledge the South as a separate foreign power.

This interesting part of the programme was voted down, much to the disappointment of the occupants of the Galleries.

At one o'clock, the august body arose to receive their distinguished guests.

First appeared the Vice President conducted by the Sec. of the Senate & followed by the chaplain, senators, cabinet, count de Paris, Duke de Chartres, Judges of the Supreme Court Foreign Ministers, Officers of the Army & Navy headed by Gen McClellan & invited guests.

After a prayer by the chaplain, the Farewell Address was read.

During the reading, we had ample time to enjoy the scene before us. The assemblage of distinguished men listened with reverence to the words of our gentle father.

The Gen & deputy old Commodores with their white locks brilliant epaulets & shoulder stripes. Among whom we recognised Gen Totten, Com. Shubrick, Com. Wilkes, Gen. Casey & others.

The ladies galleries, filled to over flowing & particularly brilliant from the bright scarlet so much worn at present. Near us sat Mrs. McClellan her face bright with pleasure at the applause which greeted the entrance of the Gen..

Mrs. Wilkes, fair & gentle, Mrs. Corning dignified & courtly. Mrs Crittenden handsome & stately, Mrs Harris & the wifes & daughters of many other distinguished senators graced our corner of the gallery.

The Secession Flags were displayed in the old House of Rep., but the crowd was so great we could not get near enough to see them.

As we left the steps of the Capitol, we were introduced to Mr. Willis, the collector, I was surprised to see a tall red haired individual in place of the slender, dark eyed man I had imagined him.

Savannah is said to have surrendered, but the news is not yet confirmed.

Gen. Curtis has driven the Secessionists entirely out of Missouri & has taken Bentonville in Arkansas.

I see, by the *Intelligencer,* that Dr. Bachs & Prof Price have been elected associate members of the University of Kiev in Russia. The same from which Father received a diploma a few days ago with a very complimentary letter from Baron Stoeckl, ambassador from Russia.

February 28, 1862

Our reception day, among other guests, we had a visit from Mrs. McClellan. She is very agreeable, sprightly in conversation & very good looking. The cardes de visite of her do not do her justice.

Miss Chase was also here. She is tall & slender & her soft brown hair waves away from a face expressive of strong character & intelligence. I think she is very attractive, though free from diffidence, she is modest & does the honours of her Father's house very gracefully.

Miss Hamlin, the daughter of the vice President, is not as pleasing in her appearance, but has a good sensible face.

Every one who came brought long faces – a large number of the troops have been ordered to Virginia & an engagement of the whole army is expected soon.

Nashville was occupied on the 24th by Gen. Buell with 10,000 troops.

The excitement there the Sunday previous was intense. The news of the success of the Northerners reached the inhabitants just as they were going to church – they immediately dispersed to their homes to prepare for speedy flight.

We have not been able to learn much about Mr. Bell's family a paragraph in the Newspaper informed us that Mr. Yeatman had been advised to claim the rolling mills which were destroyed when Fort Donelson was taken. One of the managers of the mills who was captured, reported the illness of John Bell, as well as the intemperate habits of Breckenridge.

March 4, 1862

General Smith lectured. He seems to be a true earnest man although fanatical.

Immediate emancipation was, of course, his theme.

A Matinee at Sec. Chases.

Miss Chase received her guest with graceful dignity. Gen McClellan was there for a few moments. Mr. Day was very agreeable. Gottschalk concert in the evening.

March 7, 1862

Reception day.

A number of people here, among others, Miss Goldsborough. She has reason just now to be proud of her Father.

March 8, 1862

Went to inquire about Mrs. Casey. She is not expected to live through the day Gen. Casey may be ordered off any moment. We met a number of ambulances conveying the sick from the other side of the river. Every thing seems to indicate a speedy movement of the troops.

March 9, 1862

Sunday.

Saw Com. Subrick on my way to church in the afternoon. He was excited by the news that the iron clad steamer *Merrimac*, which has been fitting up in Norfolk harbor, had sunk one of the vessels of the blockading squadron, destroyed a second while a third was aground.

March 10, 1862

Monday.

The time anticipated by some with eager beating hearts, by others with sad forebodings, has come at last. The grand movement of the troops took place to day. We did not see them go, but Dr. Cox told us, this evening, that the procession was three hours in passing the hotel where he was staying. He said there was no shouting. The faces of the men were determined as though they meant to do their duty, but grave with the thought of the severe struggle before them.

The Southerners are said to have evacuated Manasses for fear of being attacked in the rear.

Poor Gen. Casey, I am glad to learn has not been obliged to leave his wife.

Capt. Davis is in Baltimore on his way to Wash, as became of dispatches from Capt. Dupent, he telegraphs that St Simons & Brunswick Ga. & Fort Clinch & St Mary's Florida are taken by the fleet.

Leesburg has been evacuated by the Southerners.

March 11, 1862

Tuesday.

Manassas has been evacuated. The immense Southern Army is gone. Where, no one knows.

Our troops' last night were at Centreville.

Gen. McClellan at Fairfax Court House.

News has been received from Roanoke Island that Gen. Burnside is preparing for another expedition to the main land. It is thought by some that the Southern army has gone to meet him.

The cities of Fernandina on the Georgia coast & St Marys Florida, have been taken by the expedition under Capt DuPont. or rather have been evacuated by the Southerners.

The town of Fernandina was particularly well defended & the possession of its batteries commanding all the windings of the ship channel rendered the approach of an enemy vessels almost impossible had the courage of the Southerners equaled their advantage of position. They fled precipitately without attempting any resistance.

Com. Buchanan is said to have been the commander of the *Merrimac* in her attack upon the Government vessels.

March 12, 1862

Wed.

It is rumoured to day that the Burnside expedition has been surrounded by the army lately at Manassas & entirely destroyed, but there does not seem to be much foundation for the statement.

The President & organizers have divided the Army of the Patomac into 4 corps:

1st corps of 4 divisions. Gen. McDowell commander. 2nd of 3 div. Brig. Gen. Sumner 3rd of 3 div. Brig. Gen. Heintzelman 4th of 3 div. Brig. Gen. Keys. A 5th army corp to be commandey by Gen. Banks will be formed of his own & Gen. Shields late Gen. Lander's division.

As Gen McClellan has to be the field in person, he is relieved from the command of all military departments except the army of the Patomac. Gen. Halleck is to have command west, Knoxville Ten. & while there the county lying east of Halleck department & west of the Patomac department to be called the mountain dept. is given to Gen Fremont who has been restored to favor.

The latest report of Gen. Bank's division on the upper Patomac is that the Southerners have evacuated Winchester.

March 13, 1862

Last night, we attended some private theatricals at Lord Lyons.

Carlotta Gerolt, Madam L., Mrs. Vilette, daughter of the Smith, Sec. of Interior & Miss Long, were the principal actresses the actors were mostly members of the English legation. Lord Lyons had fitted up the ballroom of his house as a theater & spared nothing that might add to the pleasure of his guests. Mr. Russel took part in the Fernades Furioso. & did remarkabley well.

Lord Lyons seemed to enjoy the plays heartily. Mr.?, artist of the London news, was stage manager.

We have just had a visit from a Dr. Newbury who was at Fort Donelson immediately after the battle. The wounded, he said, had been removed from the scene of action, but the dead were still there. It was terrible to see the deceased, limbs & gastly bodies of the brave men who had perished in their country's cause.

Dr. Newbury was on board the steamer with many of those who had been wounded – One, a mere boy, died with his mother's name upon his lips & one poor fellow, who had received a ball in his brain, repeated incessantly "charge on, charge on."

No special news from the army.

Gen. McC. is expected in the city this evening.

Capt Buchanan who was in command of the *Merrimac* will probably have to lose a limb. He was severely wounded in the knee.

Excursions to Mannassas is just now the order of the day.

March 17, 1862

Monday.

The river has been filled with boats loading at Alexandria with soldiers, their destination is unknown.

March 20, 1862

Tuesday.

Went to day to Alexandria to see the embarcation of the troops.

We were first obliged to go to the Provost Marshall & sign a pass solemnly swearing thereby that we were true & loyal citizens of the United States & would in no way render aid or comfort to the enemy.

The office of the Marshall is in the house formerly occupied by the G.

As we passed through the elegantly finished rooms once thronged with the gay & fashionable, now filled with soldiers & rough men, we could not but give a sigh for our former hostess & her vanished splendor.

The day was rather too cool for enjoyment on the water, but as we approached Alexandria, boat after boat passed us, laden with soldiers & the air rang with their enthusiastic shouts as we greeted them.

They seemed to be in excellent spirits.

Alexandria seemed like a great military camp. Soldiers in the street, soldiers in the houses, blue coats everywhere & heavy army wagons rumbling along unceasingly.

One officer told us 20,000 men had arrived on Saturday. No provision had been made for their accommodation, but several churches were thrown open for them to lodge in.

We concluded to visit Fort Elsworth & on our way there passed the old church Washington regularly attended. Those grey old walls saw the beginning of our republic, were they to witness its downfall?

Fort Elsworth is beautifully situated, commanding a most beautiful view of the surrounding country. We saw it in the Spring before its completion. The works are very finely finished & the accommodation for the officers & men excellent, although the condition of some of the tents was far from inviting in appearance, as little attention seemed to have been paid to neatness.

Several of the guns are rifled. They were quiet & harmless enough looking, but it made one shudder to think of the death & destruction those iron monsters are capable.

Two pretty little brass guns interested us particularly, they had seen service in four or five of the Mexican battles.

They seemed to be pets as they were polished with great care.

The Fort is upon a hill & as we descended toward Alexandria, our eyes were charmed by the appearance of a cavalry camp below us. Nothing could have been more picturesque; the tents, the drill, the piles of redlious blankets here & there, the sunlight dawning brightly over all the slopes of the hill, with its groups of soldiers formed a beautiful tableau.

Not the least interesting part of the scene was the sight of a large tree not far from us. We watched its stately head sway from side to side, fall to its fate with dignity. Like a great human soul in misfortune, it fell, but noble in its falling. Lord of the forest still, though low in the dust.

April 19, 1862

Saturday.

Since I last wrote, success has every where crowned the mens' arms

In Tennessee Island no. 10, commanding the Mississippi, or at least one of the most important forts on that river held by the Southerners, has yielded, after a prolonged siege, the combined forces of Com. Foote & Gen Pope.

Pittsburg Landing has been the scene of one of the greatest battles yet fought. Gen Prentiss army was surprised by the southern forces & driven from its positioning, but the timely arrival of Gen. Buell with reinforcement saved the credit of the North & our army has regained its position.

The loss on both sides is heavy. Gen Johnson one of the principal confederate generals has been killed & Beauregard lost an arm.

In Virginia, Gen. Shields has been wounded in an engagement at Winchester.

The Northern forces encamped a little out of the town & the inhabitants – who had professed loyalty as long as the union soldiers were about though they had evacuated the farms – notified the confederates who attacked them. The engagement was severe, but the Southerners were obliged to beat a hasty retreat.

The army under Gen McClellan is now opposite Yorktown the scene of one of our revolutionary battles. News from there is awaited with great interest as the Southerners are strongly fortified & seem determined to make great resistance. Jef. Davis himself is said to be there.

From the valley of the Shenandoah, we hear of new victories, Mount Jackson is ours & several small towns.

Gen McDowell has advanced on Fredericksburg & from last accounts was only prevented from crossing the river by the destruction of the bridges. The confederates have evacuated the town.

An expedition was made up the Rappahanock a few days since, by two or three gun boats, nothing was seen of the confederate forces & the inhabitants left in the towns eagerly welcomed the Northerners.

From Com. DuPont, we hear that Fort Pulaski has been taken.

The siege was conducted with consummate skill. The Fort would have held out much longer as it was well garrisoned & provisioned, but a breach in the wall exposed her powder magazine which a few more shells might have ignited. Com DuPont expressed his thanks to Gen Hunter for allowing some of his men to take charge of some of the land batteries.

In North Carolina, Gen. Burnside is besieging Fort Macon.

England has been in a great state of excitement since the affair of the *Merrimac*. The superiority of iron clad vessels seems now to be fully established. Great curiosity is felt just now to know the object of French minister's visit to Richmond. It is supposed he went there to see the F and their monopoly of tobacco.

We had a visit from Mrs. Gen Heintzelman yesterday. She is a pleasant little woman. Her husband is at L. He was badly wounded in the battle of Bull's run, but has entirely recovered in helath. His arm is useless however.

We have an addition of Mr. Pallins & family to our family. We have heard indirectly from Mrs. Bell, she is in Nashville. Mr. Bell is in Memphis. He sorrows for the desolation brought upon his country, but does not regret the step he has taken.

April 21, 1862

A.M.

Father came home late Saturday evening & reported that the city was intensely excited. Regiments were moving about, drums beating & the streets filled with people.

Yesterday morning, we learned that Gen. McDowell had been outflanked & that the Southerners were moving upon Washington. This report was contradicted in the evening, however.

The panic was caused by a strategem on the part of the Government, to discover whether the troops, the rescue corps about Washington, were ready for a sudden attack. They were not completely prepared so the lesson was not unnecessary.

April 24, 1862

Thurs.

Received a letter from Dr. Woodhul. He is with the army at Yorktown. He says the rebels are so near that all military orders have to be given quietly as possibly, no reveille sounded, no drums beaten.

More than one shell had burst within a few feet of his tent. The men were making most excellent roads as well as strengthening their position.

April 25, 1862

Friday.

Went to the Navy Yard. Went on board the *Yankee* she is a small vessel with two or three guns.

A French vessel had just arrived from Richmond with M. Mercier — the object of his journey thither is not known

May 1, 1862

Went last evening to a party given by Mr. Seward to the French officers. I was introduced to four or five of them & found them sprightly & agreeable.

May 26, 1862

Sunday seems to be the day for panics.

Yesterday, the city was thrown into a great state of excitement by the news that Banks had been driven across the river.

Jackson was said to be in possession of Harper's Ferry & great fears were entertained that he would come upon Washington.

Gen. McDowell's troops have been ordered back for the defense of the city.

May 28, 1862

Wednesday.

The seventh Regiment of N.Y. is in Baltimore.

The excitement in the Northern cities is immense. Gen McDowell is blamed in some quarters for Gen Banks' retreat, as he withdrew from him a number of his men. Gen McClellan is now within a few miles of Richmond.

The Southerners have evacuated their extensive defenses at L. & gradually orchestrated, giving fight. Considerable clashes at Williamsburg.

A fleet of gun boats proceeding up James river towards Richmond met with a reverse & Com. Rodgers was slightly wounded. A terrible battle is expected before long.

We had a visit from Prof Barnard last week. He has been in Norfolk all winter. He said the college with which he was connected in Oxford Miss. was entirely broken up & the buildings occupied by soldiers.

Of several hundred of the young men who had been under his charge, ten percent had been killed at the battle of Manassas. He said the army at Richmond was greater than ours. That the Southerners were full of courage & hope in their cause & were ready to fight desperately.

We have received a letter from Mr. Harris, giving us an account of the passage of the Gulf fleet up the Mississ & the taking of New Orleans.

He says it is impossible to imagine the horrors of the scence. The air was filled with shot & sheel & the shrieks of the dying are above the noise of artillery.

Mr. Harris was on board the *Pensacola* one of the first vessels to advance. The fleet had to pass the guns of this large & perpetually defended forts, while they at the same time, encountered the floating batteries of the enemy.

Just as they were congratulating themselves upon their hours most of the difficulties in their way, the southerners set fire to the ships about N.O. & a number of vessels came drifting down the stream – their masts heads one sheet of flame.

In spite of all the danger encountered, the loss on the Federal side was very small & the meeting of friends after the battle was touching in the extreme.

Cap. Farragut has proved himself a gallant commander & his letter to the Government is characterized by the modesty which also accompanies his merit.

As the fleet approached N.O., the warfs were crowded with the inhabitants gazing with wonder upon the intrepid little vessels what had so humbly met the horrors, prepare for their reception. A few handkerchiefs were waved in welcome, but the owners thereof were immediately shot down by the mob.

From the West, we learn that a severe battle is expected at Corinth. Beauregard is determined not to yield the place without hard fighting.

We have heard from Mrs. Bell. She is in Nashville. She says "do not believe any of the reports you hear about my husband."

It is said Mr. Bell is to be sent on here as one of two peace commissioners who are to negotiate terms with the Government.

May 30, 1862

Friday.

A call from Gen. Casey's daughters. They have heard from their Father. He was in good spirits when he wrote, but feared a severe encounter at Richmond.

The young ladies leave early on Monday for the North.

June 2, 1862

Monday.

Yesterday was clouded with the news of the terrible battle at Richmond. The Southerners attacked Gen. Casey's division, which gave way &, for a time, victory seemed to be in the hands of the South. But the Confederates were finally driven back into Richmond.

The slaughter on both sides is said to be terrible.

Gen. Casey is reported to be severely wounded, but Gov. is very reticent & it is impossible to know any thing certainly of the fate of our friends.

I feel very sorry for Gen. Casey. He is an old man & suffering so much from the death of his wife that any serious wound may prove fatal. He must be mortified too, that his division was the only one that gave way. He has been drilling troops all winter, sending them off as soon as they were ready for service & was finally ordered -- very suddenly -- with a body of raw recruits. He is a good Gen. I hope justice will be done him.

I took tea last night with Mrs. Hodges.

Mrs. Rodgers was rejoicing that her husband was not in the battle, but said she had no doubt he had paced the deck of his vessel all day with compunction that he could not have a hand in the affray.

Mrs. Marcy, the Mother of Mrs. McClellan, had been there with a note from the President, giving her the contents of the telegram from Gen McClel. It contains nothing more than I have mentioned.

No further particulars have been received to day. The paper contains only the telegram of the Gen. The news from the west is that Corinth has been evacuated.

Little Rock, Arkansas, is in possession of the Union troops.

June 3, 1862
Tuesday.
Gen. Casey's daughters were here this morning.

They came to thank Father & Mother for their invitation to come to us with their Father.

Gen. Casey is unhurt, but feels very badly about the behavior of his division. It is said. Will has just come in with the N.Y. papers. The battle took place at Seven pines, about five miles from Richmond. Many of Gen Caseys officers were disabled by illness & his troops were all more or less affected by the malarious atmosphere of the country, being fresh from the North & consequently not acclimated as were the other regiments.

Gen. Jackson is in retreat before the forces of Gen. Fremont.

June 7, 1862
Saturday.
Had a visit from Mr. Holt. He talked more than usual but said very little about the country. He thought it terrible that the insignificant race of negros should be the means of such ruin to the country. He is a good man I hope he will be our next president.

Gen. Casey's daughters have left for the North.

June 8, 1862
Monday.
Went to Mrs. Peales yesterday before church. Saw a poor woman who had come to Washington to learn something about her husband. He has been taken prisoner in the last engagement at Winchester.

June 13, 1862
Friday.
A visit from Mr. Welling. He thought the anticipated battle at Richmond would be probably the last great encounter we should have.

A guerrilla warfare might be maintained for ten years or more.

In the course of conversation, Father asked Mr. Welling if he knew Mr. Gibbs, the author of a hoax which had recently appeared in the papers concerning a petrified animal formed on the side of a hill with one set of legs shorter than the other.

Mr. W said he did not like such jokes that ridiculed the doctrine of final causes, a good doctrine & worthy of respect. Father of course believed in the doctrine, but thought it might be carried too far. He did not believe in being called to admire as beautiful designs of a Divine Providence what after all were only petty imagining of men

Mr. W said in his opinion, Philosophy argued that there was no design in nature, that things are as they are, from a simple necessity of their being. because an eye sees there was no necessity for supposing it was made for the purpose of seeing.

Father said that since, should he construct an instrument for seeing according to the known rules of optics, he should form one similar in all essential respects to the human eye, he could not but conclude that said eye was originally designed for the purpose of sight.

He said he was certain of the existence of our soul, at least in the universe, with a mind of his own & from this one fixed indisputable fact be reasoned from analogy, there were other minds like his own & then to the great controlling Intellect of the Diety.

Mr. W. spoke of the mind of the Hon. Mr.Mccan of Kentucky, the ablest man now in the senate. He had been a boatman until twenty one years of age.

Dr. Hays has just come under the window to tell us all the churches in the city are to be taken as hospitals.

June 14, 1862

Saturday.

A visit from Mrs. Calvert & Hon. Mr. Mallory of Kentucky. Mrs. Calvert had heard from her daughter, she was at Richmond. She married a son of Judge Campbell we saw her last spring just after the difficulties with the south commenced, she was very disconsolate then at being separated from her betrothed.

The papers contain the official report of Capt. Davis, our Cambridge friend. He gives a description of the naval conflict opposite Memphis. The "rams butting each other" seems to strike Father as very comical.

Cary had a letter from Mr. Harris yesterday. He was in New Orleans with a sprained ankle. He said he did not know the future destination of the fleet. The *Pensacola* would be left at N.O. as she was too much injured for use.

The report about the churchs has been confirmed. We are to have service tomorrow however. Such extensive preparations for the wounded excites some fear, either that bad news has been received or that the conflict at Richmond is expected immediately.

Some say Gen. McClellan is fighting them to day.

All Gen Fremont's wounded, 180 men, to be brought on here. Had a visit from Mr. Frank, a member of Congress this evening. He contradicts the report that the churches chosen for hospitals were selected on account of the disloyal sentiments of the parish & congregation.

June 16, 1862

Monday.

Our church has been spared.

The President told Dr. Gurley yesterday it should be left undisturbed as long as possible.[29]

I went in the afternoon to Dr. Halls to see the flowers. Service was over when I reached there. Most of the congregation had collected around the church & many persons were weeping bitterly at the loss of their church.

I could not give them much sympathy, as I thought their tears might better be shed for the poor fellows who were soon to be there.

Our servants were stopped on their way home from church by a train of cars with the wounded from Virginia.

Margaret said it was sad indeed to see the poor fellows, many of them with their arms & legs shot away. They were taken to the nearest churchs & public rooms as no arrangement had been made for their reception.

Many private houses were also thrown open to them while kind hearts & hands ministered to their comfort. The crowd around one of the churchs was so great that two, died from want of air. They were Father & son.

June 21, 1862

Saturday.

Baron Osten Sacken came to bid us "good bye." He has been appointed consul in N.Y. The little man told us to sell his horse for him if we could.

We thought this rather a singular commission to entrust to young ladies. We have been busy this week dressing dolls for a private fair for the benefit of the wounded soldiers.

June 25, 1862

Wednesday.

Went to the fair. It was very pleasant

---

[29] Though the Lincoln's never became a member of Dr. Gurley's church, the church to which Mary Henry was a member, Lincoln attended the church often and Gurley acted as the Lincoln's pastor throughout their time in Washington.

The Misses Kennedy had draped their dining room with flags where three tables one covered with flowers, one with Ices, & a third with fancy articles attracted purchasers.

In the garden, back of the houses, two tents had been spread & colored lights suspended from the trees.

All in attendance were invited guests.

Many of the Foreign Ministers were present. I had a very pleasant little talk with Madam Girol & the Brazilian minister.

They gave me their versions of the old story of the three wishes, both of which differ a little from ours.

Madame said she had long ago given up wishing, she was content now to let things take their course.

Her kind, merry face when she said this certainly looked as if the little Demon of Discontent had never obtained much power over her.

Gen. Pope was called away before the end of the evening on army business.

June 26, 1862

Went to the Kennedy's again. Found only ten or twelve people there besides ourselves. Dr. Rankin, who has charge of the hospital once Epiphany Church, told us he would be happy to show us his quarters any day.

June 27, 1862

Attended a party at Mr. Hodges given to the bride of his son.

Talked most of the evening with Eliza Wilks, but had a pleasant little chat with Com. Shubric & Mr. Stevens.

The party was very small. Jack Gillis asked me to go & visit some of his injured friends with him. To go mainly from curiosity seems unfeeling.

Learned from the Mr. Kennedy his daughters had made $300 by their Fair.

This morning we had a visit from Mr. Tyler. He said if Gen. McClelen's army was routed, Washington must fall into the hands of the Southerners. There was nothing to prevent Gen. Jackson's descent upon the city.

Mr. T. is a warm sympathizer with the South so some allowance must be made for his statements.

June 28, 1862

Rumors of a great battle, nothing certainly know. We have heard again from Mrs Bell. Sadly she says, "there are times when it is easier to die than to live." We have also heard from Dr. Woodhull.

I thought to the future of the army near Richmond. He said the shells of the enemy were falling around him while he wrote & one not long before had killed a poor soldier, whos Mother had left the camp only a few hours before, having traveled all the way from Boston to visit her son.

Father heard to day that Sec. Stanton[30] was to be replaced by Gen. Scott

June 30, 1862

The wounded were coming into the city all day yesterday. I counted 20 ambulances pass the church. 1500 are said to have arrived.

Had a visit from Mr. Welling. He thinks the prospects of the country very dark, very dark. He says we may fight until both sides are exhausted, then pause, only to renew the conflict.

Dr. Hays is now in a hospital at Georgetown, he told us to night he had had a visit from Miss Dix.

The news to night is that the White House has been evacuated by our troops.

We have lost all we gained in S.C.

James Island is again in possession of the Southerners.

Gen. Hunter wished to send his negro regiment there, but the white officers refused to serve with their black "brothers" one soldier was sent home for refusing to attend their dusky majesties.

It is rumored that two of the Foreign Ministers have interfered to put a stop to this war.

England's aspect is still menacing, Lord Palmerston's condemnation of the order of Gen Butler that all the women in New Orleans to the soldiers should be treated as harlot was very severe[31].

It is difficult to understand the state of affairs near Richmond On Wednesday Friday & Saturday the fighting was severe with heavy loss on both sides.

Gen. McClellan is now between the Chickahominy & Pamunkey rivers & has obtained possession of a point which is said to command Richmond.

He made a very difficult flank movement on Friday to reduce the extent of his line which was 25 miles in length so that his army is in a better position now, but his loss on Friday & Saturday was very heavy. He has not enough troops.

---

[30] Secretary of War. Stanton was never replaced.

[31] Once capturing the southern city of New Orleans, General Benjamin Butler issued an order referred to as the "Woman Order," which instructed his troops to treat any woman in the city who insulted them "as a harlot." The order sent shockwaves around the globe. Butler's order acted as a rallying cry in the South and nearly served as the tipping point for Britain to enter the war on the side of the Confederacy.

Government has issued an order for an addition of 300,000 to be raised from the different states. I should think the fate of the Richmond army must be decided before these are fit for service.

Gen Shields is to have charge of the new recruits I believe.

Gen. Rodgers has gone down the James river as far as the chickahominy in order to keep open communications with the army in case of an attack on the right.

We have had a French clergyman with us for two days.

Taddy Lincoln, the President's son was here yesterday to see Will about a buggy for his pony.

He seems to be quite a bright child. He took pains to inform the girl who answered the door who he was. He has learned his own importance it seems. Mother went with G on Monday to Columbia college, now a hospital.

One of the wounded a mere boy interested her very much He was only sixteen years of age. Cary has been collecting books to day to send to him.

July 3, 1862

Thursday.

Mr. Welling has just left us. He saw the Count de Paris to day.

The Count says that the army before Richmond is full of hope & courage, but out numbered by the Southerners, who have three times as many men.

He arrived in Washington to day & Mr. Welling thinks he has seen enough of the war for the present. The papers announced, yesterday, he had taken a prisoner.

Mr. W. asked Father's opinion of the President's plan for liberating the slaves. Father approved of colonization[32]. He thought the experiment ought to be tried. Tut to liberate the negro, before they are ready for freedom, or ever in this country, was certain death to the race.

The state of Finances was discussed. Mr. W. said the currency had deteriorated 10 per cent or to use the popular phrase was "10 per cent above par."

---

[32] A predominate belief held by many in this era, regardless of geography, was that blacks and whites could not live in harmony together. A solution to this supposed problem was to colonize Liberia, a nation founded in part by nineteenth century American leaders, Benjamin Butler stated that Lincoln, in 1865, firmly denied that "racial harmony" would ever be possible in the United States. In addition to Liberia, new evidence now suggests President Lincoln made attempts to colonize freedmen in British Honduras after the Emancipation Proclamation took effect on January 1, 1863.

Sec. Chase has declared the war must be carried on, it cannot stop even if we have to pay $100 for a breakfast.

Father says in the time of the Revolution, paper money went down to 1,000 for one.

Mr. W. says Mr. Pearce is suffering very much from gout.

Father has been giving us a speech of Lord B since Mr. W left. It is rather prosy, but closes with some favorite lines of Father's which he is now reading with great gusto.

July 4, 1862

The Nation's Birth Day. 86 years old.

Loving America, still compared with the grey heading countrys of the Eastern world.

Laugh low little children, restrain your mirth on this her holiday.
She is young, but the Fever heat of war is upon her.
Do you hear her heart beats? They are quick & heavy.
Will she die? God only knows.

1,048 wounded have come in to day. They were engaged in the battle of Friday.

We went to the steamboat landing this evening, after most of them had been brought off the boats. Saw two or three who had been slightly wounded. One poor fellow was without an arm. We hoped to learn something of A.W. & other of our friends, but could hear nothing.

We were amused by some contrabands[33] who came off one of the vessels. Their importance & the air of conscious elegance with which one of them sported an old cap off her mistress was very comical.

The expression of one of them touched me.

She was pressing her ebony babe to her bosom with a mother's fondness & a timid anxious look, as if the comfort & security of her old Virginia house was illy paid for by her long coveted liberty.

We have passed the day very quietly.

All the bells in the city rang out a merry peal at noon & again at sundown, but with the exception of a few rockets, there have been no fireworks.

Father amused us at the breakfast table by telling us that for sixteen years he suffered from cold in a certain part of his northern limbs. In consequence of both drawers & shorts being rather short, but one happy

---

[33] Civil War era term used in the United States military to describe escaped slaves.

day, the bright thought struck him that by lengthening the former, the difficulty might be obviated.

Could a philosopher with his thoughts in Heaven attend to any thing so subject as the calves of his legs?

Father says I must insert this in his memoir if I can write it. I jot it down in my journal. Instead, Mother says I shall not, as is a reflection upon her.

Mother is writing to Mrs. Bell to night. She has spent many a pleasant Fourth with us, we have missed her to day.

Father says Mother should not monopolize the paper & pens & has scribbled a letter to his "old wife" which she will not let me read[34]. He has seized it & torn it up much to Mother's vexation. He looks more like a mischievous school boy just now than a philosopher.

There is very little news from the war quarter to night.

Gen. McClellan is now on the James River about 15 or 20 miles from Richmond. His force is by no means sufficient. The Count de Paris Duke de Chartres & the Prince de Joinville have arrived with dispatches. They have endeared themselves to their comrades by their affability.

Capt. Farragut has passed Vicksburg & is now in communication with Davis & Gen. Halleck so the whole river is open.

The Intelligencer contains a letter from Gen Hunter, saying he considered himself authorized in organizing his negro regiment by the orders given to his predecessor, Gen. Sherman. That all loyal persons were to be employed for the Government as he should see fit. No mention being made of the color of the person.

Mrs. Hunter does not approve of the proceedings of her husband.

July 5, 1862

A visit from Mr. & Mrs. Bates. Father & Casey have gone to escort them home.

Mr. Egleston has been here to tell us about Dr. Hay's hospital. He has charge of the one in Georgetown. 100 came to him to day. He has room for 100 more.

Epiphany church is full.

We are to go up to the observatory on Monday evening to make bandages.

The flank movement of Gen McClellan in the face of the enemy is spoken of as a great military achievement. His front extends over a line of thirty miles & he had, besides, to guarde the railroad to White House. His forces are now more compact, although 25 miles from Richmond. He was

---

[34] This appears to be a joke, as Joseph Henry married Harriet Alexander, his cousin, at the age of 23. No additional evidence exists of a previous wife.

prevented from taking a position on the James river before, by the presence of the *Merrimac*.

July 10, 1862

Thursday.

Mrs. Valtre, daughter of Sec. Smith, is to have a fair to night for the benefit of the hospitals.

No additional news from the army.

Gen. McClellan's flank movement in the face of the enemy seems in some quarters to be considered a very brilliant achievement. Our loss is great.

July 12, 1862

Saturday.

We passed yesterday at Bladensburg. We went to attend the commencement of the Agricultural college.

We left home in the early morning train.

Mrs. Calvert sent her carriage to meet us at the depot. The little shed used for that purpose hardly deserves the name, however. I remembered it well, for several hours passed there with Father & Sec. Thompson[35], two or three years ago, had impressed it vividly upon my memory.

It was when the college was first organized & Father & the Sec. had been called upon for addresses. We had expected a certain train to stop for us & convey us home but it voyaged past us apparently unconscious of our existence, so we were obliged to wait for one more accommodating.

The Sec. was a rough specimen of humanity, but apparently kind hearted.

The young collegians acquitted themselves well. Their speeches were followed by an address from the Rev. Mr. Pickering & Mr. Underwood, the President of the college.

A ball in the evening was pleasant ,but we enjoyed rambling over Mr. Calvert's beautiful place more than anything else.

Mr. Mallory & Mr. Holt came out shortly after tea.

We did not see Mr. Calvert in the morning, he was obliged to attend a meeting of members of congress called unexpectedly by the President.

We reached home at noon to day. Mr. Welling was our escort.

July 14, 1862

Monday.

---

[35] Jacob Thompson, Secretary of the Interior under President Buchanan. Served as Inspector General of the Confederate States Army.

Went to visit the camps with Mr. Lee of Princeton. Crossed over the Long Bridge --- a rail road has been laid over it for the benefit of the soldiery ---- visited several forts & returned by the aqueduct bridge.

We also stopped at Arlington House[36]. A number of the trees have been cut down, but the property does not seem to be otherwise injured. Several companies of soldiers, some drilling in the lawn in front of the house. The country every where looks very desolate, fences have been destroyed & no trace whatever is left of civilization.

There seem to be very few men left for the defence of the city . All who can be spared have been sent to reenforce Gen. McC.

The Forts are in excellent condition. Neatly furnished & kept in good order. A long low building attracted our attention, which we were told was a hospital for horses.

July 17, 1862
Thursday.

Went to Epiphany church to hear Miss May sing. She had been asked to do so for the pleasure of the sick soldiers. It is the first time we have been in the hospitals. We were very much pleased with the appearance of the men. The room looked very pleasant with its rows of iron bedsteads covered with white quilts. The men are improving rapidly.

Miss May sang in the gallery. There had been a flag raising & a treat of ice cream also before dark for the amusement of the soldiers.

July 19, 1862
Saturday.

Went to the Baptist church hospital with Annie Kennedy. A little drummer boy interested me. He was only fifteen years old.

July 20, 1862
Sunday.

Went to the hospital again in the Baptist Church to take a book to the drummer boy. The wounded there are rapidly recovering.

July 21, 1862
Monday.

Two Cubans passed the evening with us. Some fears are entertained that Southerners may cut off communication with the army. They are said to be collecting in considerable numbers on the James river below Gen McClellan.

---

[36] Home of Robert E. Lee, he abandoned the home to fight for the Confederacy.

July 26, 1862

Saturday.

The guns at the Navy Yard paid their tribute to the memory of Martin Van Buren. The ex president was buried to day.

July 29, 1862

A letter from Mr. Harris.

He says Com. Farragut is in rather a bad position.

Vicksburg will not yield, the canal cannot be dug which was to head off the river from her & the water of the Mississippi is now so low the fleet cannot return.

Went to see Hase's hospital in the hotel at Georgetown. The men seemed well attended. One poor man had been terribly wounded, a ball having passed into his cheek, out again through his shoulder & out of his back. He was doing well, thanks to the good nursing of Dr. Hase.

I felt very sorry for one poor home sick fellow, his sick mother had written a letter to the doctor entreating him to use his influence to procure her son a furlough.

August 2, 1862

Saturday.

 Read to Father from Russell's Journal in India, Father said the great desert principally owing to the great extent of level plain with no deviation to condense the moisture the air might contain – the atmosphere continually growing hotter as it approaches the tropics. "Very little moisture the air must contain, I should think, for the most of that derived from the Pacific must be condensed by the mountains of Asia & that from the Mediterranean by the Atlas Mountains & the ranges in Tripoli."

Father spoke of Hail stones - Said he had discovered how the nucleus was formed. He filled a glass globe or bulb with water & placed it out in the cold air, as the water froze, the bubbles of air retreated from the exterior which was of course first affected by the cold to the center of the globe & there, finally, formed the foamy white appearance of the nucleus of the hailstone. The rings sometimes observed in hail stone were a repetition of the same process.

August 4, 1862

Monday.

A very remarkable Aurora. Father has enjoyed it greatly. The flashes of light rolling up to the zenith were very beautiful Father noticed a considerable effect produced upon a small electrical apparatus he has in the parlor.

August 5, 1862

Tuesday.

We are all troubled to night about the Drafting. 300,000 men are called for in addition to the 300,000 volunteers already demanded.

The States are ordered to proceed to drafting, I suppose immediately.

Very little is known now about the movements of the Southerners at Richmond.

There is a lull in the storm, but the quiet is portentous. The usual rumors that the Capitol is in danger are afloat, but we pay, but little heed to them.

August 6, 1862

Wednesday.

Gen. Casey has just left us. He said his position was a false one in the battle of Seven Pines, He had in vain remonstrated against it. He had crossed the Chickahominy, was in advance of the army & to use his own expression, "like a wedge in the enemys country."

The sides of his division entirely unprotected.

The engagement was on the 31st. Two days his men had been busy digging rifle pits & forming abatti. He was on the alert, for he learned through a reconnaissance that the cars had been moving rapidly to & fro on the Richmond end of the rail road all day on the 30th & some of his pickets had captured one of Gen. Johnston's aids.

On the morning of the 31st, his pickets were attacked. He, at first, thought this would prove a slight skirmish, as several such had taken place the day before, but he was quickly undeceived. A vidette was sent to inform him the Southerners had arrived in force.

He quickly called in his labourers, stationed his men in the rifle pits & behind the abattis. On the Confederates came, bravely unshrinkingly.

The artillery mowed down long lines in their ranks, but these were immediately closed over. Seeing he must lose his guns, Gen Casey ordered a charge boldly & well did the men do their duty driving the enemy back 200 yds.

Overpowered, at last, by superior numbers, Gen Casey was at last obliged to fall back upon Gen Couch's division. This gave way & retreated to the line commanded by Gen Heintzelman which would also have yielded if it had not been for the timely reenforcement of Sherman.

August 29, 1862

Sykesville[37]

Friday.

I have not written in my journal lately because we have been very busy preparing to leave home.

In regard to war matters, there has been little to record -- nothing was known for some time of Gen McClellan's movement, except that he had left his position after the battle of Malvern Hill & was expected to join Gen Pope.

We left home for this place yesterday.

In the cars we met an intelligent officer who gave us an account of the battle of Malvern Hill. He seemed to think it the most desperate that had yet been fought. He told us the southern troops had possession of Mannassas & would probably drive the Federal troops behind their entrenchment at Alexandria. He said our men were worn out with fighting & sickness.

The news to day is that Gen. Lee, with his cavalry, had not only taken Mannassas but Centreville. Gen Pope & Gen Burnside are beyond Mannassas & must cut their way through Gen. Lee's forces in order to reach the main body of the army.

Gen. McClellan has been in Alexandria for a day or two. He had an interview last evening with the President. He has again been made commander in chief of the army of the Patomac.

August 30, 1862

Saturday.

Gen. Pope's official dispatch was in the paper this morning He is again in communication with the main body of the army.

The Southerners have evacuated Mannassas & fallen back from Centerville.

Gen. McClellan's army at Alexandria has advanced to the assistance of Pope.

Went to the village with our host, Mr. Bear. He says the rocks split only North & South, East & West. Father does not agree with him. He thinks the Potato rot is due to too much heat & moisture when the potato is fully ripe Father thinks these concomitent circumstances, but that there is a veritable disease in the potatoe.

September 1, 1862

Monday.

We awaited the arrival of the paper with great anxiety. It contained Gen. Pope's official dispatch. Mannassas seems destined to hold a

---

[37] A community in northern Maryland.

conspicuous place in this war. The whole body of the southerners engaged Gen. Pope's army there on Thursday, not far from the scene of the battle of last year.

Jackson was driven back towards the mountains on Friday & Pope remained master of the field, but receiving reinforcements during the night, the Southerners again attacked the Federalists & drove them back to Centreville on Saturday.

Franklin & Sumner have joined Pope there, so he is now strong in men & position. Our loss in the recent battles is said to be 17,000 in killed & wounded, on Friday we lost 8,000. Mr. Pace writes that the little Falls bridge has been taken down by order of Government authorities, for fear an attempt may be made to cross there. The city was in a state of intense excitement on Friday & Saturday.

September 2, 1862
Tuesday.

A beautiful morning after yesterday's rain.

The Secessionist report that Banks has been taken.

Lee was stationed at Fredericksburg. We are looking forward with eagerness to the arrival of the mails.

September 4, 1862
Thursday.

Father left yesterday for Wash. The news from there is of thrilling interest.

The report that Gen. McClellan has been made commander in chief of the army of the Potomac is false. He has command of only one division. Gen Howell is in command of the whole.

Our troops have been driven back & are now in the forts about the city & in Alexandria.

Pope & McDowell are in disgrace & Gen McClellan is in charge of the defenses of the City. No cars have come from Harper's Ferry to day. I hope Father will come before those from Baltimore cease to run.

The Company is afraid to send out trains lest they may fall into the hands of the Confederates who are advancing rapidly. Fredericksburg is theirs.

September 5, 1862
Friday.

Went to a country ball at the hotel in Sykesville. Expected to be much amused therewith, but was uneasy about Father.

The Hotel looks upon the rail road & I took my station at the window to watch. Hour after hour passed, but still no train.

At last, a distant whistle, a low rumble made my heart beat nearer & nearer. It came, but in the wrong direction -- a burden train, shot by us, laden with soldiery, their arms flashing in the moon light. Then loud shouts as they passed feebly echoed by the men & boys on the platform.

What did this retrograde movement mean? Are the enemy advancing so rapidly that Baltimore was in danger? The moments seemed long now. Would the train never come!

The dancers kept time to the fiddles in the Dinner Hall. The moonlight fell softly & through the trees on the bank opposite. Would the train ever come?

Hark was that a whistle. I was not mistaken this time.

The distant rumble grew louder, a dull red light gleamed through the trees. The Iron Horse stood smoking & panting by the platform & Father was by my side. It was the last train that came out.

The City is much less excited than might be expected under the circumstances. Father saw Mrs. Gen. Franklin. She is greatly incensed against Pope who accuses her husband of having disobeyed his orders.

No fears were entertained at head quarters of a further advance of the enemy at present.

September 8, 1862
Monday.

No mails. We can know nothing certainly of the movement of the Enemy. Some of the farmers are driving their cattle to places of greater safety. We are cut off from all communication with our friends. We shall leave as soon as we can procure a conveyance.

September 9, 1862
Tuesday.

The Confederate pickets are within four miles of us & spies are said to have been in the village yesterday. A party of Cavalry were entertained at a farm house about two miles from here last night.

We are surrounded by secessionists here.

Mother is troubled & nervous. She will be glad to get away. The hills before me in their quiet beauty. I am off for a ramble. We are to take tea with the clergyman of the place this evening

12 p.m.

Just called in to prepare for our departure. Father has hired an open wagon to take us to Ellicott's Mills. It will be here in an hour.

September 11, 1862
Thursday.

We found our ride to Ellicott's Mills very pleasant. The road lies through such a beautiful country.

We had four miles to go before we reached the turnpike. Just as we left Sykesville, we were mot by two rebel scouts who asked us whether we had met any Federal pickets[38]. They were ragged and forlorn in dress.

Our little wagon was well crowded with our trunks & ourselves, but bore the load well.

We were told we would probably meet the Federal pickets on our way, but we saw nothing of them.

Spent the night in Baltimore at the _____ Hotel.

Saw Gen Wool who came into the parlor with several other Officers. He stood by the centre table for some time reading telegrams. He looks very infirm & his eye is dull & listless. There is very little of the fire of a soldier about him.

Col. ____ spent part of the evening with us. He said he knew nothing of the movement of the troops at Washington or of Gen. McClellan's intentions. The secessionist in Baltimore, as well as the unionists, were in great alarm, lest Jackson should come upon Baltimore. The city could be very easily shelled from their fortifications and would certainly be destroyed should such an event take place.

A company of cavelry started on a reconnoitering expedition. We saw the officers preparing in the Hall (one of them had been my neighbor at the supper table) & heard the clatter of the horses hoofs on the pavement as they rode away.

If it were possible to forget the nature of their errand, they must have enjoyed the ride as it was a beautiful moonlight night.

Gen Wood has charge of this region as far as Harper's Ferry I believe.

We left Baltimore in the early train. Passed the night in Philadelphia & reached here at 3 o'clock to day. We are about 15 miles from Phil. in a pretty rural spot, but I miss the hills.

September 12, 1862

Friday 12th.

A cloudy day. Spent the morning on reading one of Cooper's Novels aloud.

September 13, 1862

Saturday. Philadelphia in a state of great excitement. Hagerstown in possession of the Southerners the enemy advancing into Pennsylvania.

---

[38] A "picket" was a sentinel, serving as the eyes and ears of the army. They were posted very close to the enemy and were responsible for noting any movements.

Every able bodied man ordered to arm & equip himself. for the defense of the city. A number of troops sent to Harrisburg.

September 15, 1862

Monday. A battle at Middleton, not far from Frederick, the southerners defeated.

Gen. McClellan had command of our forces. The number of killed & wounded is not definitely known, but the Confederates seem to have suffered more than our troops.

The enemy is retreating. Col Reno is killed. Frederick was taken some days ago, but is now abandoned, the confederates having bought out all the merchants paying them with Confederate scrip, but not injuring property.

The troops was in a deplorable condition when they entered the town, ragged and almost starved.

A gentleman before we left Sykesville told us he saw some one of their captains on horse back with spurs strapped to their bare heels.

About 700 Marylanders were added to their forces before they left. Others came to enlist, but were discouraged by the appearance of the troops. Philadelphia is very jubilant over the victory.

September 16, 1862

Tuesday. The news to day is that Harper's Ferry is in possession of the Southerners.

Gen. Miles[39], who was in command there, was killed.

September 17, 1862

Wednesday.
Another battle near Frederick results unknown.

October 19, 1862

Willie died on Friday[40] - was buried yesterday.

December 6, 1862

Sat.

---

[39] Dixon S. Miles was a career United States Army officer who served in the Mexican-American War and the Indian Wars prior to the Civil War. He was mortally wounded as he surrendered his Union garrison in the Battle of Harpers Ferry.

[40] William Alexander Henry, born in 1831, was the brother of Mary Henry and served as a clerk and copyist for the Smithsonian's library. Henry died of jaundice after returning from a vacation with his family.

Father asked me to write down all that I remembered of Will's death, I could not do so before.

He died on Friday, Oct. 17th 1862.

On Friday a week before, a note came to Princeton for Father from Mr. Rheese, which I opened as Father was with Mother and Carry in New York. The note was about Smithsonian affairs, but mentioned, casually, that Will had been slightly indisposed.

Uncle and Will advised me not to forward the letter, as Father was to be in Princeton again in a few days and it was not worth while to trouble Mother about Will when he was probably better by the time the letter reached us.

I had been greatly disappointed at not finding Will when we reached Princeton & troubled for fear, the change from the pure air of Princeton to the malarious atmosphere of Washington might make him sick, but still Mr. Rheese's words did not cause me much uneasiness.

On Tuesday evening, as we were at tea, Carry came in, much to our surprise, alone. Father & Mother she said had received a telegram on Sunday morning informing that Will was very ill. They could not leave until evening.

On Monday, Cary's anxiety was relieved by a telegram & afterwards by a letter, saying Will had been very sick, but that he was then convalescent & there was no need of returning home.

Another letter came from Mother the next morning, Wed., telling us Will was still very sick.

I left the next morning, Nell & Cary yielding to the desire expressed in Mother's letter, to the opinion of the physician & Uncle's advice, remaining until frost should make it safer for them to return home.

Thinking Will still convalescent, we all thought it wrong for them to risk their health when there was no necessity for so doing.

Mrs. Blaney was my traveling companion, Dr. Blaney met us at the Depot & kindly took me home.

Clemy De Burt opened the door for me. I asked how Will was. He said, "his voice is failing."

I went up stairs, into the dining room, the house looked vile & desolate. I dreaded to have Mother come in. It was some time before she came, but when she did, her face reassured me. She did not seem frightened about him.

Father also, when he came in shortly after, did not appear alarmed. After a little while, Mother said I might see him, I was not prepared for the change in him. It was a terrible shock, but the smile he gave me was inexpressibly sweet. I can never, never, forget it.

His hand was so thin, so damp & cold, I thought he was dying. I had to kneel down & lean my forehead on it to hide my tears.

He stroked my hair said "she looks well," "See her tomorrow" I was afraid to stay longer for fear of tiring him.

He was very restless after that, requiring to be moved from one bed to another every 10 or 15 min. Hannah & Henry, the Watchman, carrying him like a child. The Dr. had left some medicine to quiet him, but it seemed to have the contrary effect.

About one o'clock, we left him to Hannah's & Henry's care.

Towards morning, he was very much worse. We sent for the Dr. as soon as possible. He said perhaps we had better send for Nell & Carry. We telegraphed immediately.

When I went in to him, he was lying on the bed in Mother's room. Henry was fanning him. He motioned to me to take the fan said "Henry sit down --- tired" He spoke with great difficulty we could hardly understand him. Henry left us, them & Father & Mother, went in to breakfast.

He had been quiet for some time & seemed to be sleeping. I sat motionless for fear of disturbing him. His breathing frightened me after a while, it was so very peculiar & his eyes were only half closed. He roused up when Mother came in, I think it was about this time Dr. Elliot came.

He administered a dose of medicine at Will's own suggestion, which he thought might quiet him.

When the Dr. came out of the room, Mother & I went in. Will lay quietly for a short time & then started, suddenly, upright with a wild look in his eyes, crying out "Oh they are chaining him. They are taking father!"

Mother held him down with difficulty, while I ran to call Father.

He was himself again in a few moments & asked to be moved into the next room. Then to a couch in the same room, the corner room. He was quiet a little while there & Father went into talk to him. He said, "my son, life is very uncertain. We know not what the issue of your illness may be You must trust in the mercy of God in Christ."

Will pressed his hand, said, "I know. I do. I wish I was as well prepared as you my Father."

He heard Mother's step then, & said "not now, some other time," fearing to pain her.

Father asked if he would like to see Dr. Gurley. He said, "yes."

Father asked him shortly after if he would not like to be shaved. He seemed very eager for it, I think because he thought it would please Father.

Mr. De Bust was sitting by his bed, then, he asked him if he would go for the barber, insisting, first, with his usual thoughtfulness upon knowing whether he had had his break fast.

After that, he was moved from bed to bed continually, answering all our entreaties that he would remain quiet with his plaintive "move me" "Please move me" "Please, wont you move me?"

I left the room at last, thinking the fewer there were there, the more chance there would be of his sleeping.

I placed myself where I could see him & hand Mother what she wanted when he was not being moved. We were giving him stimulants. Every now & then he would look at his hands & feel one with the other. I had not been long out of the room before he called me. He wanted me to bathe his head with cologne. I did so, while mother prepared his stimulants.

At one time, he was a little delirous, refusing to take any unless Mr. Bust gave it to him or unless Mr. De Bust said he must.

He called again & again for Mr. De. B. so we sent for him. He was quiet then & took the Brandy & Ice Cream Mother had prepared for him.

Mr. De Bust raising him up, seemed to choke him. He fell back on the pillow & ceased to breath for several seconds. I thought he was dead. A deep sigh presently told us he was not.

I heard Father & Dr. Elliot in the entry & called them.

When Dr. E. came to his bed side, he was better. The Dr. told him to hold out his arm at full length, he did so.

When he came out, the Dr. told us he had still considerable strength & might yet be spared to us – this was only 1 half hour before he died.

The Dr. promised to be back in an hour, he had other patients & could not stay with us.

Mother & Hannah then made some change in Will's dress & yielding to his entreaty of "move me" "Please move me just once more" laid him upon the large bed in the corner room. Father opened the window & said "look out Will. See what a beautiful day it is?"

He did look out & said eagerly "yes! yes!"

Father went into the next room then to talk to Prof. Baird & I followed to hear what he was saying about Will.

Hannah called "Miss Mary he is calling for Mary, Mary Henry." I ran back to his bed side. He said "put it under me, all under me" mean the sheet I suppose & his clothes all had become disordered by his restlessness. For when Mother smoothed them, He seemed satisfied. I bathed his head with cologne & putting my lips near his ear sang to him in a low tone. Choosing the chorus to a children's hymn:

For well I know that Jesus died For sinners such as I
What does all the world beside That I should prize so high

He grew quiet as soon as I commenced to sing. Mother went away then to get him something, leaving me alone with him.

I continued singing some time in a low voice, thinking he was asleep, but his breathing soon frightened me as it had done in the morning. It was growing slower & slower.

I went into the next room to call Father & Prof. Baird. Prof. Baird took his seat by the bed side to feel his pulse. I knew by his face that he thought Will dying.

We put hot ____ to his feet. His mouth was partly open, Mother put Brandy between his lips. He swallowed two or three teaspoon fulls & his pulse, for a few moments, grew stronger.

Then Father drew Mother away, she broke away from him & came back presently crying "why don't some one call Willie! Where's Willie!"

I had taken the cup & spoon from Mother & was on the opposite side of the bed from Prof Baird. Will's breath was growing slower & slower.

He swallowed one more spoon full of brandy. He breathed two or three times more softly. I could hear nothing then & asked Prof Baird with my eyes if he were dead. Prof Baird bowed assent, but I put one more spoonful of brandy in his mouth thinking it might not be so.

Mother & I closed his eyes, the expression of his face was exquisitely peaceful. It was about 11 o'clock when he died.

December 13, 1862

It is almost three months since I have made any entries in my journal, excepting the sad one of last Sat.

When I last wrote, Phil. was in an intense state of excitement, fearing the city might be invaded.

The ship of State, seemed driven master less before the adverse winds of Fate. Gen McClellan was called to the Helm once more. The battles of Antietam & South Mountain reassured the wavering self confidence of the people & again the cry "onward to Richmond rose from the conquering unionists.

A brilliant raid of the Southern Gen. Stewart next excited the admiration of friend & foe. Making the entire circuit of our army, carrying off horses, cattle, food & clothing, he vanished as quickly as he came.

Leaving our astonished soldiers grasping their muskets only in time to hear the retiring clatter of his horse's heels.

Skillfully had the Helmsman guided the Ship of State. Bravely had he headed the adverse winds & waves of Fate. But the vessel was at Anchor now the Nation, impatient, could not understand why her sails should not always be filled, her prow always cutting the waves of Victory. Forgetful of the repairs her storm beaten ship required. The helmsman was denounced.

Gen McClellan was deposed & Gen. Burnside given the command of the army of the Patomac.

On the eve of a great battle for which he had been preparing for weeks & which he had hoped would decide the affairs of the Nation, it was a bitter trial to the brave officers to be thus unreasonably deprived of his authority. When he received the unexpected tidings, his only words were "I was so certain of success."

Burnside superseded his friend with great reluctance McClellan, was closeted with him for several hours before he left the camp, giving him all the information & such knowledge of his plans as he thought might be useful to him.

The parting of the Gen., with his men, was touching in the extreme. They crowded round him to shake his hand & eager for some parting words & when his receding form made them realize they were losing their beloved commander, they ran to him with tears & lamentations, crying "come back to us McClellan! come back to us McClellan!"

The army has since been on the Rappahannock, opposite Fredericksburg, which is in possession of the enemy.

The news yesterday & the day before was that our army had crossed the river, fired the city & that the Southerners had retired.

Congress has commenced.

The President's message is flat.

The principal point in it is the renewed recommendation of the second clause of his Proclamation, relative to the gradual emancipation of the slaves.

Sec. Seward in his report recommends several methods of preventing the too great inflation of the currency. One is by taxing bank note issues, another by forming bank companies for the issue of Government notes, in other words, a great national bank with branches. Gold is now worth 30 per cent.

Photograph of Joseph Henry, 1879 by Henry Ulke

Father has grown touchingly gentle since Will's death. He speaks of him quietly & cheerfully, but we can see that it is telling upon him. He has given us several talks lately upon architecture. He was the first to introduce that study in Princeton college. He had models of temples made & other facilities contrived for the improvement of the pupils, but afterwards gave up the department to Prof Dod. Will enjoyed a similar talk last summer.

The lectures have commenced. We have had two from a Prof from Toronto, entitled "Unwritten History."

The insolent lecture committee applyed for the room, but were refused.

Will was very useful to Father lecture nights.

I commenced a head of Father to day in clay. Father looked in upon me about noon & seemed much amused at the singular mass I expected one day to look something like him. He left his work one bright day last week to have photographs taken for me.

December 15, 1862

Monday.

Yesterday was a day of excitement. We learned, after church, that the fighting at Fredericksburg had been very severe. 5,000 of our men killed.

Gen Bayard, a promising young officer, lost his life. He was to have been married next Thursday to Miss Bowman, daughter of the superintendent at West Point.

From nine o'clock until after three to day, we heard the distant booming of cannon. It is conjectured that a division of troops under Gen Slocum sent to reenforce Burnside may have been intercepted by the enemy.

I met M. Gurley on the Avenue this afternoon. He said he had just come from Willard's Hotel & had seen a wounded officer brought in. He was a tall fine looking man, but was very badly injured in the head. He said we had been caught in a trap & badly whipped.

The Star to night, says that our loss is greater than was first announced, that our men are not yet within the city, but have only taken the first line of fortifications on the other side of the river. Our loss is estimated at nearly 10,000. That of the enemy, very small.

We met Mrs. Harris this afternoon. She was with Mrs. Gen Sumner. The poor lady was nearly frantic, her husband, two sons, & son in law being all at Fredericksburg. She cannot expect them all to escape. ----- We have had another lecture from Prof. Wilson on "Unwritten History."

December 18, 1862

Thursday.   Our troops have been driven back across the river. The retreat was made without loss, but the numbers killed in the attempt to take the town & fortifications is immense; 10,000 wounded & dying strewed the battle field. It is terrible to think so much blood should be shed in vain.

Dr. Parker was here to day. He said Gen Burnside, Franklin & others had sent a petition to the President, protesting against the crossing of the river, but in spite of their remonstrances, they were ordered to do so by the President & Sec. of War.

The rebels seem to have lost but little. This battle of Fredericksburg

PHOTO: Union soldiers prepared for burial, following the Battle of Fredericksburg.

seems to have been the most bloody yet fought.

We met Mrs. Harris on the street yesterday, she was with Mrs. Sumner her husband, two sons & son in law were also in the fight. She was almost wild with anxiety.

We had a visit from Madame de Linburg & Miss Pleasant. The latter spoke with great affection of Will, she saw him often with James B. Henry.

December 19, 1862

Friday 19th.

A visit from Mrs. Hunter. She had heard indirectly from Mrs. Bell. Col. Bell was in Richmond, he had gone there to negotiate for peace. Mrs. Bell will probably lose all her property.

December 20, 1862

Sat.

Father has gone to the club.

The news to night is that Seward & Chase have both resigned & the rest of the Cabinet will probably follow their example[41].

It is said that Gen. Burnside has also tendered his resignation. Halleck is blamed by the President for the misfortunes at Fredericksburg. Blair also is said to have resigned. --- Mr. McIntyre has just left us. He came last night from the army opposite Fredericksburg where his brother is lying sick. He said he came in a train of cars with the wounded. He could not endure the distressing spectacle inside the cars & mounted on top of one of them. He was there obliged to seat himself upon a coffin & was in constant fear of breaking in upon its dead occupant.

The groans of the poor suffers below him was harrowing in the extreme. Most of the wounded are to be brought to Washington.

He said he went to an eminence from whence he could see the position of the enemy's fortifications & was completely astonished that any attempt to take them in ways the proposed should ever have been conceived.

---

[41] December 1862 may very well have been the Lincoln Administration's most difficult month. At the commencement of the Civil War, few could have imagined the level of bloodshed that would soon follow. Ownership of the war fell straight upon Lincoln, resulting in the Republican Party suffering substantial losses in the 1862 mid-term Congressional elections. The following month, two of Lincoln's cabinet secretaries resigned, the Secretary of War and Secretary of Interior. The outgoing Secretary of War, Simon Cameron, was forced to resign in shame following revelations of an alleged corrupt bargain he made with President Lincoln for the position. Speaking of the outgoing secretary, a Pennsylvania congressman stated, "That man would steal a red-hot stove."

Three tiers of fortifications half encircle the city, the river flowing in front, of course, when our men crossed, they were at the mercy of the southern guns which fired on them from the front, the right, & the left.

"In to the jaws of death rushed" our brave thousand at the senseless command of those, who refusing to listen to the protest of their brave hearts in command, thus recklessly sacrificed the blood of their country to their witless impetuosity & ambition.

Mr. McIntyre said the soldiers seemed but little affected by the loss of their comrades. They have grown reckless & indifferent.

We learned to day that all Mrs. Gen. Sumner's relations escaped. Our troops have captured Kingstown N.C.

December 21, 1862

Monday.

Admiral Davis was here last evening. He is going back to Cambridge to spend the Holidays.

We had a visit also from Mr. Wyncoop.

Dr. Stone, the sculpter, walked home with us from Bible class. He is a physician now in the Patent Office Hospital

He does not seem to admire the new statue of Franklin by Powers. When we asked him how he liked it, he said, very vainly, he did not think it equal to his own.

He said he could never forget the material of which the statue was made. It troubled him to think such an immense amount of marble should be supported by two such slender columns as the legs. Father was pleased with the criticism He said our ideas of proper proportion & beauty in architecture must be modified by our consciousness of the material employed.

An entirely different style being required for iron columns from that used in marble buildings.--- Another lecture to night on "Unwritten History," the last of the course.

The lecturer came in to our part of the building, after the lecture. also Gen Casey, Dr Bacon, Prof Hopkins, Mr McPherson, & his bride.

December 22, 1862

Father read aloud this evening an account of a discovery of a man who had succeeded in forming an organic substance out of inorganic[42]. It troubled me somewhat, for I thought if organic substances were thus

---

[42] Later proven to be untrue. The idea of "spontaneous generation" was a false school of thought which taught that life could be created from inorganic matter. During the mid-1800s, this doctrine was used to serve as an evidence for evolution.

produced by combinations of inorganic, life might at last be developed from these & what seemed to confirm this idea was the experiment of a man who had taken eggs of certain insects.

December 24, 1862

Christmas Eve. We are missing Will.

Father has just come in with a book for Carry Scott's Poetical Works. A box of drawing instruments & some books of Architecture for us.

December 25, 1862

The happiest part of the day to me has been sitting at Father's feet & hearing him read *The Lady of the Lake*. I enjoyed not only the beautiful poem itself, but Father's intense enjoyment of it.

It has been a day of pain in spite of all our efforts. I am thinking to night of a Christmas several years ago, the first time Will had money of his own, when he put 30 or 40 dollars into Mother's hands to buy presents for us.

December 27, 1862

Saturday.

The club meets here to night.

Will was of so much assistance to Father on such occasions.

Baron Gerolt has just passed through the hall.

The disasterous affairs of Fredericksburg is now attributed to the tardy arrival of the pontoon bridges sent to Gen. Burnside from Harper's Ferry & Washington, preventing him from crossing the river until the enemy had time to collect their troops.

A misunderstanding seems to have existed between Gens Burnside & Halleck, each thinking the other had given orders about the forwarding.

The secretaries are reinstated. The President having refused to accept their resignations. We had a visit from Mr. Henmant last evening. He has been absent for four years in the northern part of the continent. Father thinks highly of him.

PHOTO: Pontoon bridges laid across the river by Union troops, prior to the Battle of Fredericksburg.

December 29, 1862
Monday.

The city is in a state of excitement, on account of a raid of Stuarts cavalry at Accotink 12 miles from Alexandria. The enemy was repulsed, but succeeded in capturing quite a number of army wagons & ambulances beside 40 prisoners. ---- The wounded Fredericksburg sufferers are coming into the city daily, the hospital inmates are said to number 13,000.

Mrs. Smith's dinner to the sick soldiers seems to have passed off well. She was presented, on Christmas, with a gold watch & diamond ring as a reward for her charitable exertions. The Sec. also received a beautiful gift from his employee of a silver service.

Gen Banks has superseded Gen. Butler as command of the Department of the Gulf.

Jef. Davis has issued a proclimation announcing that retaliatory measures will be used against Gen. Butler & his officers for certain acts of theirs said to be in violation of the usuages of war[43].

---

[43] President Davis' proclamation announced that captured officers of Butler or the general, himself, "be declared not entitled to be considered as soldiers engaged in honorable warfare, but as robbers and criminals, deserving

Gen. Butler's whole career seems to have been anything but conciliatory.

December 31, 1862

We received a letter yesterday from Rear Admiral Farragut, containing his photograph. He promised it to us before he left Washington.

Father has just returned from a visit to Mr. Murdoch. He wanted the lecture room of the Institution for his readings which Father was obliged to refuse. He asked him, however, to deliver a course of lectures before the Institution upon locution.

It is rumored now that the whole army of the Patomac is about to return to Washington. I suppose to start anew.

It is supposed now that France will certainly interfere in our affairs. Mr. McIntyre was here last night & also again to night. He is going to his brother who is still sick with the army near Fredericksburg.

Prof. Hopkins has been here also.

He was turned out of his place last winter under an unjust charge of disloyalty & has not yet been reinstated. Poor man, I feel very sorry for him.

This the last night of the old year. I treasure the hours as they go. The last of the year in which we had our Will, It is so hard to commence the new year without him.

January 1, 1863

We watched the old year out & the new year in. Nell & I sat in Father's Study until the heavy boom of a cannon told us the old year was dead. I shall not soon forget that sound, it was the last of the year that knew our Will.

The day has been beautiful, We have received our friends as usual, we were glad to see among the cards left at our door that of Mr. Schleiden, we are very glad he has returned from Europe.

Mr. McIntyre, came in for a few minutes before tea.

Mr. Welling has just gone. He says it is the impression among the Diplomatic Corps that France, to day, acknowledges the Southern Confederacy, that Mr. Slidell is received as minister.

The President signed the proclamation for the Division of the State of Virginia to day, in spite of the opposition of the Cabinet[44].

---

death; and that they and each of them be, whenever captured, reserved for execution." See Footnote #31 on June 30, 1862

[44] President Lincoln's Cabinet were evenly divided regarding West Virginia statehood. The concern, from those who opposed statehood was that the government lacked the constitutional power to subdivide a disloyal state they argued had never truly left the Union.

The prospects of the country are very dark.

January 3, 1863

Saturday. Prof & Mrs. Sandoz came to night.
The Prof. has gone with Father to the club.
A visit from Mr. McIntyre & Father.

January 5, 1863

Mon.
We had a visit last evening from Admiral Davis, also from Mr. Wynkoop.
Mr. Baer & his daughters came to day. A lecture this evening.
After lecture, Gen. Casey, Dr. Bacon, Mrs. Peale, Mr. Sommers, Mr. McKnight & others came in.

January 7, 1863

Wed.
A visit from Madame Gerolt & daughter. She was very kind in her expression of sympathy for us.
Carlotta is soon to be married to a young Prussian officer.
Father brought in a book to day containing an article upon Architecture. He was commencing to read it aloud when Madame G. came in to the parlor. In a conversation with her, he said that when he was seven or eight years of age he left his home to live for a time with his grandmother in the country. He returned to the city from a different direction from that in which he left it & the house appeared to be on the wrong side of the street so that now when he looks back all his life before seven years of age seems to him to have been passed upon one side of the street & the rest of his live spent in the same house upon the other. He mentioned this to show the permanence of an impression upon the mind.
Another lecture from Prof Guyot.
Mr. Erlich & wife came in after the lecture.

January 8, 1863

Count Pataleas passed the evening with us.

January 10, 1863

Saturday.
Father & Prof Guyot have gone to the club.
I have not had much time to read the papers this week, as the house has been filled with company.

The excitement is great in regard to the siege of Vicksburg, but it is very difficult to know certainly the state of affairs. As far as we can learn, the fighting has been very severe.

Gen Sherman appears to have done well.

Father said to day, to Prof Guyot, that he had never been much of a politician until his attention was directed to Meteorology – that led him to study climatology, the productions of the earth & political economy & He had come to the conclusion, several years before, in Princeton, that we could hardly hold together as a nation more than 25 years longer.

Our prosperity, he thought, had been due to our great extent of country, to the quantity of food, enough & to spare for all men, but now we could spread no further the extent of arable land in the West was not as great as supposed.

The struggle for life was commencing, we were increasing with fearful rapidity as every year each member of society must interfere more & more with every other member so that the government ought to be proportionably strengthened.

We needed good men now, not many, & the encouragement of great foreign immigration he thought a mistake.

France has not yet recognised the Southern Confederacy.

There has been a severe battle at Murfreesboro, Tenn. Gen. Rosecrans being in command of our forces & Gen. Johnston leading the confederates. Victory was in our favor, but the loss on both sides was terrible.

Gen. Banks & Com. Farragut are Gen. Sherman's assistants at Vicksburg.

The Monitor, the gallant antagonist of the *Merrimac* has gone down with nearly all her crew. She foundered at sea off Cape Hatteras.

January 24, 1863

Saturday.

Prof Guyot & Madame Sandoz left us on Thurs. We have enjoyed their visit very much.

Prof Guyot is perfectly charming, he gave me several long talks.

Prof Hosford has been with us for two weeks. He is lecturing now upon "Munitions of War." He has gone this evening with Father to the club. I think our friends have enjoyed themselves.

On Saturday, we had some very pleasant gentlemen to dine.

On Monday, the gentlemen went to a party at Mrs. Hooker's. After the lecture on Tues., Dr. Bache[45] & Admiral Davis dined with us & also a

---

[45] Dr. Aledander Dallas Bache, an American scientist who was responsible for surveying – in great detail – the nation's coastline.

young Mr. Rodgers from Phil., who is here, attempting to get an appointment to a cadetship at West Point.

On Wednesday, Prof. H went to a party at the National while the rest of us: Prof Guyot, Madame Sandoz, Father, Mother, & I spent the evening in a round game played with cards & counters.

Father made a great deal of merriment & I think enjoyed the game as much as any of us.

Thursday, as I said before, our friends from Princeton left us. It was the saddest 'farewell' we has ever spoken. We have learned the uncertainty of human life. The war news of the two weeks has been the failure of the siege of Vicksburg & a battle at Galveston . Our fleet there was attacked by rebels & several vessels destroyed.

It is said that the army of the Patomac have made another unsuccessful attempt to move upon the rebels, having been stopped by the bad condition of the roads.

January 26, 1863

I took dinner yesterday with Mrs. Hodge. She very kindly asked me to go home with her after church, Mrs. Rodgers was looking very well, her baby is very pretty, it is five weeks old.

Mrs. Rodgers was of course delighted at the arrival of the *Weehawken* at Fortress Monroe without injury from the storm she encountered on the coast.

The *Intelligencer* says Capt. Rodgers has done more for the country in restoring confidence in our iron clad navy, after the sad loss of the *Monitor*, than if he had gained a hard fought battle. He is a gallant, noble officer & worthee of all praise.

Admiral Davis took tea with us last night.

John Porter has been cashiered & dismissed from the service.

Mr Frank, a member of congress who was here to night, told us that but for a single vote his sentence would have been death. His fault was disobedience to certain orders of Gen. Pope during his engagements with the enemy in Virginia in the latter part of Aug. & prompt compliance of which would, in the opinion of Gen Pope, have Saved his army from defeat.

Gen. Burnside arrived in Washington on Saturday morning, & at his own request, it is said, was relieved of the command of the army of the Patomac. Gen. Hooker is to take his place.

Mr. Capon took dinner with us to day. He said a regiment of New York troops had mutinied at Falmouth, but had been immediately surrounded & reduce to subjection.

The state of affairs is terrible, great dissatisfaction is felt with the President's course of conduct in many parts of the country.

I hope we are not to have civil war among ourselves.

Another movement against Vicksburg is in progress under Gen. Grant.

Prof. Hosford gave another lecture to night on Projectiles.

January 27, 1863

Tues. The Common Council of the City of New York has held a meeting to express disaprobation of the result of the trial of Gen. Fitz John Porter & to request his counsel to furnish them with a full copy of the evidence they have tendered to the Gen.[46]

The hospitalities of the city & a public reception in the Governor's room, so that the people may testify their high appreciation of his courage & ability.

Gen. Franklin & Sumner have both resigned. What are we to do for generals?

The *Star* says the reason why Gen. Burnside has requested to be relieved was because Gen. Hooker refused to act in concert with him. In the last forward movement, the artillery was caught in the mud & Gen. Burnside wished to move upon the enemy without arguing that if artillery was useless to our troops on account of the state of roads it would be equally so to the rebels.

He called a council of war. Gen. Hooker opposed the advance. Gen. Burnside accepted the trust confered upon him with reluctance & resigns at his own request. He was a warm friend of Gen McClellan. The state of affairs seems to be darkening rapidly.

In my humble opinion, we have every reason to fear anarchy at the North as well as the South.

Mr. Capon was here again to day. He says the President ----

January 28, 1863

Wed.

Dr. Schuck & his son are with us. They have been to the Capitol this evening. The House is voting upon the bill for arming the negros.

Prof Hosford was on the floor for a while with Mr. Frank, who said he was going to vote for the bill, though he did not seem very much in favor of it.

---

[46] Lasting between November 1862 and January 1863, the court-martial of Fitz John Porter was a major event during the American Civil War. Major General Fitz John Porter was found guilty of disobeying a lawful order, and misconduct in front of the enemy and removed from command. The court-martial was later found to be unjust and overturned, and Porter was reinstated in the United States Army.

Gen. Couch & Smith are to take the places of Gens. Franklin & Sumner.

The President has appointed Father one of the commissioners to examine the Mint. Gold is now worth 1,55.

Our paper currency will soon be worth very little.

The New Yorkers have presented Mrs. McClellan with a beautiful furnished house in that city as a testimonial of respect to the Gen.

We practised our German with Prof. Hosford after his return from the Capitol. He speaks the language very fluently. He amused us with a description of some of his adventures in Germany & Switzerland.

Speaking of the monotonous, life passed by the peasants of those countries he said. He asked an old woman living in one of the mountain passes how far she had ever been from her home. She said she thought she has been as far as two hours walking could take her.

Speaking of the Alps, he said he had been taken by his guide to the top of the Sonnenberg to see them. He had been left there with some traveling companions before sunrise, daylight came, but no alps. The great mountains were not to be found. Just as they were turning away, thinking the guide had deceived them, certain clouds in the valley & above them seemed to Prof Hosford to congeal – he had not noticed before that, they were motionless, with here & there dark specks. They were the glaciers. The alps that now broke upon him in all their beauty.

January 29, 1863

Thurs. 10. A.M.

Prof Hopkins has just been here. He has received a letter from his son who is under Gen Foster at New bern. He writes that the army there is about to make a movement further South & should they do so, there will be hard fighting.

January 30, 1863

Friday A.M.

Father saw Gen. Franklin yesterday.

He said he did not know, but he might be called before a Court Martial as well as Gen. Porter. He says the army is terribly dispirited; Father also, so it Mr. Bancroft, the historian, who was terribly blue about the country.

Last eve, Mother & I went to Mrs. Peale's. Father & Dr. Parker stopped for us on their way from Gen. Loffen.

Senator Salisbury[47], who behaved so disgracefully in the Senate a few days, since has apologized for his offence & will not be expelled. I was mortified. I feel an interest in his fate, having met him last summer & found him agreeable.

Father, after our return from Mrs. Peale's, read us a letter from one of the Turkish Cadi to Mr. Layard, commencing "My illustrious friend & joy of my liver."

Then came a discussion upon the study of words & language between Prof. Hosford, which I have not time to write out.

"Oats, a grain which in England is generally given to horses, but in Scotland supports the people."

Pronouncing the Dr. & old wag we went to bed.

11 h. P.M.

The Prof did not have many people at his lecture on account of the storm. Gen Casey came in after lecture. He says Gen. Franklin is to be court martialed next week.

Mrs. Gilles was here this morning with her son who came from Fredericksburg a few days since He says 11 more Officers of the Army of the Patomac are to be removed.

January 31, 1863

Mrs. _____ has presented Father with a self-lighting gas burner, which has excited our great admiration. Mr. Corneilius has presented one to Mrs Lincoln & Mr. Stanton also. It is very ingenious & pretty. He also gave Father an apparatus for producing an electrical spark, which Father has taken with him to the club to night.

The discussion of the bill for arming of the negros still continues to create great excitement in the House Mr. Wickliffe made a long speech

---

[47] Senator Willard Saulsbury, Sr., Democrat from Delaware. Saulsbury was a fervent critic of President Abraham Lincoln, opposing the war in general and the suspension of habeas corpus specifically.

Apparently intoxicated, Saulsbury verbally attacked the President on the Senate floor in what John Hay described as "language fit only for a drunken fishwife." Senator Saulsbury called Lincoln "an imbecile" and stated that the President was "the weakest man ever placed in a high office." When Vice President Hannibal Hamlin called Saulsbury to order, the Senator refused to take his seat. Finally, the Senate's sergeant-at-arms approached to remove Saulsbury from the Senate floor when the Senator suddenly brandished a revolver, placed it against the sergeant's head and said, "Damn you, if you touch me I'll shoot you dead!" Eventually, Saulsbury was calmed and removed from the Senate floor.

yesterday, in which he said one man, named Hunter, had tried the experiment of raising a negro regiment, but had failed.

He asked if we were prepared to admit that we could not put down the rebellion without calling in the aid of the negro. He would not heckle about the rank of Gen. Sambo or Gen. Hunter.

This bill might enable Gen. Sambo to outrank Gen. Hunter.

To day, Mr. Wright of Penn. spoke in favor of moderation & forbearance. He said there was never greater need for a spirit of concession than at this time. No man knew when he went to bed at night whether when he arose in the morning the Government would be in existence.

If the measure, obnoxious to a majority of the people of the country, were passed, the Government could not endure.

In every point of view, the negro bill was impolitic & uncalled for.

Should it pass, we should, in all probability, lose Maryland, Kentucky & West Virginia, besides running the risk of demoralizing the army now in the field.

He had been told by officers of the army that if black soldiers were enlisted, they would consider it a reflection upon the army & resign.

The question of interest before the Senate now is "Emancipation in Missouri."

That state has applied to Congress for pecuniary aide in freeing her negros. The *Intelligencer* is very indignant about the Porter Court Martial.

Foreign Intervention still threatens us, but Europe does not seem to regard favorably Pres. Davis' retaliatory proclamation, denouncing death without mercy upon Gen. Butler & his officers, issued immediately after the Presidents' Emancipation proclamation.

Gen. Butler is to be reinstated in Command of the Gulf.

February 3, 1863
Tuesday.
11h. A.M.
Dr. Loney came last night. He is to lecture on Wednesday.

Prof Hosford gave the last of his course last night.

Prof Hosford saw Gen. Butler yesterday. It is said he is to take Stanton's place as Secretary of War.

The bill for raising 150,000 negro soldiers has been passed. It was proposed by Mr. Stevens & modified by Mr. Casey, so as to exempt the states of Maryland, Delaware, Kentucky, Tennessee, West Virginia & Missouri from its operation & prevent negro officers from commanding white soldiers.

Admiral Davis came in after lecture. Mr. Welling was also here. He seems to think if we could have a great victory now, we might hope for peace, As the South might then be willing to yield us Virginia & the North content to establish a boundary line.

February 4, 1863

The news to night is of shining interest.

The blockading squadron in Charleston harbour was attacked on the 31st by a small fleet under Com. Ingraham -- two of the vessels were sunk, 4 set on fire & the rest driven away.

Dr. Loney's lecture was not very well attended on account of the cold. After lecture we had a visit from Mrs. Wiling & Ingraham from Boston & Mr. Brown of Phil., a lawyer & son of Brown the novelist.

February 7, 1863

A visit from John Young.

We have spent the morning in directing notes for Prof. Hosford. He is to show his bread making process to a number of influential people on Monday evening. Hoping thus to have it introduced into the army.

Mrs. Shulie was here about 2 h., the mingling of kindness & severity in the old lady's manner amuses me.

Dr. Loges was here to dinner.

Prof. Chase made an engagement with him to spend the evening with Miss Chase. He says the young lady has a little dog very much like ours.

Father, Mother & Dr. Loney left this morning for Philadelphia. They will return on Tuesday or Wednesday.

February 10, 1863

Tuesday.

The Prof.'s bread making passed off well. Many officers of high rank were present; Gens. Heintzelman, Barnard & others.

Miss Dix came in to tea. She looked very much fatigued.

Mrs Merrick did not forget us.

Senator & Mrs. Foster went into the lecture room with us. The latter gave us a very kind invitation to visit them. a number of our friends came into our parlor after the lecture.

February 13, 1863

A visit from Alfred Woodhull, John Young & Mr. Harris. It was very hard to meet -- Alfred Herbert's footstep in the entry sounded so much like Will's.

February 14, 1863

Saturday. Father & Dr Loney have gone to the club. Prof. Hosford has gone to the President's to exhibit his bread making process.

Father at the dinner table to day amused Dr. Loney with an account of his first pair of boots:

The cobbler who had the honour of making the aforesaid article was somewhat of a wag & as Father could not decide between the respective merits of the round toed & squaretoed, the two styles of boots then in vogue, concluded to make one of each sort -- greatly to his satisfaction, who I believe never decided which was the most beautiful the square or the round toe. He did not give quite all the story, one of his school companions, becoming enamored with the boots put them on one day & ran off with them, but was soon discovered by his tracks in the snow, the round toe & the pointed toe were unmistakable.

The only thing of political interest this week is the attempt of France to negotiate peace between the North & South. All such propositions have been indignantly rejected by Mr. Seward.

We have heard from Mrs. Bell through her daughter in law who is in the city. Her circumstances are more comfortable than we supposed. Mr. Bell is with his first wife's children. ---- Gen Thomas Thumb & his tiny bride are at Willards. The wedding caused great excitement in N.Y.

March 7, 1863

3 weeks have passed since I last wrote. Within that time very little of importance has occured in regard to war matters.

Vicksburg still remains in possession of the Southerners.

Congress has adjourned or rather closed its session.

The Conscription Bill has passed the House of Rep., by it all persons between the ages of 20 & 45 are liable to be drafted. The law is very general in its provisions, the only office holders exempted being the Vice President, the Heads of Departments & the Judiciary.

We had a visit from Prof. Agassiz. The beautiful symplicity of his character is in charming contrast with his noble bearing. He was with us several days. He has been appointed Regent of the Smithsonian.

Dr. Parker was interested a very curious specimen of natural History. The head of a man reduced to almost the size of man's fist, the bones having first been removed. It is to be brought to the Institution for inspection.

MA & E.A. came on Saturday last. We sadly missed the greeting Will always gave them.

Miss Dix was here on Sunday.

Prof. Hosford left us on Tuesday.

Mother & myself, to day, attended a meeting called to form a new boys home.

March 13, 1863

Miss Hamilton was here this morning. She is the granddaughter of Gen. Hamilton. She is dark eyed with dark glossy braids of hair & exceedingly agreeable manners.

Gen Casey's daughters came in while she was here, to ask us to spend the evening with them very quietly.

There were no ladies there, but ourselves.

Dr. Bacon came for us with an ambulance. We were well jolted as the streets have been completely ruined in that part of the city by the heavy army wagons.

March 16, 1863

We passed last night with Mrs. Merrick. We went home with her from church & a storm of rain & sleet detained us. The good lady is very strong in her feeling against the Northerners, denouncing them in the most bitter terms.

We realize the sad effects of this terrible war more than ever, when we hear such kind natures as hers so transformed.

At her table sat a gentle ladylike girl, an orphan whom she treats as her child & a rosy cheeked boy waited upon us, also an object of her charity.

Sarah Hodge came to us to day.

March 21, 1863

This week has been a quiet one. I am afraid for the girls. We amused ourselves one evening in reading Frankenstein.

Mr. Welling was here one night.

To day, Sarah went to the President's reception.

To night, John Torrey has been assisting at a carousel frolic.

Father is in New York.

March 23, 1863

We had all gone to bed on Saturday night when Father arrived. We did not expect him until to night. He came home with a violent cold. His visit in N.Y. was very pleasant. He went with Capt. Davis & Dr. Buche to inspect the mode of connecting compasses on board Iron vessels

They were sent down to the Narrows in a Government vessel. They have been appointed a committee to decide all scientific matters connected with the Navy.

March 28, 1863

Have been busy all the week with the New Boys Association.

Mother & myself fill the office of Sec. jointly.

Father put my papers in the nicest sort of order for me to day, it was very kind. He is still sick with his cold.

The Alexandria girls left us on Tuesday.

Mr. Welling & Capt. have been here.

March 30, 1863

Mon. 30 A visit from Mr. Lyon of Lyonsdale. He promised me a book, his photograph & a relic. a piece of a baloon made of the silk dresses of the ladies of Charleston.

Mr. Lyon was instrumental in saving the relics of Gen. Washington at Arlington last summer. He is peculiar in his appearance, has a pair of dark eyes that twinkle under heavy eye brows & a long iron grey beard.

Father once asked him mischievously how he obtained such a handsome wife, "Ah Prof," said he, "I have a great deal of inward beauty."

Dr. Bache Capt. Davis & Father are busy with their scientific naval business.

March 31, 1863

31st. Mr. Reese, a member of the Hudson Bay Company, is with us. He has lived for a number of years in Mahenzius River, far away from civilization. & has given us many interesting facts about the Indians.

He told us to day at dinner, that if they once taste human flesh, the desire for it ever afterwards becomes insatiable. He knew one Indian who had eaten his wife & six children, the latter in sight of the Fort, when he might have obtained food.

He knew of two Europeans who had been killed by Indian women, their flesh partly eaten & the rest salted down for future use.

April 1, 1863

Wed.-- Mr. Kerr, a Scotch clergyman dined with us. He seemed to think England very favorably disposed towards us. He thought at first she was inclined to sympathise somewhat with the South because that was the weaker party.

After dinner, Mr. Kerr amused us, that is Father & myself, by repeating some of Burns poems; his scotch accent & explanations of the purely scotch words made the poetry doubly pleasurable, Father enjoyed them exceedingly.

Judge Mason came in soon, so I was Mr. Herr's only auditer. He repeated some old Scotch ballads that were very quaint & pretty.

After tea, Dr. Bache & Admiral Davis came in. They have been appointed with Father a committee to settle Scientific questions arising in naval affairs. Mrs. Bache accompanied the Dr.

Capt Hague came to play chess with me.

April 3, 1863

Tues. 3rd.

Started on an expedition to the Observatory yesterday. It is the first time we have been there this winter. We thought we should never reach there, the mud was so deep. The army wagons have completely destroyed the streets in that part of the city.

We stopped at Gen. Casey's on our way home to see Bessie. It was the first regular visit made since Will's death & I dreaded it.

Mrs. Bates was exceedingly kind, she is motherly & gentle I went to thank Miss Bates for the photograph of Father she had sent me. She was going with her sister to spend the morning in the Cemetery at Georgetown.

They kindly asked me to accompany them. I proposed taking pencils & papers to sketch. It was a lovely day & I enjoyed the expedition greatly.

The grounds never seemed more quietly beautiful. Miss Bates is determined to learn to sketch & we are to go again the next fine day.

Miss Sally Bates is looking forward with great pleasure to visiting the army. The President & others have made up a party for that purpose.

April 10, 1863

Fri. 10th. The Battle of Charleston has, at last, commenced.

The Ironclads have at last reached their destination. Com. Dupont has command of the fleet. The fortifications are exceedingly strong & we must expect sharp fighting.

To day, the Keokuk is reported to have been sunk. The excitement is great & papers are selling rapidly as a little news boy, one of our protege's told us.

April 11, 1863

Sat. 11th

A visit of Baron Gerolt. He came to see Father, but not finding him at home gave me the pleasure of his company for a while. He said his daughters & his wife were very busy preparing to go to Europe in June. Carlotta is to be married. He wanted to see Father about a paper he is preparing for the Report. Carlotta has translated it for him.

Speaking of the rainy weather we have had this winter, he said we were never satisfied in the world, even had we every possible happiness, we should still have something to wish for.

When he was in Mexico once, he thought he had at last found the perfection of weather, not a cloud to shadow the unbroken sunshine, but he soon found himself longing for rain averring for some change in the bright unclouded sky above him.

April 13, 1863

Mon. 13th. Gen. Casey was ordered off last week, but Bessie told us yesterday he was not to go.

Went this afternoon to enquire if Mrs. Rodgers & heard any thing from the Capt. He is in command of the *Weehawken*, one of the ironclads in the Charleston fleet.

She had received no letter, but was comforted by hearing that his vessel had been struck 50 times without damage & not a man on board injured.

She is of course exceedingly anxious.

Little Willie & the baby were brought in to see us.

Foster has been surrounded & defeated.

April 14, 1863

Tuesday 14th.

Miss Dix was here a little while this morning, she has hurt her foot. Mother asked her when she was coming home to be nursed? She said when the Rebellion was over. She was in better spirits than I have seen her for some time.

Foster has not surrendered. He is at Washington, North Carolina. Surrounded, but boldly challenges the Southerners to take the place. No additional news from Charleston.

Father is in the Study with the Naval Commission. He expects to leave for N.Y. on Saturday. Capt Davis & Dr. Bache have just gone. The Commission seems to have had a pleasant evening. We asked why they were laughing as they went down stairs. He said, he remarked to Capt Davis that in criticising the inventions sent for their approval, in condemning & making objection they had given exercise to their bad passions, the architects of ruin were always more successful than those of construction.

Capt Davis said, "yes, but apparently it had been the object of his life to suppress his virtues & encourage his vices, to cultivate a good stomach & a bad heart."

April 15, 1863

The carpenter came in this morning with a report that the city was in a great state of excitement, in consequence of a rumor that Harper's Ferry was in the hands of the rebels

The "star", this evening, says there is no foundation for such a report.

The *Intelligencer,* this morning, contained an account of the battle of Charleston, it is fruitless, but was bravely fought, the *Weehawken* led the fleet. She advanced boldly undaunted by heavy fire from Fort Sumter until stopped by a Hauser stretched across the channel, hung with torpedos and others forming an effectual barrier to further progress.

The scene which followed was terrific beyond description. Shells tried their strength in vain against the stone walls of Sumter, destructive missels fell harmlessly from the sides of the Ironclads, but though fighting bravely & well, the gallent commanders were obliged to turn at last & the fleet steamed slowly out of the inhospitable harbor.

Most of the vessels received some slight injury

The *Keokuk* alone received her death blow, torn after crossing the bar, she gave signals of distress & her officers & crew had barely time to leave her before she sunk beneath the waves.

So ends the great Charleston expedition so long the subject of speculation & wonder.

It is said, this evening, the fleet is to be sent to join Capt. Farragut.

Father has praised a letter I have written to Mrs. Senator Wilson, I am as happy as a queen.

April 18, 1863

Sat. 18th. Father had gone to the Club. He expected to go to N.Y. to day, but did not like to leave home when Nell was sick. She has a very bad cold.

There is a rumour to night that Suffolk is taken.

Mr. Lyon of Lyonsdale was here, while we were out, to bring me a piece of a rebel balloon he promised me.

As his photograph, he left one of an ugly old Indian. I shall tell him I am glad he put his name upon it, as I should not have recognized it, the Sun certainly does not flatter him.

April 21, 1863

Tues. 21st, A visit from Gen. Casey & daughter in the evening.

April 22, 1863

Wed 22. Received our cards of invitation to day for the ball at the Minister's, given in honor of his daughter's marriage.

A visit of Dr.----.

Went this afternoon to see Mary Felton. She is nurse in the Hospital opposite to us. We found giving out medicines the ward over which she presides, looked exceedingly comfortable & pleasant. The one adjoining hers, under the care of Miss Lowell of Cambridge, some relative of the poet was very prettily ornamented with green crosses.

Father is in New York, we miss him greatly.

April 24, 1863

Miss Dix looked in upon us for a few moments. She greatly disapproves of young ladies being employed as nurses. She was very sorry to hear Mary Felton was here in that capacity.

We expect Father to night. He went to New York partly on Naval Commission business, but also to attend the meeting for the formation of the National Academy.

We saw, by the papers on Wed., he presided. We have not received a letter from him since he left.

April 27, 1863

Mon. 27th. Father arrived about six o'clock. His visit in N.Y. was pleasant. He was appointed to preside at the meetings for the formation of the National Academy, but declined all permanent office, since being virtually President of the Smithsonian, he would have much business to transact with the Academy & could not therefore be very well one of its officers.

Father expressed to the Academy, his estimation of the great responsibility of the Institution how important it was that every member should be hard working. Should any fail to bring forth fruits, they should be excluded & their places supplied by those who hearty exertions would favor the cause of science.

Father said the giving of the oath of Allegiance was very impressive. It was first administered to him by prof. Caswell. After which, in his office of presiding, he gave it to the 33 members present. They all standing & repeating it after him.

Some objections were made to the oath, at first, on the ground that as it excluded from the Society all who had ever taken up arms against the government.

Southern Secessionists, should our country be united, would be debarred from being members, this difficulty was settled by the agreement that the oath should be the same as that of the Senate & change when that changed.

April 31, 1863[48]

Thursday 31st.

This is Fast Day. We attended church in the morning, heard a sermon not at all tended to excite humility, since the clergyman spent a least an hour in debating upon our grandeur, our extent, our immeasurable superiority over all nature, our eneffable greatness, past, present & to come.

---

[48] April only has 30 days. Mary catches this error in her dating with the inserted note: "I find I have made a mistake of a day or two in my dates this month somewhere I must be more careful in future."

In the evening, we went to hear Mr. Sunderland, who in a notice in the *Intelligencer* & other papers, had signified his intention of "defining his position," his church might be disintegrated,. Himself discharged from his Pastorate, but he considered that it was every one's duty in the present dreadful crisis to express a positive & fearless opinion.

After the Bombastes Furioso, notice of the little man, we felt anxious to hear him, but the house was so crowded we found it impossible to get inside of the doors.

May 2, 1863

May Sat. 2nd.

Read aloud this Afternoon to Father & Nell from Madame D.'s letters. She describes the Cathedral at Exeter.

Father said he had seen it & was exceedingly impressed with its beauty. He was told to take off his hat when he entered, but the injunction was quite unnecessary, he should have done so involintarily.

The Army of the Patomac has at last moved – various rumours are afloat concerning it.

May 4, 1863

Mon. 4th. Went this morning to Armory Hospital to see Mary Felton. While I was there a comotion in the street called our attention & going to the door we saw passing, a number of rebel prisoners walking two abreast with a federal soldier on each side of them.

They were mostly dressed in Virginia homespun & seemed to be labouring men rather than soldiers: some of them appeared to be very feeble. 800 are said to have been brought in to day, but I think the number must have been exaggerated.

Gen. Hooker has crossed the Rapahannock in several places & is moving "onward to Richmond. There has been some terrible fighting, but it is impossible to found out whether we are victorious.

Mrs. Olmstead stopped at the door this evening just before tea & told us we had been successful, but that our loss was great.

10h. P.M.- Henry, the watchman, has just come in; he says it is reported in the city that gens. Sickles & Sykes are both killed.

Father had gone out with Mr. Patterson, an Irish gentleman travelling in this country & intensely interested in our affairs.

Later -- Father has just returned. He went to see Mr. Sumner with Mr. Patterson & had a very interesting interview with him. He said one thing that surprised me much that he had strongly opposed the retaking of Fort Sumter & had told the President that such a measure would certainly bring on the war.

Father said a number of ambulances had been sent down to the warf for the wounded from the Rapahannock.

From the great reserve in regard to our supposed victories, he seems to think with me that they may possibly turn out a defeat.

Still later -- Father has been reading scraps of Johnson's poetry, much to our mutual enjoyment. He likes his poems very much. It is almost twelve oclock.

May 5, 1863

Went this morning to the News Boys Home. A flag was floating from one of the windows in honour of our victories.

Are they such, I wonder:

Mrs. Bliss, our Treasurer, is in trouble. Her husband, surgeon of Armory Square Hospital, has been arrested on charge of having accepted a bribe.

Miss Ripley came in, her manners are graceful & gentle.

The town is filled with rumours. Gen. Couc, as well & Gens. Sickles & Sykes is said to be killed.

I am afraid our troops have suffered terribly.

A relative of one of the employees of the Institution returned to day from the scene of action -- says his company was entirely cut to pieces.

May 6, 1863

Wed. 6th.

The *Times* gives a full account of the late military operations in the vacinity of Fredericksburg.

A week from last Monday, the army commenced to move crossing the river at three places.

A few companies were sent over 2 miles below Fredericksburg to arouse the enemy & withdraw their attention from the main body of the army, which crossed at Kelly's & United States Fords about 8 & 11 miles above the city.

Those two detachments uniting, formed a line of battle stretching some distance beyond chancellor (which is about 25 miles from Fred.) & towards the river.

The most important position was, of course, on the extreme right as the enemy would, of course, attack that in order to bend our lines back & open the route to Richmond. This was given to Karl Schurtz, who, upon the charge of the Southerners, fled ingloriously with his German troops.

Gen. Berry, a favorite officer of Gen. Hooker, was sent to the rescue & acquitted himself well, preventing the further advance of the enemy.

Karl Schurtz, in spite of his disgraceful retreat, was again intrusted with an important post, again, was obliged to quit the field.

Gen Berry, crossing as before to the rescue.

This gallant officer in a third brave charge was killed.

After hard fighting, the Southerners succeeded in getting in our rear, so our lines were changed forming a triangle, Chancellorsville forming the apex., which is the present position of our forces.

Chancellor, consisting of only one house was destroyed.

The losses on both sides has been terrible in the extreme.

If many more such encounters take place, there will be no men left on either side to fight.

All that I have been writing occupied the week, but the worse fighting was on Sunday.

We are said to be victorious, but I do not see what the Southerners have gained driving us back, while the passage of Richmond is open. Our position now is said to be very strong & the men are in good spirits.

The news to night is that Gen. Sedgwick, who executed the feint below Richmond, has recrossed the river.

Gen. Sherman, who was detached on a seperate commission when the army moved, is said to have advanced within 5 miles of Richmond, burning bridges, destroying railroads, cutting off as much as possible all communication between the rebels & their Capitol.

Gen Jackson is said to be wounded, he would be a great lost to them.

Gen. Sickles is wounded, but not killed as was reported last night.

England seems to be in a bad humor just now. She does not like the seizure of British ships in neutral waters & the protection granted by Mr. Adams to Mexican traders.

Mr. Roebuck made a speech in Parlement, announcing himself in favor of putting down the "upstart insolence" of the U.S.

Lord Palmerston is in our favor.

Father has just looked up from his books to say what a wonderful thing is memory, some association of Ideas had bought to his mind a certain passage in a book he had not opened or thought of for thirty years, & now some little combination of circumstances had brought vividly before him every thing connected with the reading of it.

June 18, 1863

We have been in Princeton, that is Carry & I, to attend Mary Alexander's wedding. It passed off pleasantly & she is now making a tour of the Lakes, Niagara, Montreal & other places.

We had a letter from her to day --- We returned just a week ago to day.

We found an addition to the family in the shape of an infant which had been left at the door of the Institution. It is with us still.

Excitement has been intense the week throughout the country on account of the rebel raid into Penn.

An immense body of troops was supposed to have invaded the State.[49] & the President called for a large addition to the troops already in service.

In Phil, the tolling of the State House Bell announced the danger & the citizens hastened to enlist for the defence of their capitol.

The stores were closed & the money at the Mint & banking houses sent out of the city. All this consternation was caused by a body of calvery about 1,800 strong under Jenkins, which crossing the Patomac at Williamsport proceeded to Hagerstown & Chambersburg.

Horses, cattle, & forage seems to have been the sole object of the expedition.

Our city also was in a state of panic on Monday last.

Hooker was supposed to be in full retreat & the South, it was supposed, might be down upon us any moment.

Prof. Hossford has just been here, he gave us a description of some theatricals of our army. The number for the benefit of the medical Commission, Mr. Everett, who was present, sent their $25.00 as his admission fee.

The Scientific commission, consisting at present of only Admiral Davis & Father, are in secret counsil.

Our forces have left Fredericksburg & the two grand armies seem to be preparing for a terrible struggle in the vacinity of Bull's Run.

June 27, 1863

27th. Sat. I am sitting up today for the first time after a fit of sickness. The Rebels seem to be advancing upon Harrisburg & Philadelphia, but this is supposed by some to be a feint, their real destination being Washington.

Even the negros are being enrolled for the defense of the city. A number of troops have been sent off to Balt., as that city also is thought to be in danger. Chief Justice Taney thinks we have reason to fear an attack. --- One of the men in the Institution has just announced that the Southerners are within four miles of the chain Bridge, but this is probably only a rumor.

Prof Longfellow, the poet, is in town. He has been intending to call upon us, but prevented by the illness of his son.

June 29, 1863

Yesterday morning, Sunday, it was reported the rebels had taken possession of York.

In the evening, while we were at tea, our attention was called to signal lights at the top of the Capitol.

They were to warn the Forts to be ready in case of an attack.

---

[49] Just days from the Battle of Gettysburg, which featured 165,620 troops total from the two sides combined.

The night was one of anxiety.

To day, we learn that a large body of army wagons, about 125, were taken by the enemy within eight miles of Georgetown.

This morning, two ladies connected with the Sanitary commission were here. They were just from Alexandria. They were anxious to remove certain boxes containing stores for wounded soldiers to Balt., but were very much afraid that all communication between that city & Wash. would be cut off before they could succeed in so doing.

They said our Grand "Army of the Patomac" was nothing to boast of now, it did not number more than 60,000 men, that no one knew what was the intention of the Southerners, that the advance on Richmond might be only a feint.

It seemed probable that they intended to cut off all railroad communication with Washington & then take the place.

It is said to night that the rail road between Phil & Balt. has been broken, but that may be only a rumour.

The Northern Central has certainly been injured.

There is said to be fighting at Harrisburg to day. That city is, of course, in a state of intense excitement.

I went to dine with Mr. Gulicks this evening.

We went to the Soldier's Home where the President now resides, we met him returning with his body guard, about 20 mounted men, following his carriage.

He seemed so oppressed with care & anxiety, I pitied him sincerely.

Further on, we encountered a body of cavalry & army wagons moving in the direction of Rockville, about 12 miles from Georgetown, where the southerners are said to be with a force of 10,000 men. They were fully equiped for war.

There are signal lights again from the Capitol, what they portend, we know not.

Gen Mead has been given the command of the army, Gen. Hooker not proving himself equal to our present emergency & Gen Butler has been appointed Sec. of War. Two important moves in the game we are playing, whether for or against us time must tell.

Trains of cars have been running all day from Alexandria, heavily laden with Government stores. Everything valuable is being brought away from there, I suppose for fear of an attack.

Father & Mother have just come in from the city. Father saw a young man at the book store who had been sent this morning with stationary to the army now at Frederick, but was taken prisoner at Rockville.

He said the rebels were in force there.

They were well dressed and mounted. They released him on parole. The people in Rockville were all secessionist & were entertaining the soldiers with generous hospitality. Should our Northern men take their place, perhaps they would be found to be equally loyal.

June 30, 1863
Tues.

Various rumours are afloat to day, but it is difficult to know what to believe.

The Rebels at Rockville seem to be a body of cavalry under Gen Stuart, on their way to join the main body of the army which is supposed to concentrating some where near Gettysburg.

Paid a visit to Prof Matill in his room this evening & watched him make a casting of a South American idol.

Father read Chalk on the war after tea. He likes his views very much.

July 1, 1863
Wed.

Mr & Mrs. Peale & Mr. Welling spent the evening with us.

In speaking of the improvements which may be made in the city, Father said when he first came here, he had taken great interest in the matter & had made great efforts for the carrying out of certain plans for beautifying the city, but met with so little encouragement from the mean, self-interested motives & petty party spirit of men in office, that he became disgusted.

It was through his influence, however, that the range of parks from the Capitol to the river were left open & so many of the triangular spaces along Penn. Av. fenced in & planted with shrubbery.

Mr. Peale, in speaking of the war, thought we had the rebels now completely in our power. If Government were to intrust him with our armies he thought he could surround & completely destroy them without the slightest hope of escape.

Father, without meaning to be personal to Mr. Peale, told an amusing anecdote of _____ speaking of the genius of Shakespere, said he did not think him at all remarkable. He could himself write as good plays "if he had a mind to," He said "if you had a mind to."

Harrisburg is still safe. Troops are rapidly arriving for its protection. Six bridges have been burned upon the Northern Central railroad.

July 2, 1863
Thursday.

Went to Mrs. Peale's this afternoon to meet Father & Mother. Miss Dix was there.

She seemed to be in good spirits & was playfully upbraiding Father for not speaking to her in the streets.

She said some of the rebels had been in the city on Monday night attending the theatre[50] & others had passed the evening with their friends.

Saw Gen. Casey, went to his boarding house to enquire if his daughter had gone, & found him sitting on the porch reading a book of Hebrew prayers.

July 3, 1863

Exciting news to night, a great battle yesterday between the combined armies of Lee & Meade near Gettysburg.

Our arms said to be successful, but two of our Generals, Reynolds & Paul, killed.

Gen Rosecrans has driven the enemy quite out of Tenn. after bloody battle at Tullahoma.

July 4, 1863[51]

The day unusually quiet.

Went to the hospital in the evening. The men had a supper given them in honour of the day. A band discoursed sweet music for some time in front of the wards.

Mary & some of the other nurses passed the evening with us.

July 6, 1863

Mon. The fighting at Gettysburg commenced on Wed. & continued on Thursday & Friday.

The loss on both sides has been terribly severe, but the Rebels are in full retreat.[52]

Their bridge at Williamsport has been destroyed & the rain has swollen the river so that the fords must be impassable.

Their retreat seems to be cut off.

Gen. Lee in this move has evidently trusted too much to the incapacity of Hooker.

---

[50] Ford's Theatre

[51] After nearly two years of what seemed like an endless war, it is noteworthy to hear the marked difference in Mary Henry's tone compared to that expressed on Independence Day in years previous (1861: *"It is Independence Day, hallowed & dear to the hearts of the American people..."*). Indeed, by this point, the war had exhausted the nation's residents of their patriotic fervor.

[52] USA losses: 3,155 killed, 14,531 wounded, 5,369 captured/missing
CSA losses: 4,708 killed, 12,693 wounded, 5,830 captured/missing

Dead Federal soldiers on the battlefield of Gettysburg.
Negative by Timothy H. O'Sullivan.

July 8, 1863

Vicksburg is ours.

I passed last night with Mrs. Peale.

The President & Secretaries were serenaded & speeches were made by the dignitaries in honour of the recent victories. We heard the distant music & shouts & Mr. Peale reported the speeches.

The President commenced his with the stupendous announcement that the 4th of July was a remarkable day, with the reasons for its being so considered & ended with the elegent expression that on this particular 4th, the Rebels had "turned tail & run."

Mr. Sewards speech was fine.

100 guns have been fired today for the taking of Vicksburg.

Mary Felton & her friend, Dr. Bowen, passed the evening with us.

Father gave us two reminiscences of his boyish days that were interesting. When he was a tiny little fellow, he crept into a baker's wagon & was let down in State Street in Albany, for the first time. He saw the big state House at one end & the cross below & thought in an agony of apprehension that he was completely surrounded by houses from which their was no outlet – such was his first glimpse of the street which the Albanians regard with so much pride.

He was once walking with one of his boyish companions & happened to enquire who lived in a certain house. "I don't know, but I'll find out," said the boy & springing up the steps rang the bell.

"Does Mr. Brown live here?" "Yes," said the man who came to the door. "I am Mr. Brown," somewhat taken aback at this information, he asked his Christian name. "John Brown" said the man, "Oh, the person I wanted to see is Jim Brown, a colored man." This did not mend matters & the young scape grace was unceremoniously kicked off the porch.

July 9, 1863

Went to the hospital to see Mary Felton.

Most of the men are convalesing rapidly, some few badly wounded, looked dolefull, with their confined limbs.

Our forces are persuing the Rebels, the river is entirely unfordable, but Gen Lee's men are said to be making a bridge near Williamsport. If they do not succeed in crossing, we must expect a very terrible battle.

July 11, 1863

Sat. 11th. Mary Felton left this morning, her place has been supplied by one of the nurses from Chester Hospital.

Reports from the upper Patomac give indication that a battle may be fought within 48 hours. Gen Lee has possession of the heights on the Hagerstown side of Antietam creek & his headquarters are in the town.

There is a rumour, tonight, that the fighting has commenced. Lee's position seems to be strong. He is acting now on the defensive. He holds the stone bridge over the Antietam at Funkstown.

The banks of the creek in that vicinity are bold & the ravine deep so that it will be difficult for our forces to cross unless we gain possession of the bridge.

Stewart Patterson has lost four fingers of his right hand in one of the recent engagements.

July 15, 1863

Wed. 15th. A visit from Mr. Frank.

He had just come from Gettysburg. Said the appearance of the battle field was still too dreadful to be described, numbers of horses lay putrifying in the sun, most of the men had been buried, long mounds marking the principal places of interment. Many were buried separately with neat wooden head boards.

On one had been nailed the bottom of the man's napsack on which his name had been painted. In the cemetary where the worst part of the fighting had taken place, he found the graves of three men from his own village lying side by side.

115

The college building was a hospital for the rebels.

He conversed with some of them. They were undiscouraged.

The village of Gettysburg was filled with the wounded, almost every house was a hospital. The incidents of those terrible three days will long be remembered in that vicinity.

Port Hudson is ours.

The Rebels have escaped. Gen. Meade & others are in Virginia, greatly to the chagrin of the Government.

July 18, 1863

Sat. 18th.

We have been greatly excited for the last days, by the accounts of the terrible mob in New York.

Railroads have been torn up, houses & other property destroyed, & the lives of many of the citizens sacrificed to the fury of men governed only by their passions.

Resistance to the draft had been expected, but no such frightful scenes as these. There has been some trouble in Boston, also in Troy & other northern cities, but none in Philadelphia.

Victory has smiled upon the union arms this week, besides the surrender of Port Hudson.

Gen. Bragg has been forced to retreat to Allatoona, Georgia, leaving east Tenn. free of Rebels & Joe Johnstons has been defeated in Miss.

July 20, 1863

Mon 20th.

Bad news from Mr. Bell. Father saw Mr. Welling yesterday, who said Mr. B. was dangerously ill. He promised to come & give us particulars.

Went to Mrs. Hodge's to dinner yesterday, saw the flag Capt. Rodgers captured from the *Atlanta*[53]. She was a very fine vessel which had run the blockade into Charleston's harbour. She had been iron clad by the Southerners & sent forth with the confident hope that she would annihilate the blockading fleet.

The flag is very pretty, white, with a St Andrews cross with white stars on a square in the corner.

---

[53] Capt. John Rodgers, commander of the ironclad monitor *Weehawken*, successfully navigated from Brooklyn to Charleston, through the same storm that sank the USS Monitor.

On June 17, 1863, he forever distinguished himself by capturing the *CSS Atlanta*. His actions won him a promotion to Commodore and earned a Congressional resolution acknowledging his success.

FLAG Naval ensign of the Confederate States Navy

The rioters are quelled in N.Y. Several places in New Jersey have been affected by the discontent & even little Princeton assumed a hostile attitude & attempted to stop the passage of troops on their way to New York.

July 21, 1863

Carlotta Gerolt was married to day. She has been engaged for several years. Madame Gerolt said she met Mr. Ward at a place on the Rhine where she had been invited to spend her first three months, after leaving school.

The 9 weeks passed under the same roof, led to an engagement which the Baron consented to ratify at the end of five years, if they should continue of the same mind, holding no interview in the interim.

Their mutual constancy has been rewarded. He is in the British India service.

Fighting has commenced at Charleston by land & sea.

The brave *Weehawken* is of the fleet she led the last engagement.

July 23, 1863

Wed. 23rd. Mr. Welling, here, says Mr. Bell very ill.

G. has gone on to see him.

July 27, 1863

Mon. 27. Saw Baron Gerolt yesterday at Mr. Kennedy's. Said the family would leave here soon.

Went to Prof. Malile this morning to learn how to cast.

The Southerners have succeeded in Crossing the Blue Ridge. After trying several of the Gaps, they forced that of Chester & are now in their old field of action.

I suppose we shall have another panic in Washington before long. The venerable Mr. Crittenden is dead.

November 14, 1863
Monday.

Nell & myself came home last Monday from the country, after an absence of almost three months.

We chose the beautiful valley of Wyoming[54] for our summer residence. It is about three miles in width & lies between two ranges of high hills, the Susquehanna, flowing through its centre.

The views in every direction are exceedingly beautiful & the historical associations connected with the controversies of the early settlers & the Indian atrocities are exceedingly interesting.

A monument is erected on the spot where perished most of the brave men who fell in the terrible massacre immortalized in Campbell's poem[55].

The first few days, Father was with us & we, that is Cary & myself, had the pleasure of going with him through one of the coal mines of the district.

We stepped upon a wooden platform & slowly descended a shaft 190 ft. in depth from the square opening at the top, until we found over ourselves in black darkness, faintly illuminated by the lamps held by our guards.

We waited a few moments to "get our eyes," to use a mining phrase, & then proceeded along a low arched way. The sides & top all of coal, as we could see only when we approached our lamps close enough to its jetty surface following the course of a narrow rail road.

Suddenly from out the distant darkness, a faint star appeared, growing brighter & brighter until the blackened face of a miner peered through the darkness. The lamp in his hat shedding a faint ray of light.

We saw more of these moving stars from time to time, until we came upon quite a collection of them, the dirty forms of the miners, faintly visible as they stood around a large grate, full of burning coal placed at the mouth of one of the air shafts for the ventilation of the mine. The hot air rising, producing an upward current which carries off the impurity from below.

We proceeded a little further to where the men were preparing to blast & then, not unwillingly, retraced our steps to an inclined plane, up which

---

[54] Wyoming Valley, Pennsylvania. In the general proximity of Scranton-Wilkes-Barre-Hazleton.
[55] Thomas Campbell, "Gertrude of Wyoming: A Pennsylvania Tale (1809)

we climbed over heaps of fine coal, until we came into a part of the mine now no longer worked.

Here, Mr Minor one of the gentlemen who accompanied us, fired a blue light & then for the first time we had some idea of a coal mine.

Before us behind us, in every direction stretched away the dusky arches of coal, supported by massive square columns of the same material seamed at regular intervals with slate, while the blazing light gave a strange unearthly look to the scene.

Suddenly, we were in darkness again, one more allumination we had & then a faint streak of what appeared very much like moonlight appeared from in the distance from what appeared to be a very small opening, but which gradually seemed to increase in size as we approached, until a lovely picture of rural beauty presented itself to our admiring eyes through the mouth of the mine. Very glad were we to see, once more, the light of day.

Wearied with our exertions, we seated ourselves on some fragments of slate & while selecting from these specimens containing impressions of fern leaves, refreshed ourselves with the contents of a basket which had been carefully carried by one of the party.

Before us lay the entrance to the mine, a succession of low arches in the side of the hill, reminders of the pictures I had seen of ancient tombs in Egypt. I told Mr. Minor so & remarking that these coal formations were older and older than the monuments even of that hoary age, he repeated these beautiful lines to an Egyptian mummy which have always been such a favorite with Father.

The remained of the day was passed in driving over the valley & in enjoying the exquisite views.

The next week Father & Cary left us for the Lakes & Niagara & Mother, Nell & myself moved from the mountain house where we had been staying to the town of Wilkesbarre, where we remained for six weeks.

We were there during the election for Governor, great complaints .were made by the Democrats that the Republican soldiers were allowed to return home & vote while the Dems. were kept away & so the election carried by fraud.

The same was said to be the case in Phil.

The Amish are mostly democrats & greatly opposed to the war, fears are entertained that when the draft is enforced they will rebel.

In my humble opinion, we have every reason now to fear civil war between the Republican & the Democrats. Our country is in a terrible state.

Far away from political excitement & enchanted by the beautiful hills of Wilkesbarre, I have barely opened a newspaper during my absence so that I know very little of what has been going on.

The repeal of the Habeas Corpus, the foundation of our own & well as English liberty could not fail to excite us, however, even there & lead us to wonder at the daring of the despotism that now rules us[56].

We have been defeated in the west, but have gained in a late engagement in Virginia, our victory seemed to have been a bloody one however, most of the wounded have been brought to the hospitals near us.

We saw two from the rebels there on Wednesday. One was shot though the head, the other the lungs. I suspect they will die. Will this miserable war never end?

Father has gone to the club tonight, before he went, he was reading a book on Swedenbourgianism by Mr. James, a former pupil of his & who has always been grateful to him.

When Father was going abroad, Mr. James asked him to purchase him some books & placing a sum of money in his hand, told him to use the balance as he chose. Father was greatly surprised to find it was $250. He purchased philosophical instruments with it, now in Princeton college.

Miss Chase was married on Thursday.

Father went to the reception in the evening. Her dress was of white velvet. She is very pretty & interesting & the groom, Gov. Sprague is agreeable. I hope their future may be happy.

I forgot to say that we met Mrs. Bell in Phil.

She has gone through much hardship while living in Nashville, but is looking well.

She told us many sad tales of the cruelty of the soldiers to the people there, but they are balanced by others equally harrowing, which we hear of the southerners.

Human nature is the same, North & South, & when men are allowed unbridled reign to their passions, they will commit outrages upon their fellow men wherever they may be.

This mutual recriminations is what separates us, making us forget we are brothers. A party of Our friends in

Kate Chase and her husband, former Rhode Island Governor and Senator, William Sprague IV.

Philadelphia made a visit to Gettysburg while we were there. They said many of the bodies still lay unburied or at least the skeletons, for only bones lay whitening.

One of them had gradually sunk until it lay at full length in a stream beside which the brave soldier had met his end.

One of the young ladies, wishing a button from a coat that lay half covered with soil was horrified when told the garment was attached to a body.

Every where in the town, marks of the dreadful affray were seen. A young girl was the only female killed[57], frightened by the storm of bullets falling round the house in which she was alone with her mother, she entreated the latter to retire with her to the cellar. But to do so they would have been obliged to pass into the open air & thinking they were safer where they were the mother refused. A few seconds after her daughter fell dead at her feet, shot by a bullet passing through the room.

Mary Virginia Wade, age 20.

She was obliged to remain alone with the corpse until the cannonading was over.

Such is but one of a thousand sad scenes induced by this terrible war.

November 19, 1863

Had a delightful walk in the woods with Mr. Harris & Mrs. Young.

Made a translation from the Magazin Pittoresque for Father of a notice of the regulation of pensions in _____ in _____. Father gave it to Mr. Welling in the evening for the *Intelligencer*.

November 20, 1863

Went to the Navy Yard to see one of the Monitors there for repairs. She is a flat boat only a few inches above the water with nothing to be seen upon her iron plated deck, but a steam pipe -- a tall pipe for ventilation, a few little holes here & there for the same purpose, which are tightly closed.

We climbed into this through a small opening & saw her great guns. One of them is a monster, the other some what smaller, but large enough to make one shiver at the thought of the damage she might do.

---

[57] Mary Virginia "Ginnie" Wade, age 20. A Gettysburg native, Wade worked with her mother as a seamstress. She may have been engaged to Johnston Hastings Skelly, a corporal in the 87th Pennsylvania, who had been wounded two weeks earlier in the Battle of Winchester. He died from his injuries on July 12, 1863, unaware that Wade had died days earlier.

The turret can be turned in any direction. 18 men are required to man the guns, how they can find the room in the confined space round them I cannot imagine.

The greatest danger they are exposed to is the loosening of the bolts fastening the iron plates, which are sometimes driven into the turret by the robust concussions causing great damage.

The quarters for the officers & men are of course entirely under water. They seem to be quite comfortable, although very small.

It is very difficult to ventilate the vessel, the pipe for that purpose we observed on deck is a new invention.

We were shown an engine for pumping in the air through the opening in the top of the Turret.

After leaving the Monitor we went on board of another vessel, which has been awaiting government order for three months. She has an apparatus for heating the steam after it comes from the boiler & so a greater amount of the power is produced from the same amount of fuel.

Capt. Blake, her commander, received a sword for gallant conduct on board the Hatteras, which was sunk by the Privateer Alabama.

In the evening, Miss Felton, the Misses Blagden, & Mr. Welling, Mr. Harris & others took tea with us.

November 21, 1863

Father read poetry to me all the evening.

November 23, 1863

Saw Mrs. Hodge after church on Sunday. She said Capt Rodgers was preparing to sail. He has been very ill during the summer.

Com Shubric is very ill with fever. Father saw his daughter, Mrs. Chamber to day, she fears he cannot recover.

November 24, 1863

Rain all day.

Father made experiments in regard to the specific gravity of oils. He said he judged whether they more less viscid by the velocity with which they spouted out through a hole in the bottom of a vessel into which they were poured.

He judged that all liquids ought to flow, they sink on with equal velocity for although some are much heavier than others, as mercury than water, the weight upon each atom as it passes out from the superincumbent atoms of the liquid is proportionally greater in one case than the other.

When reading about Specific Gravities, He said it amused him now to think how some old women that he knew when he was boy used to obtain the specific gravity of their soft soap, boiling the lye they obtained from ashes until an egg which would sink in water would swim.

He said it was a great disappointment to him that Will could not follow in his footsteps. He had manifested a great taste for Natural Philosophy when he was a very little boy, but as Father was not attached to Princeton college while he was there, his attention was turned in other directions.

January 1, 1864

The day has been cold & windy. Father went out as usual with Dr. Bache. He came home much earlier than usual on account of the cold.

He did not say much about his visits, but mentioned, tho he had been very cordially received by the Sec. of War, who asked him why he did not provide better weather for the New Year, adding the Smithsonian and the War Department find it difficult to suit everybody.

Nell was sick so we did not enjoy our calls as much as usual.

January 2, 1864

We expected Prof A & his wife.

Dr. Torrey & daughters & other members of the New National Academy, but they have not come.

January 4, 1864

Prof & Mrs. A arrived this morning they had been detained by an ice freshet.

The Academy opened to day. Outsiders will not be admited until the constitution & rules of the Society have been properly arranged.

Mrs. A rested during the day.

In the evening, Dr. Torrey arrived in about an hour after his daughter. The latter had left N.J. the same day as her father, but had passed a day or two in Princeton, the former had also been detained by the ice freshet.

Dr Hall, the Geologist, & Dr. Shoreg, the mathematician, are also staying with us.

January 5, 1864

Tuesday. The gentlemen of our party went immediately after breakfast to the meeting of the Academy.

The room appropriated to the use of the Savans is opposite to the gentlemen's gallery of the Senate.

Called, or rather left cards, for Mrs. Silliman & Mrs. Lee Conte & saw Mrs. Admiral Davis. She is a quiet, ladlylike, little person -- so deaf that it is quite difficult to cary on a conversation with her.

Miss Lezzie Jackson came to us just before dinner.

The discussion at the dinner table was very interesting. The employment of disembodied spirits was speculated upon.

Prof. A. thought the knowledge & habits of study formed here were only a preperation for the knowledge to be unfolded in another world.

Spirit rapping[58] & table moving was mentioned & Dr. Strong gave some remarkable instances of the latter he had witnessed. He could not explain them, but could not doubt the evidence of his senses:

The tables were heavy & without caster - but moved with a rapidity that to him was truly astonishing.

Father told of two young ladies who had attempted table moving in his presence. He fastened the arms of one of them to her sides so that she could exert any pressure upon the table, still the movement continued.

He pinioned the arms of the other in the same way & the table remained motionless. The young lady was exceedingly astonished to discover she had been using pressure of which she was entirely unconcious.

Prof A. said he had weighed his hands in the position they then were, lying gently upon the table with his body slightly inclined forward & found the amount of pressure equal to 30 or 40 pounds each the weight being that of the arms & shoulders as well as the hands. If he bent forward at all this 60 or 80 pounds was of course increased to a much greater amount. It was evident then that if several persons were seated around a table even though it were a heavy one the mere weight of the hands would be sufficient to move it without any voluntary pressure. The rotary motion might be due to the fact that persons in the position assumed, naturaly would lean a little more on the right hand than the left & so give an impetus in a particular direction.

A reception in the evening at Sec. Chase's in honour of the Academy

January 6, 1864

Wednesday.

Went to the Capitol with Mrs. A.

Visited the Academy. The room was well lighted & pleasant. Dr. Bache sat in the presidential chair on a slightly raised platform with a large table before him. The Savans were seated in arm chairs before him, listening to Prof. Pierce who was explaining some very perplexing looking problems upon the blackboard. We did not stay long.

Prof. Agasiz went with us to see Mrs. Douglass. The pretty came down looking very handsome. The mingling of deference & playfulness in her

---

[58] Sprit Rappings, an elaborate parlor activity in which a hostess claimed to communicate with the dead, first rose to predominance during the American Civil War and in the years to follow. Mrs. Lincoln is even said to have participated in communicating with spirits.

manner to the Prof was very pleasing. She asked his advice in reference to her boys. She lived for them & taught them to be proud of the name they bore. We gave her the love she said she preferred to admiration.

M Fallon asked us to take tea with her at the Hospital. The party consisted of Prof & Mrs. A, Prof Pierce, Admiral Davis & wife, Dr & Mrs. Bliss, Miss Lacock, Miss Lowe, & Mary & myself.

We found a table spread for us in the kitchen with a drummer boy for a waiter. We were as merry as possible and the Prof.'s declared they would not have lost such an entertainment for the greatest dinner in Wash.

I told Prof Pierce we had left him in the morning in despair he was so hopelessly deep. We wondered if might not grow to wise for himself some day & fail to understand his own problems. He laughed as he answered that "know thyself" was the most difficult problem given to man. But grew earnest and grave when we asked if there was no danger of his finding himself some day beyond the sympathy of his fellow men.

"I can never be beyond the sympathy of God. I can never be lonely in the study of the great works of the Creator. If Jesus Christ were on earth, would we care for the sympathy of man? Would we not find in him an all sufficiency?"

It was pleasant to hear a man of his caliber mention that name with so much reverence & love.

January 7, 1864

Thurs.

Judge & Mrs. Searing, Miss Bates, Mr. & Mrs. Sprague called.

A party at Sewards.

January 8, 1864

We had quite a merry scene after breakfast this morning.

Miss Soney & Miss Jackson have been teasing Prof. Hall with the pretense that they had some serious cause of complaint against him.

This morning they promised to tell him what it was. As they had really nothing we were curious to see how they would get out of the scrape.

Jane commenced by advising him to take something to make him sleep better at night, otherwise he would divulge important secrets if he were not more careful. A habit of talking in sleep was certainly very dangerous.

The poor Prof. looked completely puzzled and declared that if he had been so unfortunate as to talk in his sleep he certainly had said nothing that could give offense to the ladies.

He would call in Dr. Strong as witness to that effect.

The good old Dr. was greatly astonished when Jane asked him if he remembered what he had said to her, the morning before, concerning the remarks made by Prof Hall in his sleep.

He rubbed his hands together, but could not remember that he had said anything in regard to Dr. Hall.

Jane told him to think again. She deemed him at least a reliable man. The Dr. in vain tried to deserve the title of reliable, Dr. Hall in triumph went for Dr. Torrey who also slept in the same room with him.

The Doctor did not know what the joke was precisely, but entered into the spirit of it and accidently hit upon the very thing we wanted him to say. I asked him if he had been at all disturbed in his rest. He said, yes, by snoring & by low muttering from Prof Hall.

He was asked if he could distinguish what was said. He said not all, but he believed it was something about the bother it was to wait upon ladies at parties.

Jane pronounced her father an honest witness, a truly reliable man & told Prof Hall he might consider himself convicted.

Just then, Prof A. came in & asked us to stop at Mr. Seward's to enquire for his coat which had been lost the day before.

Dr. Torrey went out to help him look for it.

Presently, soon many peals of laughter were heard from the Prof. at the door.

He came in with Dr. Torrey by the collar. "I have found the thief, I have found the thief".

The laugh was now turned upon Jane & her reliable witness. Dr. Hall declaring his testimony could not be admitted.

Left with the other gentlemen for the Academy.

A party at Dr. Baches in the evening.

January 9, 1864

9th Sat. Made another visit to the Academy. They were busy with the election of foreign members. In the evening we had a soiree[59].

January 11, 1864

Mon. We had a delightful excursion to day.

Gen Barnard invited the Academy to visit the fortification & had a number of ambulances ready for us at 10 o'clock in the morning.

Our party consisted of about fifty.

At Fort ___, a cold collation was prepared for us which was very acceptable as the cold air had given us an appetite.

A long table was spread in a new bomb proof shelter. The commander of the fort, with his men, were drawn up in order to receive us the band playing Hail to the Chief!!.

The speeches at the dinner were exceedingly amusing.

---

[59] Party

Prof A__ arose first & thanked Gen Barnard for the pleasure of the day. Gen B. replied & called out some one else. The command of the fort was toasted. He said he was too young a man to speak before so learned a society.

That his post was the post of danger outside the bomb proof & he always wished it to be so, except on such occasions as the present.

Prof. Pierce, who was surrounded by ladies, said that outside the bomb proof must generally be the post of danger, but he had never thought he had -- with an expressive glance at the ladies -- been in greater danger than at this especial moment within this bomb proof.

The man who made the bomb proof was then called out. He felt diffident about speaking before such an Assembly, after such speech had been made & others.

Whatever he might say he was sure he could not bring down the house. Mr. Rutherford made a very pretty classic speech.

Prof Barnard made a long speech, very complimentary to Prof Agassiz to which that Gentleman expressed his pleasure at the delightful day we had enjoyed.

Corn. Hodges spoke. Other speechs follow with toasts to the President & vice President of the Academy & to Sec. Smith.

Once the dinner ended, we visited Arlington and then proceeded homeward.

In the evening, Mrs. Agassiz amused us with some incidents in the beginning of her married life:

Going one Sunday morning to her shoe closet, she found a snake coiled up in the toe of one of her slippers. Springing back in horror, she called out, "Oh Agasiz there's a snake in my shoe."

"Oh dear said the sleepy naturalist, I wonder where the others are?"

Mrs. A. retreated precipitately from the rooms.

Coming in the night before, with a number of snakes tied up in a handkerchief, the Prof. had left them forgotten upon the table & the reptiles had of course made their escape.

Another time, a jar was sent to the house containing, as she supposed, Jamaca ginger.

She placed it among her preserves & taking it down sometime after to supply her table, was horrified to find it filled with toads & snails.

She restored it to the delighted Prof who had been bemoaning the loss of his valuable specimens.

Before the Prof was married he had a bachelor's establishment in the cellar, of which was occupied by a pet bear. One evening he had invited some of his companions to sup with them.

In the midst of their conviviality, they were startled by heavy unsteady footsteps upon the stair leading from the cellar.

Presently the door was burst open & in walked the bear.

He had broken his chain pulled out the plug of a barrel of wine drank until intoxicated & then concluded to join the party upstairs!

The members thereof, objecting to his company, speedily dispersed.

With other similar stories Mrs. A amused us until bed time.

January 12, 1864

Tues.

Went this morning to the Freedman's city. This is a regular village built by Government for the contrabands.

We found them in comfortable little houses with a school, chapel & home for the infirmed and aged.

Prof A. lectured in the evening on Glaciers.

The house was crowded, a number of people came in after the lecture; among them, Mr. Lesboa, Ashkenazy, & the Austrian minister.

Ashkenazy said his name meant "the head of an ass," but that animal was not as desired in his courts, as with us.

January 13, 1864

13th. Wed. Called first at Mrs. Barnards, then at Mrs. Sewards, then at Mrs. Chase's, then went to the Capitol.

Mr. Davis was defending himself from the charge of treason. He might better have been quiet for instead of refuting the charges made against him with proper dignity he only indulged in vulgar abuse of his opponents. Another lecture from Prof Agassiz in the evening.

January 15, 1864

15th. Friday. Another lecture from Prof. Agassiz. He had described the cold period of the world when the earth was covered with ice, but had to appeal to Father for the cause thereof.

Father said it was caused by the ejection of an immense quantity of volcanic material into the ocean, producing an immense amount of vapor which was condensed for centuries into snow.

January 16, 1864

16th. Sat. The Agassizs left us to day.

They were the last except Jane Torrey of our pleasant party.

The next meeting of the Academy is to be held at New Haven.

January 25, 1864

25th. Went yesterday evening with Father to bid Mary Felton good bye. She leaves the Hospital to day.

We heard some of the men sing.

Father was very gloomy again about the state of the country.

One of the regents walked home from church with him. He said our money was depreciating so rapidly it would soon be worth little or nothing.

January 26, 1864

26th. Tuesday.

A meeting of the Regents last evening. We were in the parlor when they came in for supper.

The Vice President, Dr. Bache, Gen Totten, Mr. William Astor, Mr. Fessenden, Mr. Winter Davis, Mr. Seaton, formed the party. All them seem very much interested in the Institution.

Mr. Astor intended to resign, but he says now he is determined to continue one of the Board until he is turned out.

At the supper table, Mr. Fessenden spoke in high terms of Jef Davis and expressed his regret that he should be on the side of the rebels.

He was a warm friend of the Smithsonian & the Coast Survey.

January 27, 1864

27th. Wed. Another meeting of the Regents.

Only Dr. Bache & Mr. Davis of Kentucky came in to supper. The latter has been accused of treason & a motion has been made to expel him from the Senate.

January 28, 1864

28th. Thursday - a meeting of the commission

January 29, 1864

29th Friday - Went to a theatrical exhibition at Campbel's Hospital. The scenery & stage arrangements were made by the men & the comedy prepared by them for the occasion.

It represented various scenes in a recruit's life, ending with a drunken frolic in a Virginia inn, where the chaplain's daughter appeared as a pretty bar maid.

Her lovely little face formed a pleasing contrast to her rough companions.

January 30, 1864

30th. Sat.

Gen. Casey has just been here. Father has gone to the club.

I see by the *Intelligencer* that Mr. Davis is not to be expelled from the Senate.

The little Foundley has been with us for two or three days.

February 4, 1864

Feb. 4th. Thursday.

Father, last evening, gave me a more connected account of his life than I have ever had before

He said his grandparents, paternal & maternal came from Scotland in the same vessel landing in this country the day before the battle of Bunker's hill.

His paternal ancestor went to Deleware co., N.Y.

He was born in Albany, living there until he was seven years of age, when his Father died.

His Mother was left to her own for support and he was sent to Galway to his Grandmother.

He went to the district school until he was ten years old and was there placed in a store. Mr. ___, the head of the establishment, took great interest in him, giving him one or two floggings, which Father greatly resented at the time, but even in his anger acknowledged they justly deserved.

He was a handsome sprightly boy and a great favorite of the young men, who, as is customary in a valley store, collected around the stove in the winter evening or lingered about the door in warm weather.

He still continued to attend the village school in the afternoon, but had as yet shown no taste for books.

His thoughts were very busy in those days, however, and he would speculate in his boyish way about the mysteries of God & Creation until his mind would spin with the thoughts so big for his little brain.

One day his pet rabbit escaped from him & while he was chasing, ran into an opening or air hole in the foundation of the church which had, in some way, widened sufficiently to admit his squeezing himself through.

He followed his rabbit therefore on his hands & knees & attracted by a glimmer of light, he groped his way towards it. Found it proceeded from an opening leading into the church creeping through it, he found him behind a bookcase in the vestibul of the church, which was used for a village library.

Taking down a book - Brooks Fool of Quality, one fitted to excite an interest in a boy's mind, he was soon absorbed in its contents, spending the entire morning in the library.

This was literally the first book he ever read.

He made other stolen visits to the library.

His patron was very fond of novels which Father now read with avidity and obtaining a share in the Library, read all the works of fiction contained in it.

Commencing with the determination of reading only what was true, he at last rejected all, but what was imaginary.

He left the store when he was about 15 and I think was then employed in a watch making establishment for a short time

He did not like the business, however.

He had at this time a passionate admiration of the theater, spending all his spare money in attending it and was at last introduced behind the scenes and witnessed the different modes of producing stage effects.

He was now asked to join a society call the Rostrum -- a private theatrical association.

Entering as an obscure member, he had hitherto had very little intercourse with boys of his age - He soon distinguished himself by his ingenuity in stage matters and was made President.

His cousin, the watchmaker, left the city of Albany after father had been with him about a year and He was left without employment

He now spent his entire time at the Rostrum. Dramatizing a tale and preparing a comedy which was acted by the association and was in great danger of being ruined.

He had a slight fit of illnes and while he was confined to the house one day, a Scotchman, who was living there, left upon the table of the room Gregory lectures on Nat Phil.

It commenced with an address to the young reader trying to encite in his mind an interest in the objects about him.

He had often shot an arrow, from a boy, but had he ever wondered why the arrow left the bow, why it fell to the ground & other things. Looking into a blank wall, we saw nothing, when gazing into a stream we saw objects around us -- repeated more clear & beautiful in detail than any painting. Why is this? It is due to reflection of light, but what was reflecting of light? What is light?

Have enough thought Father, it is a queer thing I never thought of that before.

His interest was unchained, he read the book and when he came out of his sick room the whole world seemed changed to him. Every object was teeming with interest. He had, as it were, awakened from a dream.

He had before, taken very little interest in things about him. He lived in an ideal world. In the country. He could not tell one tree from another, he lived amid the fancies of his childish brain.

Now all was changed, the actual world was before him more deeply interesting than any creation of the imagination.

He at once made a resolve to spend his life in the acquisition of knowledge and going to the Rostrum, he immediately resigned his office of President and attended a night school.

Soon became the assistant of his teacher.

It was about this time that he fell in with a man wishing to introduce a new system of grammar, who employed him to go with him, partly as pupil partly as assistant.

Father spent a week or so in studying the rules of grammar & for the first time, discovered the use of it.

One whole week was pursued in then subject and then he went on his grammatical tour.

On his return, he was admitted into the Academy and studyed diligently.

He was then induced to take charge of a school in the country for a short time. He was later on probation for the first month and paid only eight dollars, but the next month had so raised him in the estimation of his employers that they paid him fifteen.

He soon returned to the academy and assisting one of the young men in attendance.

He now could pay his own tuition and improved his opportunities.

The Patron at this time wanted a young man as tutor for his sons. Dr. Beck sent Father to him.

When he rang at the door, a black man who had been sailor under his father, accosted him with "Are you not son of Billy Henry?" "Yes," said Father.

"What are you doing here? Going to be tutor to the three sons?"

"Bless you," said the old man. "You will be as great as Napoleon Bonaparte one of these days. Mark my words, I know it. You will be as great as Napoleon Bonaparte."

His sojourn with the Patron was very pleasant, he had only four pupils and was obliged to teach only a few of the morning hours. The rest of the day being at his own disposal and devoted to the study of physiology, chemistry, anatomy & devoting some thought at the time of studying for a physician and make some advance in medical studies.

At this time, the southern counties of New york paid a large tribute to the Northern counties in the use of the canal, so it was proposed to balance another - to have a great state road in the south.

So Father was approached to survey the ground. Starting with his men from West Point, they went through the woods, engineering to Lake Erie.

The Patron was very sorry to part with him & pressing his hand affectionately in parting, told him if he could ever serve him with his patronage or purse, he would be most happy.

Father acquited himself so well in his engineering tour that the Patron & others were anxious to secure him a captaincy in an engineering corps.

There was much surplus money in the Treasury then, which it was to be spent in internal improvement.

The Diary of Mary Henry: The Civil War Out My Window

The bill for the organising and of the corps, however, did not pass congress and Father, being at this time appointed to fill the vacancy of a prof. in the Academy. Gracious to the solicitation of his friends, he accepted, although against his inclination as he had become very much fascinated the life of an engineer.

He now commenced a series of experiments in Natural Philosphy. The first regular series that had been made in the country.

Dr. Hare had invented his blow pipe, but regular & systamic investigation of the principal of science had not yet been attempted.

Father, now rapidly advanced in reputation and the friend who had hitherto supported him, now commenced to look rather coldly upon the young aspirant who was growing fast about him.

He was walking sadly along, one day, when he was accosted by one of his friends.

"You aut to leave," said his friend. "Albany is no longer the place for you. You have come to the surface here, you must go elsewhere."

The call now came from Princeton and Father went on there. The place seemed very pleasant to him. There Uncle was with him.

Uncle went to the seminary & Father accepted the professorship. He had been married a short time before.

The college was then little esteemed, the number of students not 100. Father with the diffidence of himself that always troubled him when he entered upon a new position, commenced his duties with solicitude. But here were his happiest days.

Coming in the winter time, the place seemed somewhat dreary, but after a short, absence in Albany, Mother & himself returned to praise -- the spring in all its beauty.

The campus, beautiful in its fresh green & redolent with lilac. Here in this old college his time passed in the investigations so interesting to him, the fame of his magnets attracted students and the number of students at once went up to over 200.

His class was such as he liked to teach. He had been used to the noisy boys of the Academy and was at first almost embarrassed by the great attention of the apprentice students who now listened to him.

He had calls now from William & Mary College and from Virginia. The latter was one very desirable in a pecuniary point of view, the salary being their current in the country. Father did not like to abandon the college, however, now that he had become interested in it.

The faculty sent him abroad and resumed his life.

His tenure now was one of great pleasure & profit.

When this Institution was established, he wrote to express his opinion of what it should be and was then asked to take charge of it.

He left Princeton with very great reluctance & many misgivings to enter upon duties which have been arduous and not of the same interest as those which inspired him in the classic halls of Princeton.

This outlay, Father has promised to fill up.

Photo: Smithsonian Institution. circa 1864.

July 10, 1864

Sunday. Several persons were called out of church this morning exciting our curiosity and on coming out after service we were startled by the intelligence that a large body of Southern troops 40 or 50,000 in number were marching on Wash.

They had thrown the city of Baltimore into a state of intense excitement by their near approach - had cut the northern central railroad & burned Hagerstown.

These reports have all been confirmed, but there are various conflicting opinions entertained in regard to the supposed object of the enemy whether a raid, merely for purposes of plunder or a demonstration on Wash. to call off Gen. Grant's troops from the vicinity of Petersburg is still a matter of conjecture.

The quartermaster's clerks have all been ordered to report themselves for service in the defence of the city.

July 11, 1864

The city is in a state of intense excitement.

Southerners said to be at Rockville & skirmishing with our pickets. After cutting the Northern Central R.R. yesterday, they proceeded across the country cutting the telagraph wires on the Phil & Harford turnpike & burning the residence of Gov. Bradford, about 5 miles from Baltimore - this was in retaliation for the burning of Gov. Fletcher's house[60] by Gen Hunter.

At Magnolia Station about 18 miles from Baltimore, the bridge over Gunpowder Creek has been destroyed.

2 P.M. Mother just in from a shopping expedition. Says we are surrounded by the rebels - city filled with refugees from the country, coming in with wagons filled with household effects. Rebels fighting at Tenally Town.

4 P.M. Mr. Gill brings news of the closer approach of the enemy.

Mr. Shand has come to offer his services in case they may be needed in the defence of the Institution.

Says the rebels are attacking Fort Mass. on Seventh St.

We are going to the top of the high tower.

View from the top of the Tower —

The city lies before us peaceful & beautiful in the rays of the setting sun.

The broad river lost in the distance by a cloud of mist hanging low on the horizon is dotted here & there with boats, two of which have moved with stealthy eager motion into the port of the Arsenal. We are told they are laden with troops.

Dr. Hamlein & others have joined us.

A jet of smoke rises. curling off into the rose colored clouds, disappearing & appearing again, marks the scene of the conflict if there is any.

Mr. De Rust, who is looking through the glass, reports signals from the top of the soldiers Home. We look & see the signal maker with his flag.

A body of colored troops are moving down 12th, we watch them as they move slowly along, their wives & little ones crowding the pavements.

The sun is sinking lower now & shedding its last beams over a scene of such quiet beauty it seems to mock our excitement.

The shadows of the towers stretch longer & longer over green parterre below us.

Gen. Hamlin tells now to night will the attack be made. Our hearts beat quicker, we look towards the distant Capitol, the white house &

---

[60] In 1864, Union soldiers under the command of General David Hunter set fire and burned the home of Virginia Governor John Letcher. The home was located in Lexington, Virginia. In retaliation, Confederate forces in Maryland, under the command of Bradley T. Johnson, Bradford's home and burned it to the ground – destroying all his furniture, library and papers.

wonder if it possible they can be in danger. But the -little-jets- of smoke curl up lazily as before. The sun has gone down.

Gen Hamlin rises to go we follow, one by one.

10 P.M. Have been in the city, every thing quiet & orderly
The rebel force estimated at 45,000 Gen. Blair's house burned.

July 12, 1864
12th Tuesday.

Firing at 5 O'clock in the morning. Communication with Baltimore cut off.

Firing again at 1'cl clock. nothing known.

Went to drive in the afternoon with Mr. Gill - went to terminus of 14th & 7th sts. Driving first out Seventh, we came to Campbell Hospital, where at the top of a hill we were stopped by a man on horseback who forbade our going farther.

A number of people had collected here to see if anything could be seen or hear if any news was afloat.

We retraced our steps & crossing over to Seventh street encountered the President coming into the city from the soldier home in an open barouche, surrounded by a body guard of horsemen.

Just beyond the college we were stopped, as before, & obliged to return.

July 13, 1864
11 A.M.

No certain news - Rebels said to be retreating.

2. P.M. News of the retreat of the enemy confirmed.

Night. Went to drive with Father, passing the railway yard near the Inst. saw it filled with engines. All rolling railway stock had been sent to Alexandria by order of the President when the city was supposed to be in danger, but had been sent back as rebels are said to be at Falls Church.

Driving out 14th we encountered about 75 prisoners, escorted by mounted officers. Their butternut dresses were soiled & torn, but they seemed undaunted & many of them were exceedingly fine looking.

One tall Virginian amused me, he moved sturdily alone in dignified disdain without one look of the curiosity indulged in by his companions.

We encountered no other war indications, until we came to the hospital surrounding Columbia College. The poor invalids were enjoying the cool evening air, lining the banks on each side of the road.

One or two pale sad young faces excited my warm sympathy. They looked so much in need of home kindness & affection.

Farther on we encountered the vedettes & were obliged to return.

There were about 10 soldiers placed at the side of the road with two stand of arms stacked in front of them. One of the men came forward to speak to us. He told us it was certain the rebels had retreated.

Father said he was surprised to learn there had been quite a severe battle in the neighborhood. "Oh no," said the man, "only a skirmish."

"But we lost 300 men," said Father, "Oh "that is nothing," returned the man. "We don't consider that anything of a battle in these days."

Life has grown sadly cheap within the last few years.

Turning down a side road we found a soldier stationed to guard a foot-path across the fields.

Further on, another stationed upon a crossroad. We were not molested again, however, until we came to the toll gate on Seventh St.

Here we were told by a fine looking young officer that the rebels had retreated towards the Patomac & our troops had gone to Tenally Town to endeavor to intercept them.

The vedettes on Seventh St. road were much further out than last evening.

On our return, Mr. Bates called, said the Southerners had greatly enriched themselves by the raid - had carried off not only cattle & money but men & impressed them in the Southern army.

They certainly managed the affair well, Hagerstown was compelled to pay $20,000 to purchase her safety. The town was not burnt as reported.

Some fears are entertained that the force of Southerners which alarmed us, will unite with those at Falls Church & attack us from the South.

Our for fortifications are too strong in that direction to be taken.

July 14, 1864

14th Thurs.

The Blagdens here this morning. They live so near the scene of conflict we had felt very anxious about them. They first knew of the state of affairs by the news which startled us all on coming out of church on Sunday.

On riding home, they saw an ambulance & some riders coming down the avenue & supposed the family were leaving, but on a near approach found the party consisted of Col. McCook & staff in search of a place to establish headquarters.

Numbers of our Union soldiers came to them Monday & Tuesday or food & drink, but they suffered no especial inconvenience except from their fear of losing their horses.

They visited the scene of action & gave us a great desire to do so.

Mary picked up a diary of one of the rebels who was interred while they were present.

One poor fellow had been buried so hastily his feet protruded from his grave.

The nurse of her little brother, whose husband was in the employ of Mr. Blair, and now captain in the army, told them the rebels had entered the house, burnt & tore her clothes, before her face, in retaliation, they said, for what her husband had probably done in the South.

Took all the food she had for her children & then told her they would fire the house.

She was leaving it, when Breckenridge rode up & exclaiming indignantly at the brutality of the men, ordered them from the premises & placed a guard there so that she should not suffer further molestation.

Her little sons were much attached to a small donkey owned by Mr. Blair & left in their charge, which had been seized by the rebels. This, they asked Mr. Breckenridge to restore to them. He did so, but it was afterwards seized again by the rebels, declaring it was old Blair's donkey & they must have it.

Much of Mr. Blair's furniture was destroyed before Breckenridge could prevent, but he succeeded in saving private papers & silver which were carefully packed & sent to a place of safety with a card saying "for the sake of old friendship."

Breckenridge had enjoyed Mr. Blair's hospitality while planning a duel in the vicinity & had been treated with great kindness.

At the house of Mr _____, she found devastating traces of the rebels.

The furniture was entirely destroyed and the yard strewn with letters of the most private & affectionate nature.

At 2 P.M we started to view for ourselves. The first mark of the recent troubles we encounter near Fort mass -- a woman stood disconsolately by the side of the road, near the remains of a house which had been burned.

We asked her if she had suffered by the raid. She pointed to the ruins and told us that it had been her home.

A union officer came to her & asked her for some kerosene oil, supposing it was needed for the Fort - she went with alacrity for it

He then asked for lamp wick & cotton cloth which she also gave him. "What do you want to do with these things," she asked.

"Burn your house madame," was the cool reply.

The poor woman was obliged to remove her property as best she could, losing most of it. Ruins of other burned houses, felled trees, & abatties fortifying the road next met our view, until we came to a barricade completely across the road, which compelled us to turn to the right & go through a field, where we encountered rifle pits dug by our men. Beyond this, we passed several houses, burned or sacked before we came to MB's beautiful residence.

The fence was torn down, the gateway only remaining. As we drove through the grounds, we found various pieces of the presence of the Southerners.

The smouldering ashes of their camp fires, broken boxes, canteens & other things. While innumerable poultry feathers testified to the havoc which had been made among the fowle. I doubt a cock crow will be heard there for months.

The house, we found guarded. It is delightfully situated, the avenue leading to it winding through wood, a grove of magnificent forest trees, which completely hid it until a turn in the road brought it to view. Some of the servants were folding up a carpet & packing, some at the side of the house.

A number of carriages containing visitors were at the front. We went round to the back entrance, picked up some hard tack, a song book, a pack of playing cards & some other trifles left by the rebels.

We drove through the grounds to a lovely spring & then passed out into the high way again by a different road from that we came. Every where we found signs of the rebels' tin cups, ashes & other things.

As we came on to the turnpike, we saw some persons in a grove opposite to us. We joined them & found some of the rebel graves.

Several large square pits filled with straw had been prepared for the burial of others, but were left unfilled in the hurry of departure.

Further up the road, we found some of the rebel wounded under three or four miserable tents.

In the first of these, we found the surgeon -- a fine looking officer who had been left in charge of them.

His frank, noble, undaunted bearing interested us greatly.

We asked if he was a prisoner. He said he thought he ought not to be considered such, as he had volunteered to remain with the wounded. His dress was rough & worn, but he proved an exception to the rule that a taylor makes a gentleman.

We asked if they had food. He answered, proudly enough, that had been left to supply their wants up to that time.

In the next tent, two poor fellows lay shot through the head.

One seemed to be dying. He lay with his eyes closed, breathing heavily.

His features were delicate & regular & his forehead, where the bullet had not reached it, as fair as a girls'. They both lay on the ground with only a little hay under them.

A bright looking little fellow was switching off the flys.

We asked him if he had had enough to eat. "Yes," he answered merrily, we always have that around you Yankees up here."

We left the two poor, unconcious fellows with heavy hearts.

There were 8 or ten in the next tent - one badly wounded in the leg, but looking happy & contented as he lay on the grass switching away the flys with a spray of leaves.

Outside the tent was a merry little officer, one of those who had volunteered to take charge of the wounded.

He cut off his rebel buttons for us &, when we objected, said with a laugh, he would capture some union ones.

"How long do you think it will take to make me a good union man?" he asked of a bystander.

"A great while, I should think," said the person addressed, "As you say you would shoot your own Father were he on this side."

Near the next tent, a poor fellow was pouring water over a wound in his head, by him was another of the volunteer nurses.

He said he had remained because he could not leave his Lieut. & asked us to go into the tent to see him. He was lying on a blanket with clean linen & shaved. His appearance in strong contrast with his surroundings.

His companions were dirty enough. Their uniforms were all dirt under their – whatever they might have been originally.

On our way home, we visited a house which had been riddled with balls from the Fort. Some rebel sharp shooters had been stationed here & protected by a pile of stones at the corner of the house. One of them had picked off an officer. It was afterwards occupied by our troops.

Our rifle pits extended from the house to the road, a distance of about 40 ft. They consisted of holes dug in the ground with a slight embankment of earth in front.

An Englishman, called in the evening, had also been at the scene of conflict. Had found upon the walls of one of the houses he visited numerous rebel inscriptions. On a marble top table, the only article of furniture left in the parlor was inscribed "This house is sacked in retaliation for the many homes made desolate in Virginia."

On one of the bedroom walls, "our complements to the ladies, sorry not to find them at home."

A note picked up on the stairs contained an apology & the regrets of the officer in charge to the young lady of the house for the destruction of her wardrobe.

A music book lay uninjured & beneath some lines addressed to "my mother in Heaven" was written "Sacred to an orphaned rebel."

The following is the purport of a letter addressed to the President found in the yard:

Dear Uncle Abraham,

We like the way you fight. We hope you will be reelected. We have come this time to show you what we can do. We will return & give you another lesson. We have inlisted for 40 years of the war.

Yours,
The biggest rebel in the country

July 18, 1864

18th Passed Sat. night at Mrs. Peale's.

Miss Wheeler came in - said the secessionists of the city of Baltimore had been aware of the intended raid of the southerners & many ladies had gone in the train captured at Gunpowder bridge, provided with refreshment & when the train was stopped & the cry of "the rebels, the rebels" startled the passengers they were recognizing their friends & saluting them by name.

Gen. Manydier was on the train with his wife & a young friend.

He had not been able to obtain a pass to leave Wash. & had put on his uniform to show his right to do so, but fortunately wore over it a linen coat which with his unmilitary appearance quite deceived the rebels & that passed by him with no supicion of his military importance, only demanding his watch & purse.

These, Mrs. Manydier, had tucked fully hidden on her person as soon as the cry of "the rebels" "the rebels" was heard.

They announced on opening the car door they did not intend to molest the ladies.

Gen Franklin was put in a buggy & driven some distance but at, on awakening about twelve o'clock, was surprised to find the sentinals left to guard him had fallen asleep.

He thought at first they were feigning, but they proved not to be, & slipping by them over a fence, he escaped into a wood nearby.

There he concealed himself in a gully, covering himself with leaves & remained until the next night. The rebels were round & near him all day searching for him. Coming out of his place of concealment when the coast was clear, at a late hour of the night, he met a countryman, with a load of hay bringing food secretly to his horses which had been concealed in the woods. He told his story & hiding under the hay was taken to the man's house where he remained until a messenger dispatched to Baltimore returned with a detachment of men for his protection.

Yesterday, Sunday, took tea with the Kennydy's.

They had visited the scene of the late contest & brought back various relics.

Great indignation is felt at the conduct of the Government.

Mr. Welling thinks the Presidents hope of a realection is entirely destroyed. It seems our excitement was caused by a very small force, the number of troops actually engaged in the feint on Fort Stevens did not exceed 500 men.

The whole force in Maryland is supposed to have been about 30,000, headquarters of Gen. Early, was on the farm of Mr. Higgs, adjoining that of Mr. Blair & the number of troops which bivouaced here seems to have been between one & two thousand.

About 500 appeared at Beltsville in the vicinity of our friend, Mr. Calvert's place.

Firing of a gun or two to induce our forces to believe they were enforcing there & then marching off towards the Montgomery road to join another detachment of the enemy, leaving the people in an intense state of excitement.

Our forces supposed them to be in the vicinity of Beltsville until the next day.

A skirmish was said to have taken place there, but it consisted only of the two or three shells thrown by the enemy to deceive us.

Miss W. told me her friend who had left her children in & was so uneasy about them found them not only well but highly delighted by the visit of the rebels they had played upon the piano & amused them generally.

There were other forces operating in the outskirts so that the total force in our vacinity seems to have been about 8,000.

Their duty seems to have been to create a diversion, while the remainder of the 30,000 were carrying off booty from Maryland.

The numbers of men, horses, cattle & other items carried off was immense. Horses & cattle in great numbers were driven to the barracades by the countrymen in our vacinity, but were refused admittance by the guard who had orders to allow no one to enter the city & fell an easy prey to the enemy, who had not even the trouble of seeking them.

The excitement of our friends in N.Y & Phil, while we could not be heard from, has of course been intense.

Gold rose to 290 & has gone down again. Went to buy stocking this afternoon found them $1.00 a pair.

July 19, 1864

Went to drive with Mrs. Douglass. Her husband's sons have lost all their property, which was in slaves & they are entirely dependent upon her. She spoke of them with the greatest affection

Many admiring glances were cast upon her as we rode along. She is amiable & exceedingly desirous, as she says, that every one should love her. Only she added naively, "I wish it sometimes & try for it so hard I defeat my own object."

The President has ordered another draft of 500,000 men.

Atlanta, Georgia, said to be taken by the Southerners.

Johnson in command of the rebel forces.

July 20, 1864

20th Wed. The papers are down upon Hunter for his neglect to defend the Shenendoah valley.

He had been intrusted with the guardianship of this great highway of Virginia, but left it to make an attack upon Lynchburg.

He burned a number of bridges & other things, but was too slow in his movements to take the place.

The rebels learned his approach & were reinforced before he reached it.

He was obliged to retreat before them & instead of stopping in the Shenendoah valley, passed into western Virginia, leaving said valley open to the enemy who abandoned the pursuit & maid the raid into Maryland which has caused such excitement.

Gen. Sigel was at Martinsburg, but his force was very small & would have been captured if he had not anticipated the movements of the enemy.

Gen Hunter in his retreat from Lynchburg, burned the Military Institute at Lexington with its valuable library & chemical apparatus.

Gov Letcher's house was also destroyed by order of the Gen. .

Mrs Letcher, only being allowed 10 min to save a few articles of clothing.

The Sacking of Washington College was done with his knowledge & permission though not exactly by his order.

The lady principal came to him & intreated him to interfere, but received a preemptory refusal. The North is very indignant at the supineness of the Government in not preventing the repeated raids of the rebels.

The pursuit has been abandoned. They escaped through Ashby's Gap last Friday.

Their train was more than a mile long, long trains of cattle & other booty had been sent before them. The new Treasury Sec., Mr. Fessenden, appointed in place of Sec. Chase, seems to be already in difficulty. He went to N.Y. to negociate a loan of $90,000,000 but has failed.

July 22, 1864

22nd Yesterday, Col. James F. Jaquess[61] came to see Father who said he had just returned from Richmond.

---

[61] A circuit riding Methodist preacher from Illinois.

He had gone there in his own private capacity to endeavor to make peace.

The President had given him a letter to Ge. Grant, who passed him through the lines.

He had an interview with Jef. Davis, who represented to him that the North was fighting for what it considered a question of vital importance to the Government of the country, but that there was much kindly feeling for the South & that money & food would be sent to them immediately if peace were concluded.

President Davis told him, he knew the loss of life & property had been immense in this war & could not be too much regretted. He had done all in his power to prevent the outbreak of the rebellion, but that now, no peace could be concluded without the recognicion of the Southern Confederacy.

Their forces were in condition They had killed more of the Northerners than their losses numbered.

He believed fully that they would be successful. He pressed his hand warmly at parting and assured him the effort he had made had been truly appreciated.

Davis looked well, better even than when he left Wash., but had lost one of his eyes from disease of the optical nerve[62].

Col. Jaquess was accompanied in his benevolent expedition by James R. Gilmore the author. The rebels, or a small part of them, have been attacked near Snickers Gap & obliged to destroy some of their plunder.

Sec. Fessenden having failed to obtain a loan from the banks is endeavoring to negociate one with the citizens.

Gold 262.

The Englishman called to say good bye.

If he at all represents the English people they are not very favorable to the North.

July 23, 1864

23rd Sat. The Northern papers still down upon the Administration for the late raid.

Great mortification felt & want of confidence in the power of the Government to put down the rebellion. Another informal effort made for peace by J N Sanders, C.C. Clay & J. P. Holcombe from the South at Niagara. They requested safe conduct to Wash. in order that proposals for peace might be considered.

They were not formally authorized by the authorities at Richmond.

---

[62] Plagued by a lifetime of health problems, Davis suffered from a chronic eye infection that made it impossible for him to endure bright light. Eventually, the CSA's only President was forced to endure an eye amputation.

Horace Greeley & Mr. Hay the President's sec. went to Niagara to confer with them by consent of the president who, finding the southern delegates were not official, were obliged to ask the President for orders.

He sent back the following, as this precluded all discussion announcing. as it does beforehand terms of peace. The self-constituted delegates retired, thanking H. G. & Hay for their efforts & stating that although the south might be weary of the sad desolating struggle & might long for the return of peace, still she would not yield to terms which would compromise her self respect.

Atlanta has not been taken as supposed, but seems to be in a fair way of falling soon. The Loyal Citizens of Maryland have presented a petition to the Pres., asking that the recent losses be assessed upon the sympathisers with the south. It is sincerely to be hoped the pres. will not yield to so unjust a demand.

July 26, 1864

Tues. Great battle at Atlanta a loss of 2000 on our side & about 6,000 on that of the enemy[63].

The city is not yet in our possession, but we have gained the outer fortifications. Mrs. Peale returned yesterday from a visit to the army before Petersburg with Mr. Seward & family. She seems greatly impressed with the strength of our forces & the probable success of attempt to take the city.

She said to Gen. Grant, "If you take it Gen., you will be in the White House," "Far be it from me madame to desire any such honour," he replyed[64]. There are rumours of another intended raid by the south.

July 30, 1864

30th Sat. Another fright. Some of soldiers returning from the pursuit of the...

[65]"Executive Mansion, Washington, July 18, 1864. "To whom it may concern: "Any proposition which embraces the restoration of peace, the integrity of the whole Union, and the abandonment of slavery, and which comes by and with an authority that can control the armies now at war against the United States,

---

[63] Actual causality numbers: C.S.A. losses – 5,500, U.S.A. losses – 3,641
[64] Ulysses S. Grant was elected president roughly four years later.
[65] A newspaper clipping stuck to the page of Mary Henry's diary. Though the clipping obscures the text of her entry, it offers additional insight to the war and the Union's terms of a southern surrender.

will be received and considered by the
Executive Government of the United
States, and will be met by liberal
terms, on other substantial and
collateral points, and the bearer or
bearers thereof shall have safe conduct
both way. "Abraham Lincoln."

...have caused great excitement in Tenally Town the inhabitants supposing them to be the Southerners closed their stores & prepared to depart.

Father came in at noon to say their alarm was not quite unfounded.

The Southerners are said to be again in possession of much territory. Gen Hunter at Maryland Heights

August 2, 1864

Aug 2nd Took tea yesterday at Mr. Kenedy's.

He had intended to start on a fishing excursion, but the rebels have possession of the road. Mr. K thinks the Southerners are in large force now.

The former raid was probably to supply this larger army with food & other items.

All publication of news has been forbidden by the Government. So we are completely in ignorance as to the movements of the armies.

August 3, 1864

3rd The silence imposed by the Government is at last broken & we learn that the rebels are advancing upon Harrisburg.

Mr. Welling says this force is the same that visited us before. Our troops, having ceased persuing them, they returned to give a blow at Gen Hunter's forces at Winchester, forcing him to retire to Maryland Heights.

August 4, 1864

The rebels are reported to be leaving the state, Gen. Averil in persuit.

Chambersburg said to be burnt.

Carey has gone to Oxford. Father to New Haven, so we feel quite lonely.

The magnificent seige of Petersburg has failed & with it the hopes entertained of the grand results of the summer's campaign.

Anticipated with such eager expectation.

The mines were sprung & the outer defences of the city were taken, but the negros failed in duty & the day was lost.

Thousands of our men, dead, cover the soil of Virginia bloody, fallen.

Battle after battle has desolated our homes & wrung our hearts with anguish. Mown down by the deadly fire of the southerners, opposed by them, steadily & well, what have we accomplished & found very with pain & difficulty to the gates of Petersburg.

Now after weeks of inertia, the hopes of the country lie as low as the walls our powder mines shattered. While the bulwark of the southerners rise stronger than before.

August 6, 1864

The excitement of the last raid has hardly subsided, but alarming rumours are again afloat.

Gen. Grant & Gen. Hooker are both in the city, as Mr. Bates informed us this evening and fear an attack upon the city

August 8, 1864

8th Mr. Tyler was here last evening. Sherman's forces repulsed at Atlanta. The paper commencing to call loudly for peace.

August 27, 1864

Father went to see Chief Justice Taney. He thinkd Pres. Lincoln will be reellected & that there will be revolution afterward.[66]

August 29, 1864

29th Princeton. Left home this morning. Came on with poor Mrs. Dod, who has lost her son another victim to this terrible war.

August 30, 1864

30th Father came to night from Phil.

Mother & Nell at Germantown. The democrats rejoicing over the nomination of Gen McClellen.

---

[66] A Maryland Democrat, Chief Justice Roger Taney's comment demonstrates the level of animosity openly displayed toward President Abraham Lincoln by top government leaders. On October 13, 1864, the clerk of the Supreme Court announced that "the great and good Chief Justice is no more," after having served for more than twenty-eight years as the Chief Justice of the Supreme Court. President Lincoln made no public statement.

THE BEGINNING.

ELECTION of M'CLELLAN!

PENDLETON, VALLANDIGHAM,
Vice-President.   Secretary of War.

ARMISTICE!

FALL OF WAGES!

NO MARKET FOR PRODUCE!

Pennsylvania a Border State!

INVASION! CIVIL WAR! ANARCHY!

DESPOTISM!!

THE END.

1864 presidential election poster, postulating the negative consequences that would follow, should the McCellen and the Democratic Party win the White House.

September 6, 1864

Shelter Island.

Arrived here last Saturday evening in company with Father & Carry. Prof. Hosford's country establishment is an antirevolutionary abode and has been in the possession of his wife's family almost from the first settlement of the Island.

It has been raining hard yesterday & to day, but we have enjoyed the excellent & ancient library of the house exceedingly.

Last night, Prof. Hosford gave us some interesting anecdotes of Webster[67]. Mr. Feller saw him not long before he died at Marshfield.

Webster had sent for him. Webster asked him if he would prefer talking in his library or to take a drive. Prof. Fellon chose the latter.

As they went out, Mr. Webster remembered he had not ordered dinner &, asking Prof. Fellon to accompany him, going together into the kitchen he gave miniscule directions for the preparation of meal.

He was very particular about his food & several of his favorite dishes.

They drove over a very fine country & stopping at a very extended & beautiful view, Webster said that many years before Fletcher's mother, he always thus spoke of his first wife. She sat where Prof. Felton then was & expressing her delight at the prospect & her conviction that no other spot in the world could be so delightful for a place of residence, He immediately commenced the negociations which ended in the purchase of Marshfield.

At a turn in the road they encountered an old man of 80

Farther on, they came to the family grave yard. Webster pointed out the graves of those he had loved & here said he, "I shall soon be laid myself." He died but very short time after this.

On retiring, he told Prof. Felton the stage would arrive for him at an early hour & added play-fully "as Mr. Webster will not be in a fit state to appear, he will bid you good bye from the window."

In the morning, as the Prof. passed down the yard to the stage, he saw him for the last time as he put his night-capped head out of the window to bid him farewell.

Father's first impressions of Mr. Webster were anything but favorable. Father went to see & endeavored to impress upon him his news in regard to the will of Smithson. Webster listened in silence for some time & then replied that he believed Smithson had no such refined ideas, "when he used the terms increase & diffusion of knowledge he only meant by to enforce his words."

He then spoke rather disrespectfully of scientists in general. Father asked if he formed his opinion from the men of Cambridge and being annoyed at his manner let the deplomatist see that he at least deserved & demanded respect.

---

[67] Daniel Webster (1782-1852), US Secretary of State & Senator from Massachusetts.

He was sufficiently affable before the interview closed, but Father entertained so disagreeable impression of his visit that he did not enter his presence again until he was compelled to do so.

In the year ____, England invited the U. S. into the World's Fair. The matter was turned over to the Nat. Inst. & a com. of arrangement appointed.

Webster caused some trouble by acceding to the request of the people of Northampton that the goods should be sent there & otherwise interfering with the arrangement of the Com. & Father requested to wait upon him.

As before, he was very ungracious, but Father, who had nothing to fear or ask from him, told him very plainly what he thought of his proceedings & again elisted from him the respect which was his due.

He met him afterwards at dinner, but did not have any further conversation with him until he was invited with him to meet Hosseth at the Presidential mansion.

Webster cared little for the foreigner & Father & himself spent the most of the evening together.

Previous to this, Webster, in a speech prepared for the laying of the corner stone of the new wing of the capitol, had endeavored to give a history of the advance of science since the older part of the building had been erected. He sent this part of his speech to Father for correction who found so many mistakes that he rewrote it & sent it to Webster -- it was adopted by him verbatim.

Webster could be merry enough at times. Once, when wishing to pass through a crowd unknown, he knocked his hat over his eyes went reeling from side to side of the pavement & singing & half drunken song passed entirely unrecognised.

September 7, 1864

New York.

Arrived here on Monday eve.

Had a very pleasant visit at Shelter Is. The Island is about 5 miles wide & 4 or 5 broad. The Indian name is Manhaset ha ha Cushewamack -- Island sheltered by islands.

After leaving Prof. Hosford's, went to Rockaway to visit Mr. Dickerson's family, the house was in full view of the ocean, the beach being only a few yards from the house.

A sand bar has been forming within the last few years which has greatly interfered with the bathing.

We went yesterday to visit central Park. It is exceedingly beautiful. Every thing has been done to render it so in the way of bridges, water &

Sheep grazing in Central Park, during the 19th century. Central Park was created in 1857.

rocks, the great want is trees. Some have been planted, but years of course must pass before they will be any addition to the landscape.

Met Mrs. Eames in the cars, she said there was a great revulsion in feeling at the North in spite of the victories which have lately crowned our arms.

One of the hottest among her republican friends had remarked the day before that he was by no means certain he was willing to give his last cent to free the negro.

Certainly we are beggining to feel the effects of the war.

Mrs Eames had been obliged to give $10 for a pair of coarse shoes for her little girl. Prices have gone down, however, somewhat, with the fall of gold. It stands at 190 now it has been as high as 275.

During our life in the country we, for a while, almost forgot the intensely interesting state of affairs.

We return to the city again to find everyone excited & interested in Sheriden's movements. He has driven the Southerners before him, down the valley of the Shenandoah and is now in the neighborhood of Richmond. Should he follow up his victories with a successful effort there, we may hope for peace, but if the army goes into winter quarters, the Southern army now weakened and probably dispirited by the fall of Atlanta, will have time to recruit.

Mrs. Eames said we had not received positive information within the last few days and some rumours were afloat that we had experienced a repulse.

Father went to Boston on Tuesday.

Nell is staying with Prof. Barnard. He was installed President of Columbia College on Monday.

Every one is of course deeply interested in the approaching presidential election. The coming contest will be between Lincoln and Mcclellan. Neither men fitted for the office. There seems little choice between them. Lincoln is a bear and totaly incompetent and Mcclellan merely a military leader, no statesman. If the latter were elected, the Southerners might return. if the former we may fear a rebellion at the North if the war does not speedily close.

Either must become in time the scape goat for the numerous train of ill which ever follow the track of the chariot of war. In these sad days the President holds no enviable office.

September 7, 1864

Went last evening to a festival at Mr. Beecher's church.

We were introduced to Mr. Beecher who said as Mr. Cuyler presented us, "the daughters of Prof. Henry that name is a passport anywhere."

Mr Beecher is a stout, good natured looking man very much like a fat boy. There is a certain mirthfulness about him which is pleasing if one could quite get rid of the feeling that it is assumed for effect.

His features are heavy & are more suggestive of good dinners than of intellect or great spirituality (My cousins accuses me of unkind criticism.)

He made a speech during the evening. It was not one of his brilliant efforts, my memory has retained very little of it.

One thing was worthy of note, He said it was "the object of the North to free the negro, not to pamper him. To lift from the heavy burden of slavery so that he might stand forth a man. If he could sustain that yoke could he not, when emancipated, from it go forth even as his white brother to work and warfare. Is he too weak for this, then let him go down."

Go down to what Henry Ward Beecher? To slavery again, or to be trodden as the dust under foot? To be hunted to the far corners of the earth as a burden and a curse? Strange philanthropy which thrusts upon these ignorant children of Nature a freedom, in many cases undesired, and casts them upon the cold charity of a selfish world.

Children in helplessness, Men only in enlarged capacity for suffering. Were it kindness to tear a child from a parent protection, though that guardianship might perchance have been stern or even cruel only to leave the little one to perish from cold & starvation. Truly the tender mercies of the abolitionist are cruel.

Have passed the day at Central Park. Nell seemed benefitted by the pure air, but very tired. There has been a temporary rise in gold today on account of rumours of a defeat.

September 8, 1864

Sat. Went to see Gardener's picture[68]. It is the reading of the Proclamation by Mr. Lincoln. Mr. Seward has just interrupted him to substitute the word _____ for _____. Sec. Chase is on the right of the President, somewhat in his rear standing with folded arms; before him Stanton is seated. The other officers of the cabinet are grouped about him in various attitude. The president himself is seated. I have given a very lame

---

[68] The painting was actually the work of Francis Bicknell Carpenter.

description of the picture. The likenesses are all good, but all of the distinguished gentlemen seem very indifferent to the great matter under discussion. It will be on exhibition for a short time in N.Y. and I suppose will eventually be purchased by Government and placed in the Capitol.

First Reading of the Emancipation Proclamation of President Lincoln, an 1864 oil-on-canvas painting by Francis Bicknell Carpenter.

January 2, 1865

I have been absent from home for four months and now on this, the second day of the new year, resume my journal.

Since I last wrote, the Presidential campaign has been decided & Abraham Lincoln appointed to another term as the head of the nation.

Sherman has made a victorious march through Georgia, Atlanta & Savannah owning his power.

Grant sill remains in the vicinity of Richmond.

The old Chief Justice, so long the friend & supporter of the Institution, has ended his day[69].

---

[69] Chief Justice Roger Brooke Taney (March 17, 1777 – October 12, 1864). Appointed by President Andrew Jackson, Taney is best remembered for delivering the majority opinion in Dred Scott v. Sandford (1857), that ruled, African-Americans, having been considered inferior at the time the Constitution was drafted, were not part of the original community of citizens and, whether free or slave, could not be considered citizens of the United States.

Mr. Dallas, Mr. Dayton Minister to France, Park Benjamin the author, & other distinguished men in the military & civil service of the country have also departed

The old year goes out weeping for some of the noblest of the country's sons. Weeping too for the peace which cometh not.

The recent victories serve but to cast a momentary & lurid light upon the clouds wich unvail in coming years.

Yesterday was New years day. We heard a sermon in the morning from Dr. Gurley & passed the evening quietly at home reading, Dr Thomas Browne's Religio Medici. Speaking of the numberless animals brought to life by the power of the sun, Father said that at the time Dr. Browne lived the spontaneos generation of animals by the heat of the sun was believed in & that now that supposition had been revived & much discussed.

Organic matter, when boiled sufficiently, it would seem to destroy all animal life when put away in air tight vessels exposed to the sun would after a time be found filled with animals.

Other experiments had been tried to prove whether these curious manifestations of animal creation were produced from eggs or by spontaneous generation.

In connection with the same subject, he said his own frame & being had from his earliest years been a subject of wonder to him & had puzzled his childish brain, sometimes almost to the verge of insanity.

He quoted this pretty little stanza:
"Bubbles upon a sea of matter born.
We rise, we break & to that sea return."

January 3, 1865

Prof. Agassiz came in last evening while I was writing.

The meeting opened this morning. There were only twelve members present.

After dinner to day, Prof. Agassiz read us a poem sent to him by Longfellow with some bottles of wine on Christmas eve.

Father & the Prof. differ somewhat on polittical matters.

Father thinks the term of the Presidency ought to be longer, perhaps for life, also the many offices under Government ought to be of longer durations or some means adopted to put an end to the system of office seeking so injurious to the country.

The elective franchise, he thought, ought to be limited.

Prof. Aggassiz thought it ought rather to be extended.

Father contended that a certain amount of property was needed to make a man sufficiently interested in the Government to vote.

The Prof. acknowledged that the property qualification gave more stability, but it was a stability he despised. He thought our great mistake lay in the insufficiency of public instruction. We ought to educate our lower classes better to fit them for voting.

Dr Torrey & Mr Leslie have just arrived.

Mr. Nystrom a Swede, has come in to spend the evening

January 4, 1865

The gentlemen have just left for the Academy.

At breakfast, the conversation turned upon the state of the country. Both Mr. Leslie & Prof. A. seemed to think it had never been more prosperous.

That the energy of the people now called out would at the close of the war need only to be turned in new direction to benefit the nation.

The slumbering citizens had been aroused and the nation "manured" to bring forth a glorious harvest.

Father said the country was now expending the recourses it had been laying up for ages. Apparent prosperity, the country enjoyed, but still the breakfast before them cost twice as much as it would have done two years before and should the war continue much longer, he would not have a cent to leave his children. That the nation was incurring an immense debt at the rate of 20 millions & a half daily.

Mr. Leslie acknowledged that individuals might suffer, but still the nation at large was the gainer.

Prof. A. said in support of the newly developed envy of the nation that the congress, before the war, would never have voted such immense sums as it now does for the public interest.

Literary & Scientific Institutions might now hope for larger appropriations. Father attributed this increased liberality to the inflation of the currency. Money had grown cheap & was easily parted with.

Sec. Blair & his son have caused some excitement by an attempt to visit Richmond. It is supposed to hold a conference with Jef. Davis. Gen. Grant refused to pass them through the lines not being authorised so to do by the President.

January 9, 1865

Jan. 9th. The Savans all left us on Saturday.

Prof. Pierce was with us Thursday & Friday.

We have with us now Mrs. Seldon from the South.

She succeeded in passing through the lines with great difficulty.

Gen. Sheriden telegraphed to Father to ask if he would receive her. She has been showing us to day some of her southern articles of dress. The shoes she had on were of coarse leather. She paid 90 dollars for a brass thimble. Prices of other articles were in proportion.

Fremont is to be minister to France.

January 16, 1865

16th Everet is dead New England's pride has fallen. How many of our great men have passed away within a year & how few there are to take the vacant places.

January 18, 1865

18th Fort Fisher has fallen & the Nation rejoices over another victory over the rebels.

Gen Terry, the hero of the action, is now the lion of the day. Gen Butler is in disgrace for not _____ the Fort. His severity and cruelty have placed him without our sympathy.

Fort Fisher is a few miles from Wilmington & commands the entrance to the Cape Fear River.

January 20, 1865

Have been making calls all day.

The city greatly excited by the report that Mr. Blair has gone on a second expedition to the South. The result of his first visit from which he has only just returned is doubtful, but it is generally believed that Pres. Davis consented to negociate peace if the President would receive his commissioners.

Whether we are deceived by another fake hope, our hearts beats more quickly with the thought that the beginning of the end of this terrible war approacheth.

We find an entirely new set of faces have taken the place of our old acquaintances since our retirement.

Wilmington it is said has fallen into our hannds.

January 25, 1865

I record in my journal to night one of the momentous and saddest events of lives. The burning of a large portion of the Inst.

The fire originated in the insersion of the pipe of a stove which had been put up in the picture gallery into an air chamber in the wall, instead of a flue.

The man in charge had been told to be particularly careful and Father had inquired of several times if he was sure all was safe. The fire must have been smoldering several days, but did not break out until yesterday, shortly after three o'clock.

I was sitting reading in the Library, reading and surprised at the sudden darkning of the room went to the window and finding a thick cloud of smoke or mist obscuring the view, I hastened from the room to discover the cause.

One of the gentlemen from the Inst. met me saying "the building is in flames you have but five minutes to save your property.

We immediately went to work packing books & other items. First clothing and then Father's Library.

The house was soon filled with people.

The furniture was soon removed and placed under military guard outside of the Inst. We were soon informed that our end of the building was no longer in danger so we stationed ourselves at one of the windows to watch the progress of destruction.

Truly it was a grand light as well as a sad one, the flames bursting from the window of the towers rose high above them curling round the ornamental stone work through the archs & trefoils, as if in full appreciation of their symetry, a beautiful friend tasting to the utmost the pleasure of destruction.

The capping of the square tower near us soon fell, filling the air with smoke & cinders.

On the highest tower which still stood, flames roared, above it the anemometer turned, steadily recording the wind while it fanned into greater fury the fires beneath.   Faithful in its dumb creation to the last.

Thousands of spectators had collected in the grounds - and a body of men kept mounted guard around the building, driving them back as they approached too near.

As the first mounted to the upper room of the tower, where Fathers papers were kept. It was very hard to see them come floating down. To feel that in the space of an hour was thus destroyed the labor of years.

When the east end of the Inst. was pronounced entirely out of danger, the furniture was restored and every one except the inhabitants of the building ordered to leave, a military guard was placed at the door to prevent intrusion and in our carelessly disordered rooms, we gathered to learn the extent of our calamity.

Numerous friends came in to offer sympathy and assistance and to urge us to leave the dismantled house for the night, but we prefer remaining as the fire was still burning and our property not entirely free from danger.

Father & Mr. Rheese escaped very narrowly. The roof the office fell only ten minutes after they left.

They had time to save very little – all the recorded letters of the Inst.

The report, almost ready for the press & others were destroyed, a drawer of articles on meteorology collected for a number of years by Father, prints & observations & reflections of his own was destroyed.

They were writing in the office when the crackling of the flames above them warned them of the danger, placing cloths over their mouths they endeavoured to obtain the papers of value, but were nearly suffocated by the smoke.

We are in some what better order to day, but are wearied out with the effort to restore our property to proper places.

My one great effort was to preserve Father's books. If we had left them upon the shelves they would have been uninjured as it is, I am afraid many of them are lost.

January 26, 1865

Another busy, tiresome day has passed in the endeavor to produce order out of confusion. We find of our articles destroyed, but much less injured than we expected, owing to the kind care of our friends

The apparatus room, the picture gallery, the Regents rooms & lecture room were destroyed.

I went this morning to visit the scene of destruction. All Smithson's personal effects, all Dr. Hare's philosophical apparatus, the Stanley Indian Gallery of portraits have all perished.

We entered the apparatus room first.

The dismantled walls & towers rose high above us reminding us of the ruins of some English Abbey.

Mr. Welling was my companion, we picked our way over the cinders & burnt bricks through the lecture room to the Picture Gallery.

The remains of the dying gladiator lay scattered about, we picked up a few pieces, but they crumbled in our fingers. The blue sky above us formed a beautiful roof, but we dreaded storms too much not to be glad to learn that something pleasing to the eye, but a protection to the museum of curiosity below us to be immediately erected.

Father is himself again to day.

The warm sympathy of the Regents & friends of Inst has been very grateful to him Mr. Patterson told us the Senate was discussing a very important bill when it was announced that the Inst was on fire and immediately adjourned.

The Supreme Court abbeys its session.

People came from George Town to witness the conflagration. The loss of his letters is a very great trial to Father, but he has hardly mentioned it, thinking much more of the library & private papers of Bishop Johns, entrusted to the care of the Inst.

Father's letters were written with very great care & were in answer to questions upon almost every subject. They had been all prepared with the greatest care, not a letter ever left the Inst but a copy of it was taken.

It is next to losing Father to have them go. It is a calamity I have no resignation to meet.

It seems so very hard to save our furniture and other things which are so valueless in comparison with when we would so gladly give them in exchange.

January 31, 1865

The bells have been ringing to day & guns firing in honour of the passage of the bill for the anti slavery amendment of the constitution[70].

Admiral Davis here to night, warm in his sympathy for Father.

February 4, 1865

We are reduced to order again after the fire and were it not for the meloncholy view, would find it difficult to realize how much that is valuable has been destroyed.

The loss to the Inst is estimated at $20,000, not including the roof, which Father thinks is well destroyed as it was badly constructed and must have taken fire some time.

Better now than later, when more valuable material would have been collected.

Father bears the misfortune with the utmost patience & sweetness, one remark in a letter to Dr. Torrey this morning touched me.

Speaking of the loss of papers he said, "A few years ago such a misfortune would have paralyzed me for future effort, but in my present view of life, I take it as a dispensation of a kind and wise Providence & trust that it will work to my spiritual advantage."

The entrance of peace commissioners into our lives gave us a hope on Thursday & yesterday that we might be approaching the end of the war.

Sec. Seward & the President went to Fortress Monroe to meet them, but to day we learn all is in vain.

Mr. Welling was here last night. He said it was only a maneuver on the part of both Northern & Southern politicians to satisfy the peace party & others of both sides & prove that the war must proceed.

February 28, 1865

This month has passed in little else than making & receiving calls and in attending the meetings of Congress.

I am sorry to say I have made, but one entry in my diary. This has been an important month in the way of success to our arms.

---

[70] On January 31, 1865, the House called another vote on the 13th amendment, with neither side being certain of the outcome. Every Republican supported the measure, as well as 16 Democrats, almost all of them lame ducks. The amendment finally passed by a vote of 119 to 56, narrowly reaching the required two-thirds majority. The House exploded into celebration, with some members openly weeping. Black onlookers, who had only been allowed to attend Congressional sessions since the previous year, cheered from the galleries. – *C□□□te□□ W□k□□e□□□*

Sherman has covered himself with glory.

Charleston is ours Savannah & Wilmington - we may hope now for a speedy termination to the war.

On the 22nd the city was illuminated in honor of the recent victories. Although it was a stormy evening we went out to see the public building in their brilliant array. The Navy Department pleased us most it was brilliantly lighted partly with colored lamps.

Strings of flags were suspended diagnilly across the front of the building while larger ones draped the columns of the porch below.

A list of all the victories gained by our arms was on the west side of the building.

The Treasury Pattent Office & Post Office looked as if translucent as the light shone upon their white walls.

In the fashonable world this has been an unusually gay month. Morning & evening receptions balls & parties have occupied both night & day. The closing entertainment of the season was given by Mrs. Sprague a Matinee dansante. A saloon draped with pink & ornamented with chandeliers of flowers was erected for the German.

Supper was at half past seven.

Father has been as busy as possible since the fire rewriting his report. & others.

Cary & I spent the greater part of the morning in making calls & then went to the capitol for a book.

Met Chief Justice Chase & Father in close confab.

The Justice gave us a very cordial greeting and asked if we had a load of literature. Mrs. Chase of Providence is with us.

March 1, 1865

Went to the Capitol with Mrs. Chase, a discussion in the Senate in regard to treaties with the Indian races.

The appropriations for Father's report passed.

Went to Mr. Mills' studio his son was just finishing a bust of the President.

Father had a cast of his face taken.

We expect Dr. & Mrs. Gray of Cambridge to night. They came to attend the Inauguration.

March 3, 1865

Columbia & Augusta have yielded to Sherman. Johnson is concentrating his forces & we may expect a terrible battle before long which it is supposed will decide the contest.

The Southern army is much weakened & as they still refuse to arm the negros we have the advantage of them.

Columbia was burned by the rebels as the evacuated it. It is raining fast I am afraid we shall have a wet day for the Inaugeration tomorrow.

March 4, 1865

The important day which makes Mr. Lincoln the ruler of our country for another four years has passed. It commenced with clouds & ended in sunshine a prophetic omen we may hope of his new career.

Mrs. Chase & myself went at seven O'clock to the Capitol in order to secure seats in the Senate gallery.

We found the doors closed, but having sent away our carriage in the confident supposition that we could obtain admittance the door keeper took pity upon our desolate condition and admitted us. It was raining hard.

Several senators passed us on their way to their breakfast after sitting up all night.

Senator Morgan gave us a cheerful "good morning" in spite of his wearisome vigil. Admission was not obtained to the Senate until eleven O'clock The galleries were then crowded with ladies to the complete exclusion of the other sex. The Senate convened & transacted business until twelve when the secretaries entered followed shortly after by the Judges of the supreme court in their black robes headed by Chief Justice Chase. Then came the Diplomatic corps in their brilliant court dresses. The members of the House & distinguished individual occupied the remaining space among the latter we noticed Admiral Farragut & Gen. Hooker.

It was an impressive scence.

[71]The first ceremony was the inaugeral of the new vice President as chairman of the house, preceded by a farewell address by Mr. Hamlin, in which he thanked the senators for their courteous behavior to him & asked pardon for any offences he might unintensionily committed.

Mr. Andy Johnston then made his speech which was radical in the extreme & more like a stump oration than an address such as was worthy of delivery before the imposing audience assembled there.

Near the close of his speech, he turned to receive the oath of office administered to him by Mr. Hamlin & kissed the Bible.

He made a few more remarks & then received another oath of allegiance to the country. This was of some length and was repeated word for word after Mr. Hamlin.

Its puport was that he has never indulged a thought treasonable to his country nor ever would nor had ever lifted his hand against her promising future fidelity. He then took his seat in the chair vacated by Mr. Hamlin. His address has been delivered from the desk immediately below the chair.

---

[71] Compare with Mary's April 14, 1866, assessment of Andrew Johnson

The new senators & those newly elected received the oath coming up to the platform of the Speaker's chair as their names were called.

The President was seated immediately below the desk, his ushers on either side of him Mr Foster & _____.

The marshals who were distinguished by bright yellow scarves, ornamented with blue rosettes now proceeded to clear a passage down the front aisle for the President & his suite.

Mr. Lincoln moved slowly between the ushers towering above his neighbors, but with a look of weariness & sadness upon his face, which made me pity him.

The Secreaty, the diplomates & the Judges followed with the members of the House.

The galleries emptied themselves quickly & a general race was made for the most available places for a sight of the inaugeration ceremony.

Fortune favored us with a comparatively good situation near a window, overlooking the platform which had been erected for the purpose on the East portico of the center building.

We could see the marshals surrounding the President & the top of his head and what was truley worth beholding, the mass of human beings crowding the area and park below.

Their shouts announcing the appearance of the President upon the platform. Of course we could not hear a word of the Inaugeral, we abandoned our position shortly for the portico of the senate wing in which we were in order to have a better view of the crowd.

It was almost frightful to witness as the immense mass pushed through a narrow opening to obtain a sight of the procession which now commenced to move.

Women were bore along fainting, carried off their feet by the people about them. Two pugnacious dames, one black, the other white, were having a regular hand to hand fight with their fists in each others' eyes as they were carried on with the stream.

Admiral Davis joined us here with his two little girls and after watching for a short time longer the seething multitude below us, we went in the opposite end of the portico where we saw a portion of the procession.

Very much bedrabled by the mud, which was more than ankle deep, the President was seated in an open carriage with his son Tad by his side and the two ushers in front

We then went to the portico of the Library to view the procession as it proceeded down Penn. Av.

The military appeared very well from this point of view but the procession was not as a whole very impressive. The sun shown out bright & clear as the pagent proceeded to the white house. So begins our new

Presidential term. May the glorious sunshine of Peace beam on us ere its close We are all very tired after our days excursion. Dr. Gray has gone to the levee at the Presidential mansion.

March 6, 1865

Andy Johnson's miserable speech on Inaugeration day is imputed to his being in a state of intoxication.

Sheridan has taken Charlottesville.

Hon Hugh McCulloch has been nominated Sec. of Treasury.

Went to see Mrs. Douglass yesterday Miss Cameron daughter of the former Sec is visiting her. Mrs. D. was looking remarkably well and was using some amiable deplomacy to procure an invitation for a young girl who was present to be a member of a party bound for Fortress Monroe and the army.

March 16, 1865

Our party have mad a very pleasant trip to the front.

To City Pointe & Fortress Monroe.

April 3, 1865

The war department was hung with flags yesterday and the city in an excited state generally from the supposition that Gen Grant would in all probability be within the fortifications of Richmond before night.

Father & Mr. Patterson who has been with us since Saturday went to the warf for news a number of very badly wounded men had just arrived from Fortress Monroe. One poor fellow had lost both legs and one arm all were very seriously injured.

Henry Smith came to call in the evening.

He was on his way to New Orleans to join he regiment. He had been recruiting his strength at home after an imprisonment of six months at the South.

The description of the treatment he had received could not but excite our indignation.

The seemingly systamatic inhuman treatment of those taken in a war is a dark spot upon the escutcheon of the South.

April 5, 1865

Went last evening to Mrs. Peale's in order to go with her to view the illumination of the city in honor of the recent victories.

We went first to the War Department.

It was brilliantly lighted and beautifully draped with flags. While we were admiring it a beautiful crimson light was thrown upon the entire scene by some species of fire works.

The effect was beautiful in the extreme.

This was followed by white light giving the effect of frost work to the trees and afterwards by blue which was not as pretty.

The Presidents House shown resplendent with candles. The Treasury was distinguished by an immense green pack.

In front of the State Department was a transparency with these words upon "At home union is order and order is peace should Abroad union is strength and strength is peace."

The Capitol was adorned with several tier of lights encircling the dome while the white marble seemed translucent with the innumerable lights below.

There was a large transparency in front which we were not near enough to read.

The effect of the building at a distance was exceedingly fine. The National Observatory was lighted and was much admired.

A large mass meeting was collected around the Patent Office. The word union in large letters formed of gas jets adorned the front it was brilliantly illuminated as was the Post Office opposite.

We were with Mr. Seward and his daughter part of the time.

Sec Stanton House was very tastefully adorned a serinade under his windows closed the enjoyment of our evening.

April 6, 1865

Our army is in pursuit of the rapidly retreating forces of Lee in is earnestly to be hoped that they will be overtaken and the final blow given which may terminate this sanguinary war.

The mere taking of Richmond is of comparative small importance if the Southern army remains unconquered.

Mr. Seward was thrown from his carriage about 5 O'clock last evening and lay in a state of insensibility for some time.

It was feared his skull was fractured Father called there about 10 O'clock found him much better. His arm is broken.

April 7, 1865

The paper this morning does not give a very definate idea of the recent battle before Richmond

It does not seem to be as important as was supposed.

Mr. Patterson has just left us. 11 o'clock.

Richmond has fallen no particulars as yet Prof. Baird has just given the news to Father.

1 A. M. Mr. Gill has just brought in "The Star" Petersburg is ours Richmond is evacuated and our forces are in persuit of the enemy.

The church bells are ringing and the guns firing in honor of the victory.

2. P. M.

Lee and his whole army are captured.

Guns are firing and the bells are ringing out a merry peal.

Poor fellows how hard it must have been to yield. our hearts are heavy for them even while we rejoice most freely in the prospect of peace.

8. P. M.

The victory was not as great as supposed, but still is sufficiently important to be a subject of great rejoicing.

Gens Ewell, Kershaw, Button, Corse, Custis Lee and several other officers were taken and several thousand prisoners.

Sec. Seward's injuries were not as serious as at first supposed. He is much better to day.

April 10, 1865

We were awakened at 5 o'clock this morning by the usual sounds of victory, the firing of guns and the ringing of bells and before we were dressed Father came to our door to tell us Lee and his army had surrendered.

The news came at 9 o'clock last night. The correspondence bet. Grant & Lee concerning the negociated surrender was noble and generous on both sides Gen Lee, his officers and men were all paroled.

Mr. Morgen took tea with us last night and also this evening.

The conversation was entirely financial.

One remark of Father seemed especially to catch the attention of Mr. M. that property must in the next generation pass into an entirely new set of hands property holders now being obliged to pay the expenses of the war by taxation and also by depreciated currency.

Father illustrated the currency question by supposing several Islands each containing originally the same amount of gold as a circulating medium. Now if upon one of these Islands a certain additional quantity of gold were to descend.

The country would apparently be very prosperous. Every one would be rich. But the people no longer feeling the need for labor would cease their industrial persuits prices would go up the neighboring Islands would send in their manufactured articles and the products of the ground.

Gold would thus go out of the Island and the people enfeebled by indolence and their country injured by want of cultivation would be worse off than before this additional descent of gold which at first promised to be such a blessing.

Now suppose that the inflation of currency just described was caused by the issue or descent of paper money upon the Island instead of Gold, each paper dollar passing in the Island for a gold dollar. The effect would be exactly as before described. People would all be rich and cease to labor, the other Islands would send in their manufactures as before, but there would be this difference.

To the Islander the paper dollar would be just as good as the gold one as long as he traded with his fellow countrymen, but the foreign traders could make use only of the gold as the paper dollar would not be recognized in their own country and so the gold would be drained off leaving the worthless paper.

But the Island being apparently rich, the trading Ilands would trust until some some sudden demand or panic would reveal to the astonished people that their riches was but paper their prosperity a dream.

Suppose now a third case and that is our own.

This paper money is made a legal tender and the gold becomes a commodity. As before the country will seems very proserprous and the people rich as long as they trade among themselves, but when foreign goods are required the trader finds that the money to purchase them must itself be bought and the expense is so great that trade is checked.

The gold is therefore retained in the country or at least does not go out as rapidly as in the preceeding case, but how great are the evils of the inflation.

Prices must grow higher and higher as the depreciation of the paper money increases. Creditors are paid in a line.

Such was the great crash of 18 which took place just as Father arrived in Europe and turned his attention to the philosophy of Finance and political economy.

Currency which defrauds them of half their due. Saleries are found to be worth only a small portion of their former value. And the buble although it may for a longer time deceive the people with illusive show of prosperity is only a buble still and must burst at last.

Mr. Morgen said we must expect a hard time for the next ten years. We must pay by heavy taxation the expenses of the war.

Financial matters seem to be in a very puzzling state generally should Gold fall suddenly as assuredly it will if not propped up in some way thousands of merchants will be ruined as prices will also fall. Then where is Government to find its income tax. Bankruptcy will threaten the nation and with it millions more of unfortunates who have trusted in its bonds.

It is to be hoped Mr. McCollaks brains are of the best material. The Nation has grown so dizzy with the height of its fancied prosperity it needs some very steady hands to guide it.

Some house are illumined to night but it is too rainy. Some house are illuminated tonight but it is too rainy for much of a display.

I suppose peace will soon visit us now. Mr. Morgen thinks there is no fear of a war with England. Those who have lost property through the Alabama will endeavor of course to obtain remuneration for their losses from England and may embroil us if we are not careful but England will be slow to enter into a contest with us.

The Alabama was fitted up in England by the Southerners and preyed upon a large number of our vessels.

There is much bitter feeling against England on account of the merchant vessels which have run the blockade and supplied the South with ammunition and food. But these could not be urged as a reason for War.

April 14, 1865

We are all tired with restoring the House to order after the illumination last evening.

We were obliged to attend to our own lights and so did not see the display in the city. Every building was lighted from the Capitol to the smallest retail store and dewelling house and the streets were one compact mass of men, woman, horses and children, mingled together and wild with excitement and confusion

Penn. Av., lighted from one end to the other, presented a most striking & beautiful appearance.

The ruined state of the building did not allow of much display on our part, only the dwelling portion was illuminated.

This evening's event is the Rugby House to witness a grand torch light procession.

As it came up 14th St. we had a very fine view of it. Passing under our window the crowd of lights and transparencies collected in front of Sec. Stantons and were rewarded by a speech from the Sec and another from someone whom we did not recognize.

After cheers for the Union, the President, the Army, the Navy and for the brave dead and wounded the patriots moved off to the inspirating air of "Rally Round the Flag Boys."

April 15, 1865

We were awakened this morning by an announcement which almost made our hearts stand still with consternation. The President was shot last night in the Theater.

When the morning paper was issued, he was still alive, although little or no hopes were entertained of his recovery, but now the tolling bells tell us he has ceased to breath. He is dead.

Mr. De Bust has just told Hannah he died at 1/2 7 o'clock.

Deeply must the country mourn his death, for although uncouth & ungainly, he was true hearted, magnanimous and kind, and in the present crisis, ready to follow such a course with the defeated belligerants as would win them back to their allegiance to the Government and subdue the rebellion in their hearts, as well as subjugate their aims.

The South has lost in him a good & judicious friend.

His successor, Johnson heartily desires the death of the leaders of the rebellion & is in every way ultra in his views. I have not given the particulars of the disaster.

It was announced in the yesterday's papers that the President, with Gen. Grant, would be at Ford's Theater in the evening, and a large crowd collected there in consequence.

Gen Grant, however, left the city before night for N. Y.

Mrs. Lincoln had not been well & the President went to the place of amusement with reluctance, not wishing to disappoint the audience.

He was received with more than usual applause. About 9 1/2 o'clock, a shot was heard which was at first supposed to be from the stage and a man leaped from the President's box upon the stage crying "Sic Semper Tyrannis" "I have done it." and making his way to the door, mounted a horse & rode off.

The shrieks of Madame Lincoln, first announced to the petrified audience the catastrophe which had taken place. The President was found to be in a state of insensibility, shot twice through the head.

He was immediately conveyed to a house opposite the theater, followed by Mrs. L., escorted by her friends, in an almost frantic condition.

At the same time of the accident, an attempt was also made upon the life of Sec. Seward.

The assasin entered the house upon the plea that he had brought a prescription of Dr. Verdi, the physician of the Sec.

He pushed passed the servant into the room of the sick man & after disabling the attendants, inflicted several sabre wounds in his neck & then made his escape. Sec. Stanton it is said was warned of the danger and guarded himself against it. The rain is falling heavily and the bells still toll their melancholy tale.

7 P.M. The sad day of excitement is over.

The President's body has been embalmed and lies in state at the White House, while the frantic grief of Mrs. Lincoln has settled into an apathetic dejection from which it is impossible to arouse her.

The President remained unconscious to the last.

The members of the Cabinet, Mrs. & Miss Kinney and Miss Harris surrounded his bed.

Dr. Gurley was present & afterwards escorted the bereaved widow to her home. At the request of Mrs. Lincoln, he communicated the mournful intelligence to poor little Tad, who was wandering from group to group of the sorrowing attendees endeavoring vainly to find out what was the matter.

His cries, when he heard he was fatherless, were exceedingly touching. He has been the almost constant companion of the President.

Johnson has received the oath of office and seems empressed with the dignity and responsibility of his new office.

The assassins have not yet been arrested, but the evidence is conclusive that Booth--a miserable actor and worthless vagrant, a son of the great tragedian, committed the deed. That is the murder of the President.

The stabbing of Mr. Seward was probably done by an accomplice. Mr. Seward is in a critical position and has not been informed of the death of the President or of the danger of his son, who was so much injured by the assassin that very little hope is entertained of his life.

The feeling of resentment at the South as instigating in all probability the murder is deep and I fear will entirely replace the feeling of kindness before entertained for the insurgents.

The Southerners, if they have countenanced the dreadful deed, have fatally mistaken the interests of their cause.

April 17, 1865

17th The sorrow for the President's death is deep and universal. As we went to church, yesterday, we found all the houses draped with black.

In front of the studio of Mr. Baumgrass, a large portrait of Mr. Lincoln was suspended, surrounded with the marks of morning.

The church was so thronged with strangers we with difficulty made our way into the building and after standing for some time were provided with seats in the isle. The pulpit and gallery were dressed in black and the Presidents' pew was closed and clothed with the same sad emblem.

The Dr., in a short introductory address, alluded to the terrible calamity which had befallen the nation and spoke in terms of true affection of the personal qualities of our beloved chief Magistrate.

The Assassins have not yet been found. The feeling against the South is exceedingly bitter. Mr. Seward's wounds are not as serious as was at first supposed and he will probably recover. He was informed last night of the death of the President and of the critical condition of his son, who still remains in a state of insensibility. The funeral ceremonies are expected to take place on Wednesday.

April 18, 1865

Have just returned from the Kennedys, where I passed the night. I went to see Dr. & Mrs. Gurley yesterday afternoon. The Dr. said he had been called to go to the President about 7 o'clock in the morning. He found him in the house opposite the theater, lying insensible upon a bed with the life blood dripping from the wound in his head upon the clothes and the floor beneath.

The several members of the cabinet & other persons were standing around, the deepest sorrow depicted upon their countenances. The Dr. went to the bedside, but for a while was too much overcome with his feelings to perform the religious services required of him.

He went to Mrs. Lincoln and found her in an almost frantic condition.

The President died about 7 1/2 o'clock.

Dr. Gurley returned to his bedside a few moments before his decease. He made his way through the sorrowing & silent spectators & found him slowly drawing his breath at long intervals, lying as before, perfectly motionless.

A faint, hardly perceptable motion in his throat, and all was over. So still was the room that the ticking of the Presidents watch was distinctly heard. After a solemn & impressive prayer Dr. Gurley went to break the sad intelligence to Mrs. Lincoln, who was in the parlor below. She cried out. "Oh why did you not tell me he was dying?"

Robert Lincoln showed great self-possession & calmness and did all in his power to comfort his sorrow stricken mother.

Dr. Gurley went with her to the White House. Some of her expressions are exceedingly painful.

To day the remains of the good kind man are deposited in the East Room and from an early hour the streets have been thronged with people going to take their last view of him. Sally & Anne Kennedy asked me to go with them, but I thought I would rather remember him as I saw him last, at the Capitol at the inaugeration.

Carry and I are going out again soon, we feel too restless to remain at home.

Father writes that the feeling of resentment against the Southerners in New York is bitter in the extreme. One man, for an expression indicating want of sympathy, in the general sorrow was thrown over the railing of a ferry boat & instantly crushed by the wheels.

We expect Father tonight.

He heard the news shortly after his arrival in New York on Friday night.

Capt. Alexander was here this morning. He says he has no doubt that Booth is concealed in Baltimore It will be very difficult to catch him as being an Actor he is accustomed to assume all disguises.

The Capt. is firmly convinced that the assasination and attempted murder of Mr. Seward was a plot to destroy the amicable relations springing up between the North and the South through the humane policy of Mr. Lincoln and by substituting a sterner administration and harsher measures against the rebels, with increased bitter feeling to unite the South for further resistance.

Seward was Mr. Lincoln's chief supporter in his lenient measures.

The city is in such a state of excitement that the slightest-unusual circumstance attracts a crowd immediately.

Yesterday afternoon, while I was making a call, a number of carriages passed the window where I was seated, some empty, some filled, driving furiously and the street was soon filled with people moving eagerly towards N.Y. Av not one of them knowing what was the matter. In a few moments a crowd extending over several squares had collected.

After some time, it was discovered that two negro women fighting has caused the disturbance.

Traces of the assassins have been found and several supposed accomplices in the plot arrested, but great fears are entertained that the murderers will escape. A sense of insecurity pervades the community and guards have been placed around the houses of the most prominent citizens.

April 19, 1865

To day was the funeral of our good kind President.

The ceremonies of the White House were conducted by Dr. Gurley, Dr. Hall Bishop Simpson and one other clergyman whose name I have forgotten.

In the East Room the catafalco was erected in the centre of the apartament graduated semicircular platforms were arranged around this for the accommodation of the invited attendants.

The various delegations had each their place assigned Father was invited to take part with the officers of the Smith. Inst. and I went with him to the Treasury building were he obtained for me a position upon one of the porticos to witness the procession.

Only four or five ladies were admitted into the East Room.

It was a beautiful day and as the people collected at the corners of the streets at the windows & upon the roof of the houses it was difficult to realize we were not preparing for some gala festival instead of the last sad honours to the well beloved dead.

The procession left the White House about 2 P.M.

We were notified that it had started by the distant booming of guns & the tolling of bells. The sad sweet strains of the funeral march heralded its approach and soon the military escort appeared marching slowly with bent heads & guns reversed. The sad pagent was two hours in passing.

The funeral car was heavily draped with black plainly showing the coffin which was adorned with beautiful flowers. The remains were placed in the Capitol and will be open to the view of the public until Friday morning.

They are to be conveyed to Springfield.

April 24, 1865

The remains of President Lincoln left the city Friday morning.

Dr. Gurley has joined the company who escort them. The papers this morning contain a description of the manner in which the cortege has been received.

Mrs. Lincoln is quite ill and poor little Tad quite inconsolable.

Mercy tempered with a great deal severity is appropriately to be the policy of the new president in dealing with the rebels.

May 10, 1865

Since my last entry in my journal the search for and arrest of the various conspirators concerned in the assassination has kept us in a constant state of excitement.

Booth the actual perpetrator of the deed was traced to the vacinity of by our detectives. where he had taken refuge with a farmer with one of his accomplices both bearing assumed names. They had hidden themselves in the woods the day before their seizure hearing of the approach of our soldiers but had returned at night to sleep in the barn of their host.

The cavalry surrounded the barn about daylight & called upon the miscreants surrender. Harold Booth's companion consented to do so but the assassin evinced his determination to resist to the last extremity.

The barn was fired & as the flames rose to the roof lighting up every corner of the building his form was distinctly visible to those outside.

As he stood in the centre of the floor with his arms folded as the grew hotter he approached the door perhaps with the intention of cutting his way through the guard when one of the soldiers fired upon him and he fell mortally wounded.

The shot entered his neck and for several hours he lay in great agony his limbs being paralysed and his breathing extremely difficult. The only intelligible words he said were "Tell my mother I died for my country I thought I did for the best.

He asked to have his hands lifted & when he saw them exclaimed "they are useless now they are useless now."

He seems to have been a reckless enthusiast totally unprincipaled but with a certain kind of fascination which won him friends. The one bright spot in his character appears to have been his love for his mother & sister.

A number of persons have been arrested as accomplices in the murder who are now confined in the penitentiary near the arsenal. Jef. Davis Thompson, the former Sec. & other distinguished southerners are accused of instigating the deed and a large price has been placed upon their heads.

The trial of the assassins commenced to day. The court is not open to the public who awaits with intense interest the results of their examination. Judge Holt is the presiding officer. The President was interred in Springfield last Thursday.

Everywhere testamonies of respect and affection greeted the funeral cortege escorting the remains to their last resting place. The war is virtually at an end one by one the armies of the south are laying down their arms and the Southern citizens once so bitter in their hatred of the North are every where taking the oath of allegiance. According to Gen. Halleck's orders this token of submission is not sufficient for the restoration of officers of the army above the rank of colonel or civillians of certain eminence these must make personal application for pardon.

Father went to see the new President last week. He knew him some years ago having sought his acquaintance in order to disabuse his mind of certain prejudices entertained by him in regard to the Smith. Inst.

He is residing at present in the Hon. S. Hooper's house. He received Father with cordiality remarking.

You are looking thinner Prof. than when I saw you last.

His demeanor was dignified & modest while the expression of his face was sober almost sad. He is a man of very little culture and when Father knew him before was greatly opposed to all collegate & university education & in his opinion inconsistent with the true principles of democracy.

Father had with good effect endeavored to remove such unworthy prejudices. I called to day upon Mrs. Davis.

The Admiral was one of the party which escorted the remains of the Pres. to Springfield. He returned last Sunday.

They go to the 6 St. to reside very soon.

Nell has been making a visit on Phil is now in Oxford. Mrs. Mercer came to ask Father to get a pass for her to return home.

She came into town for market purposes and found that she could not return no one having been allowed to go beyond the limits of the city without a permit since the assassination.

She says Booth was in her store about two weeks before the murder. She remarked that he had very beautiful black glossy hair, but did not otherwise observe his appearance.

She also said a supper had been prepared for the conspirators at a small tavern not far from her house the night of the murder and a coffin filled with firearms sent there a few days before.

She saw the herse with the coffin pass her door and wondered that it was unaccompanied by mourners.

Mother & Carry just in from a shopping expedition. Cotton goods are going up owing to the demand at the South now that the trading ports are open again.

A large mass meeting was held last night and resolutions past to induce the Government to exclude from the Southerners who had left the city for reasonable purposes the right of return.

The Capitol at least it was urged should be kept free from the contamination of those who however loyal they might be now in profession had stained their names with treason & rebellion. A number of speeches were made.

May 15, 1865

Jef. Davis is taken.

He was captured near attempting to escape in his wife's clothing.

The trial of the assassins has continued for three days.

Went to see Mrs. Gurley yesterday who is sick.

The Doctor has returned from the sad expedition to Springfield. He was one of the escort of the President's remains. He said the display of grief they encountered every where was very impressive.

One little incident he mentioned was touching.

Two little girls came to the General in charge with a bunch of violets accompanied by a note from their Mother explaining that the little ones thought it was a pity Mr. Lincoln should have all the flowers they wished theirs to be put upon the end.

May 16, 1865

Coffin of little Willie. This was done & the Dr. brought the violets with the note to Mrs. Lincoln. Gov. Aiken has just been here.

May 20, 1865

Sunday.

Jef. Davis is at Fortress Monroe. His wife & children are with him. There is to be a grand review of the whole army on Tuesday & Wednesday of this week.

May 22, 1865

We have been as busy as the busiest sort of bees preparing to receive guests who wish to see the Review.

We have with us, Mr. & Mrs. Dickerson & child from New York and Mr. Patterson's son & two daughters from Phil.

We expect others tomorrow.

The city is thronged with strangers.

Com. & Mrs. Shubric were here just before tea with Mr. Walter. Mr. _____.

The artist engaged in the fresco painting upon the dome of the capitol called in the morning to ask Father for some pictures of electrical machines. He wished to introduce one into his decorations.

Nell has come home with Frank

We have witnessed this day, a spectacle which we must ever remember. The Review of one half of our great army. The Army of the Patomac with Sheridan cavalry. We went at an early hour to the Treasury building to take possession of a room of the Light House Board which had been reserved for us & the other families of the officers of the Board.

We made our way with difficulty through the crowded streets. Every window & balcony on the avenue was crowded with spectators, and at the upper end of the street, near the Treasury, a covered platform had been erected for the accommodation of a certain number of the eager expectants of the procession.

Our window commanded an entire view of the broad avenue almost to the steps of the Capitol. From one end of it to the other we could see the advancing columns of the men who had fought bravely & well in the defense of the Union and who would soon be busy again with plough and pruning hook, rejoicing in the Peace their hardy hands had won.

In the distance, the bayonets gleamed in the sunlight like a solid sea of silver, then we could distinguish the infantry moving with steady step, the cavalry and the artillery.

On they came in the dim distance, down the long middle of the avenue, now under our window, hour after hour, as inexhaustible & unceasing as the flow of a mighty river.

The horses prancing & curvetting. The artillery rumbling heavily, regiment after regiment. The regular company being here & there intersperced with a regiment of zouaves, their costume resembling the Turkish so much we almost expected to see the c and the crescent.

The stars & stripes and the different corps banners floated out in the sun, while here and there, beside the batteries battle flags that had been torn & stained in the service of their country.

Nothing but a shred of some of these were left.

Hour after hour the steady stream moved on until upon our wearied senses began to dawn some realization of the immense extent of the army.

Among other pleasant people, Robert J. Walker was with us & entertained us with various anecdotes of his late foreign tour of his balloon excursion

He invited a certain number of gentlemen to dine with him in the air at a certain hour. He hired a balloon & the services of a distinguished aeronaut, expecting to make the ascension in private, but found 100,000 people had collected to see him ascend.

He enjoyed his trip greatly and descended without accident.

Among other interesting items he said that on some public occasion in Ireland some mention was made of the powers of the Americans & their defeat of the English in the wars of 76 & 1812.

Wallis rose to reply and turning towards the assembly of beautiful lassies present with their lovely complexions & high eyes, he remarked that the reason the British failed in the engagements mentioned was because they did not go to work in the right way -- if they had sent over a regiment of such fair damsels the Americans would have been unable to resist & would have surrendered at discretion.

Speaking of the great emigration from Ireland, he observed that it might be well to unloose Ireland from her mooring and float her alongside N.J., since she was coming over to us in detachments.

Our party has been increased by Prof Moffet & son from Princeton & Mr. Weichaus who could not find a place to sleep & asked to be taken in. We could only provide him with a sofa.

Frank has been obliged to put up with the same sort of accommodation while three of us sleep upon the floor. We have 11 guests.

Our family, consisting of 16, not including servants.

Prof Duffinkel, Mr. Bank with two friends Mrs. T. Cryler & Miss S. Cryler passed the evening we were sorry we had no place to offer them.

May 24, 1865

Having yesterday, had a most excellent view of the procession on the avenue, we thought we should like to see it more in detail so we went to a stand or covered booth created for the Judges & leaders opposite a similar one devoted to the use of the President and cabinet with the reviewing officers.

Some of our party obtained seats in the latter, but I was one of the fortunate individuals to be immediately in front of the dignatarys.

Sherman Corps was reviewed & 60,000 men passed before us.

The view was not as impressive as yesterday but we could see the men & their officers better - The two booths I have mentioned were stationed on opposite sides of the avenue immediately in front of the Pres. House.

The field officers, alone, salute the President & other senior officers who all arose when a Brigadier General appeared.

The horses of the officers were adorned with flowers & stepped as proudly as if they were conscious of the magnitude of the occasion. As each regiment appeared, the band turned off in front of us and played until the entire regiment had passed when they fell into line again.

The Generals in command of division left the procession when the division had passed & took their places upon the Presidential stand where they were received with welcome & congratulation from the Cabinet & their fellow officers.

Our new President has a somewhat sharply cut face, but at a distance in my short sighted eyes resembled Douglass.

He returned the salutes of the officers with dignity & gentlemanly bearing.

The gaily ornamented booths with a division of the dignitaries in the center & either wing filled with gaily dressed ladies presented a very pretty appearance.

The horses of the military commanders, however, seemed generally to disapprove them & gave their riders a fine opportunity of displaying their horsemanship.

Whenever a gap occurred in the procession, the crowd would rush forward in front of the President stand & call out the different dignitaries to be driven back by the mounted guard as the soldiers again appeared.

The battle torn flags always excited the enthusiasm of the populace and several officers who passed without arms were vociferously cheered.

Gen Sherman stood all the time his troops were passing with Mrs. Sherman by his side in the front seat of the Pres stand.

A number of contrabands, mules & wagons laden with box & bags chicken & kitchen utensells, after each driver gave us some idea of the supplement of an army.

We came home about 4 o'clock, having in the days reviewed 135,000 men. So ends our four years' war.

We were told that as many men had perished, more remained and although we mourn the dead, we must rejoice that the great question of slavery which has again & again threatened our destruction is settled at last and our Union established upon a firm & sure hope with an enduring foundation.

May 25, 1865

Thursday. Mr. Patterson and party left this morning.

Mrs. Dickerson at the dinner table asked Father what he thought of the Darwinian development theory. Father said he would not say he believed or disbelieved, there was much to be said in favor of the theory as well as that of a separate creation of Man.

I strongly held by Agassiz.

Mrs. D. seemed to fear that the truth of the Bible was assailed.

Father said that the Bible was not intended to teach science in this case, however, Nature & Creation were not in conflict as it is not said how man was created.

Father said it was easy to see how different races might have originated.

The higher marriage of individuals with certain peculiarities shortness of stature, large hands, feet & other items continued through several generations would determine a race. Or certain climate might be favorable to certain peculiarities & others unfavorable thus supposing an equal number of tall and short people to settle both North & South.

Supposing the climate of the North more favorable to the tall than the short the latter would in time die out leaving a race of comparative giants.

Supposing on the contrary the climate of the South more suited to the short of stature these would live & the tall disappear, leaving a race of dwarf such as Bosfurman.

May 26, 1865

Friday.

It has been raining fast all day, but in spite of the inclemency, we went to Arlington & Alexandria.

The lawn not far from the house at Arlington has been converted into a cemetary and as far as we could see, the white headboards stretched away in regular succession neat walk had been made. It was a peaceful quiet place to rest in.

At night Father gave us one little incident of his boy hood which interested us. He said that a certain man in the village where he lived with his grandmother, It was a shoemaker I believe, annoyed him greatly by passing his hand roughly over his face, bending up his nose in the process & causing him considerable pain.

He was a slight delicate boy but determined to discover some means of self defence. He at length hit upon the following expediant his first experiment as he says in practical mechanics. At the approach of his tormentor he threw himself upon the ground and as the man stooped over him to seize him he caught hold of ancles and placing his feet in his stomach with one dexterous kick sent him over backwards. He tried the same experiment several times upon some young men who were in the habit of teasing him with the same success and greatly to the amusement and admiration of the bystanders. He mentioned during the conversation that his first ambition was to be a chimney sweeper. He had watched a certain individual somewhat his senior ascend his grandmother's chimney and was inspired with the greatest admiration for the calling There was a small space between his grandmother's house & that of the next neighbor and his clothes suffered greatly in consequence of his efforts to ascend between the two walls chimney sweep fashion.

May 27, 1865

Went to the Patent Office with Mrs. Dickerson.

The large room on the North Side is nearly completed.

Mrs. D. was very much pleased with the pompous style of the first exhibition hall I have not made up my mind whether I like it.

May 29, 1865

Monday. The Sunday School celebration for the year.

The children were addressed by the President in Lafayette Square. He called them his little sons & daughters & among other things said that each little boy was a candidate for the Presidency & each little girl might be a President's lady, so they should cultivate minds & morals so as to be prepared for any position.

Mr. Welling & Alfred Woodhul here in the evening.

Mr. W. has returned from a second expedition from Richmond bringing away his daughter. She is a great favorite of General Lee who said to her at parting, "Be careful what you say, do nothing to excite the censure of your Northern friends or their bitter feeling. You will hear much that will wound you but guard your lips, truly don't forget us."

The southern feeling at Richmond has grown more sullen & defiant since the recent proceeding against them. The trial of the Assassins still continues. Gen. Hunter presides.

It is conducted with very little justice or discretion. I fear it will be a disgrace to us.

May 30, 1865

Tuesday. The Dickerson's left us this morning. We have enjoyed their visit greatly.

June 1, 1865

June 1st Mr. Peace last night said President Johnson did not approve of the course persued in the trial of the Assassins.

Was greatly displeased at Holt & Stanton who he said had deceived him in regard to the evidence concerning the participation of Jeff Davis in the murder and caused him to issue prematurely the proclamation setting a price upon his head.

January 1, 1866

The new year has commenced with clouds and rain. We have had fewer calls than usual on account of the weather.

Father did not start on his round of visits until quite late.

January 2, 1866

Jan. 2nd The weather still cloudy & rainy.

England seems to approve the Presidents message.

Some more callers for the N. Year tonight.

January 3, 1866

The sun deigned to shine upon us to day so we started out to pay our respects to the Ladies of the Cabinet.

Mrs. Wells was not receiving in person, but her place was supplied by her neice & a lady friend who entertained us agreeably.

Mrs. McCall is a portly lady, not very refined in appearance but unassuming and good natured.

Mrs. Speed, the wife of the Attorney general, is a matronly kind individual who gave us a very pleasant welcome.

Mrs. Harland pleased us least, she was assisted in her duties as hostess by her daughter and a very pretty young girl from New York.

Mrs. Dennison did not receive. We made several other calls and have returned fatigued with our expedition.

Mr. Brown, a young man who has come to the Dist. to prosicute his studies, has just left us.

January 5, 1866

Called yesterday upon the Senator's wives.

To day went to see Lady Elmer, neice of the English minister.

She is a lady of medium height with bright dark eyes & pleasing expression, but somewhat nervous manner. We had no opportunity of conversing with her, as there were several people already with her & as all her guests were seated, she could talk only with those nearest to her.

It would have been better if she had received standing, as is the ordinary mode.

Carry & I enjoyed conversing with our neighbours & soon left.

We made a number of other calls, but not as many as we wished as it is very cold.

January 19, 1866

19th. Since the last entry in my journal, very improperly so called, we have done little else than make & receive calls.

This morning was our reception day, we have passed a very pleasant morning. Among the very agreeable people who honoured us was Mrs. Patterson, a very lovely lady whose husband is a gentleman of fortune residing here.

The symplicity yet elegance of her manners was very charming. We were all delighted with her.

She was accompanied by a long trained young lady who discoursed largely about her grand acquaintances in New York leading us thereby to accuse her slightly of snobishness.

Her long train, I am sorry to say, was slightly damaged in making her exit.

After they left Madame de Lemobrey came in it was pleasant to see an old familiar face we are obliged to form so many new acquaintances.

She was exceedingly agreeable & was joined by Col. & Mrs. Bliss & a young lady friend.

Col. Bliss is the step son of Bancroft and is exceedingly fine looking, his wife is very delicate in appearance. They had hardly left before Gen. & Mrs. Dyer made their appearance.

Gen Dyer was exceeding kind at the. time of the fire.

I must not forget to mention the visit of Mrs. Stockton, wife of Senator S., formerly Minister to Rome. She is a magnificent woman and entered the room with a grand display of silk & velvet. Rather rotund in person, she has brilliant complexion, large dark eyes & with her sparkling wit is very fascinating.

She was followed by a tall lady of pleasant appearance whose name I have forgotten, and almost hidden by the hoops of the grand dames & a youth of careful attire, tenderly twisted mustache, bowed himself into the room.

Mrs. Stockton devoted herself to Father. Mother entertained the other lady while the youth fell to my share.

The party left as they entered, in grand style, leaving with us an invitation for a matinee on Wednesday at Mrs. Stockton's.

Hetty Hodge was here among the first. She has not yet become accustomed to the disipation of a Washington winter & is very doubtful about her liking for it.

The pleasantest face of all our visitors to me was that of Miss Hooper. It is full of sensibility & sweetness. I should like to have her for a friend.

We had 28 calls in all. Prof MacClean has been with us for several days & left us this morning. He went last night with Father to the reception at Sec. McCulloh's.

The Bill establishing negro suffrage in the district passed to the House to day, greatly to the indignation of all residents therein.

What a fine influx of the dusky race we shall have, if the National Capitol is thus made a negro Ethiopia.

Grace Patterson is with us. Elle left us last Saturday after a short visit in company with young Mr & Mrs. P. We detained Grace.

January 20, 1866

A visit from Mrs. Allen, sister in Law of Mr. Foster, the vice President, & her daughter. The latter intelligent & pretty.

Father & I went over the building with them.

They were pleased with the extent of it & surprised when Father told them that all the important operations of the Inst. could be carried on between the four walls of his little office and that the rest of the building was only a clog on its usefulness.

The wind blowing & the night cold, but Father went to the club as usual.

January 22, 1866
Monday. 10 1/2 P.M.

Yesterday was our Communion Season.

It was pleasant to be present, a united family at the sacred feast, but brought back the painful longing for our dear Will.

He may have been with us though, we know it not.

In the evening, read aloud to Father from *Nature & the Supernatural,* by Horace Bushnell.

Mr. Bushnell used the word "vital forces" instead of "vital principle" to which Father objected.

The vital principle he contends is not a force, but a controller of the forces of Nature.

He read to us an extract from one of his own essays upon force, its accumulation & other things. It was written more than 20 years ago & was first read before the American Academy at one of its sessions. It seemed to me very beautiful.

Among other things, he said that in order to raise matter to a higher organization, a certain part of said matter must run down to a lower condition in order to produce said elevation; thus in the potato plant, a portion of the potato that is of the starch & others contained within it is expended in forming the materials for the plant & a portion also to supply the power for its formation so - that if a plant were to grow in the dark, it would be found it weighed lighter than the potato from which it sprung.

We had a long & intensely interesting conversation upon Nature & the Supernatural.

I wish I had time to record it all to night.

He closed by saying there was enough in this world to make us humble and trustful that the unknowable was greater than the known. That nothing could be more certain to him except his own existance than the presence of the Creator - God in the Universe, the existance of an all powerful mind controlling all things similar to our own & the best evidence to him that the Bible was what it claimed to be was its adaptbility to the wants of human nature.

January 24, 1866
In the evening train gone to Willards.

Before breakfast. - Last evening, Dr. Torrey, Dr. Barnard, Dr & Mrs Gould arrived

They came to attend the meeting of the Academy which opens this morning.

Three of the gentlemen went to the President's Soiree.

Dr. Barnard amused us with his description of some of the Ladies dresses.

Uncle has not yet arrived, we are afraid he is not coming. A party at Mrs. Freeman Clarks, one also at the Pres.

January 25, 1866

Receptions at Mrs. McCullochs & Mrs. Morgans. Our party has been pleasantly increased by the arrival of Prof. Witney of New Haven.

January 26, 1866

This is our reception day, but I left Mother, Nell & Carry to enterain our guests and went with Mrs. Gould to visit the President's family.

There were very few persons in the room as we entered.

Mrs. Patterson and her sister received, standing in the centre of the room. They have not yet become enough accustomed to their position to feel at ease but have improved since last summer we saw them, before we went away.

Mrs. P. is a delicate, modest woman and quite unassuming.

We went to the green house which is in admirable order & thence to the meeting of the Academy to hear a eulogy pronounced by Dr. Gould upon Mr. Gillis.

It was well written, although the praise of our dear deceased friend was somewhat too strong.

A large party at Mrs. Riggs.

January 27, 1866

A busy day.

Two matinees, one at Mrs. Sprague's, we did not remain long there, but after saluting the lady of the house & looking for a short time at the dansers, proceeded to the house of Mrs. Williams, formerly Mrs Douglass.

First calling upon Mrs. Grant.

Gen & Mrs Grant occupy one of the large houses near Mrs. Douglass & were both receiving.

The General's face expresses strong determination of character, but no great amiability. Mrs. G. is cross eyed & extremely plain.

We remained but a few moments & then went to see the Bride.

We found her receiving her guests with her usual affability, but hardly looking as well as usual -- her white silk dress was not becoming.

A large number of persons were present & some grave looking gentl. & equally solemn looking ladies were waltzing in an adjoining room.

Down stairs we found an elegant collasion of which we partook with great satisfaction.

Mr. Williams, Col., I believe I should call him, was a tall rather fine looking man and is said to have attracted the fair widow at first by his indifference to her charms.

Such singularity excited her interest and she asked to be presented.

The consequence was a mutual liking which in less than two weeks was consecrated by the marriage vow. She seemed very happy. Passed an hour or more there very pleasantly.

At dinner, a very interesting discussion: the Darwinian question of the development theory.

Father was inclined to believe in it to a certain extent, as it explained so very many natural fenomena, but Dr. Barnard denounced it entirely as leading to Pantheism & Infidelity.

A party in the evening at Dr. Parker's, also one at Mrs. Dalgreen's which we did not attend.

January 28, 1866

Went to church in the morning

Dr Lorrey gave us some interesting information in regard to his California trip.

January 29, 1866

Large parties at Mrs. Sherman's & Gen Grant's, both crowded to excess. I did not go.

Carry was especially pleased at the kind inquiry of Gen. Sherman about Father. He said he had seen him the day before & that he was something to see.

January 30, 1866

Went with Mrs. Gould to the Capitol.

We ascended the dome & saw the new frescoes[72].

Distance, however, we found in this as well as many other cases greatly lent enchantment to the view. The figures are of course enormous in their

---

[72] The modern-day dome sitting atop the U.S. Capitol Building was constructed between 1855 and 1866. Visible through the oculus of the dome in the rotunda is a fresco painted by Italian artist Constantino Brumidi.

Named ▨he A▨▨the▨▨▨ ▨▨ Wa▨h▨n▨t▨n, the painting depicts George Washington sitting amongst the heavens in an exalted manner. Literally translated, the work's title means, "George Washington ascending into heaven and becoming a god."

proportions and the immense extent of mouth & eyes was ludicrous in the extreme when seen near by.

We went into the Senate & heard Mr. Trumbull in a speech upon the amendment of the constitution.

Went also to the house & visited some of the Committee rooms. Went to Mrs. Harris' reception in the evening, was introduced to Gen. Thomas & other military dignitaries.

Spoke to Sec. Wells went from there to Mrs. Gen. Sherman's & saw Gen Meade there, his likeness are exceedingly good.

IMAGE: Portion of the *Apotheosis of Washington*. The banner, "E Pluribus Unum" meaning "out of many, one".

January 31, 1866

Calls all day too tired to go out at night.

February 1, 1866

Calls all the morning. Two parties tonight, but Carry is too tired to go.

March 17, 1866

The gay season is over & we have been greatly enjoying the quiet of Lent which has only been interrupted by two or three soirées at the French ministers & the President's weekly levees.

I have not mingled as much as my neighbors in the festivities of the winter, but our household has constantly been represented by the numerous guests who have been with us. The grandest affair of the season, however, was honoured by my presence viz. a ball at the French Ministers.

The house occupied by the representative of the French is the one formally owned by Mr. Corcoran.

The painting gallery was devoted to the dancers who continued with the German until nearly eight-o'clock in the morning.

For the last two or three weeks we have been enjoying a visit from Frank, Mary & the baby. The latter small individual, completely rules the household.

Mrs. Hursey called this morning to ask us to dine at Gen. Hunters on Monday.

Alfred Woodhul passed the evening with us.

March 19, 1866

Monday. Frank preached for us yesterday.

Father was very much pleased with his sermon & thought that with a little touching up it would be admirable.

Dined with Mrs. Hunter.

The General was away from home, but Mrs. H. & her neice entertained us very agreeably.

Mrs. H. reminds me somewhat of Mrs. Bill in her appearance & conversation.

A game of croquet in the evening with Jack Gillis & Dr. Tryon.

March 20, 1866

Went to the Senate with Frank nothing of much interest going on.

Saw Mrs. John Stockton in the gallery, her husband's seat is to be contested tomorrow.

Mr. Stockton came across the gallery to speak to me & was very agreeable.

In the house, one of the members was making himself exceedingly ridiculous by abusing Mr. Greeley for some attack upon him.

Something of more interest came up before we left in regard to the taxation of Green Backs. Everything concerning the currency is interesting now, since a return to specie payments[73] is a matter requiring very delicate management.

We are mounted on stilts & must be let down gently or we may cry for broken bones.

Sec. McCulloh seems well able to manage the difficult question if Congress will only allow him sufficient power & freedom of action.

The loan bill by which he wishs to purchase the Greenback floating currency & sell instead interest bearing bonds to be paid at some distant date, say fifty years or more, I am afraid will not be passed or will be so restricted & altered that the end desired will not be accomplished.

Thades Stevens is so fond of the paper money that he desires to retain it indefinately.

Sec. McCullah was violently attacked in the *Intelligencer* last week by Comtroller Clark, who endeavoured to show a great discrepancy between the Sec. Treasury accounts & the actual amount of money in the Treasury.

Mr. Clark, in his mode of calculation, has done himself great injury.

His wife was in the Senate & House this morning & greeted me in her usual kind sweet way.

Gen. Custer passed the evening with us. He is a fair haired, blue eyed man with a fine broad forehead. The last time I saw him, he was flying past like the wind, on the day of the great review, his horse having run away with him.

Brevet Major General George Armstrong Custer, US Army, around the time of his visit to the Smithsonian.

March 21, 1866

Part of the family dined at Mrs. Hodge's.

---

[73] Specie payment – The redemption of paper money, referred to as "Green Backs," in gold coins.

Father & Mother went there in the evening. I have had a head ache all day. Frank says his conversation is too intellectual for me.

The Wilkes were here in the morning.

Mr. Beaman & Mr. Alexander spent the evening with us.

March 22, 1866

Mr. John Stockton seat is contested today.

Frank, Mary & the baby left at 4 o'clock.

Lottie remains with us a little longer.

Played croquet.

Father read Schiller aloud to me. Sir Edward Bulwer Lytton's translation liked the Diver very much. Went to teacher's meeting in the early part of the evening.

March 23, 1866

Friday.

Mrs. Sen. Chandler here in the morning.

Miss Lizzy Salomons took dinner & remains all night.

Father, much amused with a piece of poetry, a criticism upon an article entitled "mind & matter." read Schiller again until late. Raining fast.

We miss baby terribly. Even Father yielded to her sway & employed a part of Sunday afternoon with Mother as assistant, playing hide & seek with her in the museum.

March 24, 1866

Saturday. We were surprised to see the sun shining this morning after last night's storm.

Capricious April seems in haste to succeed blustering March.

Miss Lizzy left us about ten I walked to the avenue with her & we were both tempted into some of the stores by the array of new goods on the doors & windows.

We were happy to learn prices are coming down. Father has a meeting of the Regents tonight who have finished with business matters & are now discussing oysters & chicken salad in the next room.

March 25, 1866

Sunday. A sermon from Dr. Gurley in the morning. Did not go to church in the evening. Father read aloud our favourite verses.

March 26, 1866

Monday. A large crowd in the Senate today in anticipation of a Presidential veto of the civil rights bill. Senator Foote is very ill.

March 27, 1866

Tuesday.

The case of our New Jersey Senator was considered in the Senate today.

That August body deciding he was not entitled to his seat. He was not treated with much courtesy as he petitioned for a few days delay, but was denied.

The message of the President regarding the civil rights bill, was read[74].

March 28, 1866

Senator Foote's death was announced in the senate today. He was one of the oldest members of the Senate & an influential conservative his loss will be greatly felt. The Senate adjourned until Monday.

March 31, 1866

Mr. Stockton called with his relative Mr. Ponlairs. He seemed cheerful in spite of his congressional defeat.

Mrs. Stockton will be greatly disappointed, as she enjoyed her winter greatly and is well fitted for the society duties of Washington.

Mr. Ponlairs was looking well. He had suffered much pecuniously during the war, but said he enjoyed as much happiness in his present small plank house that he had ever experienced in his former elegant mansion.

Mr. Stockton seemed to think the opposition in the Senate to his holding his seat was due to the desire of the radicals to get rid of his conservative vote in their purposed effort to carry the civil rights bill, over the president's veto.

Miss Terry & Alfred here in the evening to tell Lottie they were going on Monday.

April 1, 1866

A merry evening although not exactly sabbatical.

Went to Trinity Church. Col. Yates & Jack Gilles accompanied us.

We were entertained first by a wedding, the marriage of an adopted daughter of Mrs. Schoolcraft. Father had been invited to give away the bride, & has been in a strait for several days between his kindly feeling to Mrs. S. & his exceeding dislike to the part assigned him.

He at last compromised with Mrs. S. and was allowed to accompany the bridal party without taking any active part in the ceremony.

---

[74] On March 13, 1866, the U.S. Congress overwhelmingly passed the Civil Rights Act of 1866 – protecting the rights of African-Americans. President Andrew Johnson vetoed the bill on March 27, 1866.

The church was thronged with a large audience which had assembled to listen to the opera singers Hableman & Johansen, whose music was exceedingly delightful, but hardly in keeping with the sacredness of the occasion.

The sermon from the rector was a most remarkable speculation as to the future of our bodies and filled Father with pity, all the way home that the man should have made such a goose of himself.

April 2, 1866

Monday. Lottie & Miss VanAntwerp left this morning in company with Miss Terry & Alfred we went with them to the depot & saw them off & then went to the French minister's matinee.

The Wilkes are here this evening to play croquet with the Delafields. Our gentleman corps consisted of Mr. Welling, Col. Yates, Dr. Pancrast, Dr. Tryon, Mr. Gillis, Mr. Alexander, Mr. Beaman.

April 3, 1866

Tuesday A quiet day and evening alone.

The first almost this winter pleasing for its variety.

April 4, 1866

Miss Finney with Miss Cogswell & her brother from New Brunswick passed the eve. with us.

Miss F. said her uncle, Sen. Dickson, who has been dangerously ill, intended even at the risk of his health to be carried to the Senate in order to vote upon the civil rights bill..

Every conservative vote is of the utmost importance.

The bill, with its numerous clauses, is calculated to increase rather than diminish the feeling of hostility between the northerners & southerners and the hatred of the negro.

It is earnestly to be hoped that it may be defeated.

The bravery of the President in his opposition to congress where he thinks the interests of the country are concerned is truly admirable.

It is intimated that he may be impeached for disloyalty by the radicals, but he may play Cromwell upon them & arrest them before he is arrested.

April 5, 1866

Thursday.

Meeting of N. B.'s home.

Discussion of the civil rights bill in the senate.

Speech by Mr. Trumbull.

Meeting of Sunday school teachers in evening.

April 6, 1866

Friday.

Father left at half past ten A. M. for New York.

Great excitement in the senate to day.

The vote upon the veto to be taken.

Miss Dayton, Miss Johnson, Dr. Pancrast & Dr. Woodhue passed the eve with us.

April 7, 1866

Saturday. The President's veto has been annulled & the Radicals are triumphant. The civil rights bill passed the Senate yesterday.

The excitement in the galleries was intense when Sen. Morgen gave his vote for the bill, he was cheered & many of the senators went to shake him by the hand.

Sen. Dickson was not present.

This is a cold rainy day after the warm spring air of yesterday.

The house seems as dismal as possible without Father.

April 9, 1866

April 9th Monday.

11 AM -- Yesterday was stormy, but Henry drove Carry & I to Sunday School..

Missionary meeting in the afternoon, an address from Rev. W. E. Dodge.   Mr. Freeman Clark was present & was called upon for an address, but asked to be excused.

Church in the evening.

Saw Mr. & Mrs. Foster. The latter came back to me after leaving very kindly to inquire how I was provided for in the way of escort home.

Dr. Gurley gave us two good sermons.

This is a bright beautiful morning after yesterday's rain.

Sturdy little Princeton has fired a political gun in the form of a set of resolutions expressing the opinion of the citizens in favor of the representation of the Southern states in Congress.

Their approval of the President's veto of the civil rights bill & their strong disapprobation of the treatment of Sen. Stockton in which Beaton warmly joins.

The loan bill passed the Senate.

April 10, 1866

The civil rights bill vetoed by the President passed the House yesterday by a large majority.

Its tendency is to increase the estrangement between the North & South and also the hatred of the negro. By one of its enactments a premium is offered to anyone giving information against any citizen found abusing the negro, the delinquents to be tried by military not civil authority.

This offer of a bribe for the information required will probably lead, as during the war, to numberless fake accusations & many innocent persons being arrested through the avaricious spirit or malice of their accusers.

As for military trials, it is quite time that martial law should be abolished since peace has been declared.

Two letters from Father. He says Dr. Bache is in a very sad condition, but knew him & seemed for some time greatly to enjoy his conversation. He was seized with paroxysms of distress which could only be quieted by anodines & in which he called out so loudly that can be heard to a great distance.

He cried out with cursing in one of these when Father was there. "Oh I am so miserable." It is deeply trying to Father to see him in such a condition.

April 11, 1866

11th Went to Mrs. Gurley's to take care of little Emma while Mother & Mrs. G. went shopping. Mother & I passed the evening with Mrs. Peale who gave us an entertainment of ice cream & cake.

April 12, 1866

12th A letter from Father.. no further particulars concerning Dr. Bache.

Carry & I took tea with Susie Hodge. I employed myself in trimming Susie hat. Major Penrose & a friend of his came in.

We had a sweet little note yesterday from Lottie, giving us the pleasant intelligence that Harriet had united with the church last Sunday. 39 others took upon themselves the same vows so that it was a very solemn occasion I feel like giving thanks for the 39 as well as for Harriet, for each one must have some relatives who are rejoicing now for them as we are for her.

Lottie came to the Communion before, so that nearly all withwhom we are closely connected are now committed by a tie which even death cannot sever. This is a bright beautiful morning, it is growing warm again.

An interesting little item in the Year Book of facts concerning the use of glycerine instead of water for making modeling clay.

April 13, 1866

A letter from Father. Dr. Bache no better, will probably not last long[75]. Father deeply engaged in testing oil. had not yet seen friends considering duty should come before friendship or ceremony.

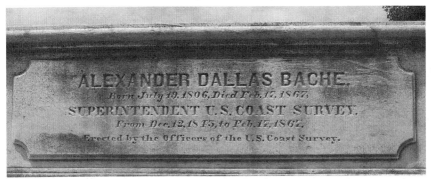

Memorial plaque affixed to the Alexander Dallas Bache Monument in Congressional Cemetery in Washington, D.C.

Mr. Beaman passed the evening with us.

April 14, 1866

This day one year ago, the President lay dead at the hands of an assassin. The public buildings are all closed in commemoration of the sad event.

We may still mourn the good man departed, but his mantle has fallen upon one who seems well able[76] to guide the ship of State through the turbulent political billows which even now when we ought to expect a calm, still threaten to destroy her.

Another letter from Father, he may be home to night.

April 16, 1866

Father arrived at six o'clock yesterday morning.

We left him, making up for lost time in the way of sleep, when we went to Sunday School.

Dr. Gurley preached.

In the evening Judge Hare came in. In the course of the conversation at the tea table, Judge Hare remarked that from the tendency of all creation to seek an equilibrium the "men down" as Father calls it.

---

[75] Bache succumbed to his illness on February 17, 1867, at the age of 60. He is buried in DC's Congressional Cemetery.

[76] It is interesting to compare Mary Henry's present assessment of Andrew Johnson to that of her initial evaluation on March 4, 1865.

All things would come to a dead level, all organisms cease to exist were it not for a sustaining as well as a creating power.

If a world could be created without a God it could not possibly continue in existance without one.

An argument for the existance of the Deity he had not met with. Father said that his belief in God was inducted. Nothing was more plain to him than the fact of his own existance, of the thinking living principal within called a soul. "I think therefore I am" reasoning from analogy he must suppose that those around him were equally endowed & finding in Nature evidences of mind of rational thought similar to his own, he could no more doubt the existence of a supreme controlling intelligence than his own.

April 23, 1866

Prof. Hosford is with us. He came yesterday morning.

April 27, 1866

Dr. Woolsey, President of Yale arrived this morning.

He is not at all striking in appearance and his bearing indicates almost too much humility.

April 28, 1866

Went to call on Mrs. Admiral Farragut also upon Mrs. Stockton.

Mr. Welling and Dr. Gurley came to dinner.

Miss Dix also was here. She has resumed her visitations of the insane hospitals and is looking better in health and spirits since she has gone back to her old duties.

We had a pleasand Dinner. Some communications from Miss Dix & Dr. Woolsey causing us some merriment.

Dr. W. does not talk much, but what he says is very interesting. His eyes are keen & penetrating and his smile peculiarly winning.

Mr. Welling expects to leave in a week for Europe to be gone about six months.

Just before dinner we had a call from Mrs. Rev. Johnson and her daughters.

After dinner we had a game of croquet.

Mr. Beaman and the Marquis de Shonbrun joining us. Dr. W. also took part in the game.

The Marquis is very agreeable and intelligent. He has come to our country to study its political economy. I met him a number of times in society last winter.

Our pleasant day closed with a visit to Mr. Bierstadt's picture of Mount Hood.

Mr. Gillis & Dr. Tryon came for us about 8 o'clock.

April 29, 1866

Sermon from Dr. McGern in the morning. He took for text the simple word "alone" as applied to the life of our Lord when on earth.

Dr. Woolsey gave us a very interesting sermon in the evening.

April 30, 1866

Dr. Woolsey left us this morning we were very sorry to have him go. Col. Yates and Capt. Crugan passed the evening with us.

May 2, 1866

An important cabinet meeting yesterday in which the President brought forward his reconstruction policy and was supported by all the secretarys.

Dennison also went with the President. Speed was not present, being out of town.

The Wilkes came this afternoon with Mr. Beaman for a game of croquet. The air was too cold to be pleasant. It is more like Fall than Spring.

May 3, 1866

Mrs. Bridge here in the morning.

Meeting of News Boy's Home Association, Church & Teachers meeting in the afternoon.

Went to see Mrs. Peale.

Father and Mother spent the evening with Mr. & Mrs. Chanler.

Father would not tell us where they had been & amused us & himself by making us play the game of 20 questions to find out.

Two French men came with letters of introduction, one of them the great grandson of the inventor of the balloon.

Evening

Three French gentlemen, Mr. Fox & Mr Besel came to play croquet.

Mr. Foote & Mr. Taylor came to see father in the evening.

Mr. F. said his wife had invented a paper making machine which would probably be very profitable as a pecuniary speculation

Father was curious to know what led her thoughts in that direction he said he must "get under her bonnet."

She is at present trying to make diamonds.

Mr. F. promised me a set if she should be successful.

May 4, 1866

Col. Yates here in the evening.

Poor old Count Gerouski[77] is dead. He breathed his last at Mrs. Eames. He was a Pole, but had lived in this, the country of his adoption, for a number of years.

His shrewd remarks upon political and other matters have been a source of great amusement to Father.

The last time we saw him was at a reading given by Mrs. May Howe at Mrs. Johnson's.

May 7, 1866

Yesterday went to church & Sunday School.

Had the pleasure of seeing Dr. & Mrs. Hodge from Princeton.

Read "Nature & the Supernatural" to Father in the evening.

Jack Gillis, Dr. Tryon & the Kennedy's here this afternoon.

Meeting of the doctors of the city who discussed nothing, but the cholera.

May 8, 1866

A visit from Miss DeLeon.

She was in Richmond during the war & gave us an interesting account of her experience. Among other things told us, she had kept an account of marketing expenses for the family as a curiosity.

Turkeys were sold at $150, butter $50 per pound and other things in like proportion.

May 9, 1866

Miss DeLeon stayed with us last night and entertained us during the eve, with a description of her travels abroad and especially her visit to Egypt where her brother was consul. She has gone to attend a lecture given by her brother for the benefit of the sufferers of the South.

Dr. Torrey arrived this evening.

May 10, 1866

The discussions in congress yesterday seemed mostly to have concerned the great question now at issue is the representation of the Southern states.

The reconstruction Com. have presented their report, one clause of an amendment to which is that all who have participated in the rebellion be disfranchised until 1870.

---

[77] Adam Gurowski (1805-1866), was an author and linguist. Being acquainted with eight languages, Gurowski served as a translator in the State Department during the American Civil War.

Our friend, the Chief Justice, I am glad to see is in favor of the immediate restoration to the rights of citizens of all who loyaly disposed.

In a letter to the Anti-Slavery society which recently held its anniversary in New York, he says that all free men are entitled to suffrage on equal terms and if this truth had been recognized in the first movement towards national reconstruction by an invitation to the whole loyal people of the states in rebellion to take part in the work of state reorganization undoubtedly the practical relations of every state with the union would have been already established with the happiest results.

He adds, "nothing is more profitable than justice."

The Anti-Slavery Society, at their meeting, did not second jis views, however, but abused the president roundly. Wendell Phillips introducing a set of resolutions in which the chief magistrate is denounced as a traitor & the headquarters of rebellion declared to have been changed from Richmond to the White House.

Congress is determined to restrict the power of the President as much as possible and has brought forward a bill introduced, I believe, by Mr. Trumbull which provides "that no salary or compensation be given to officers appointed by the President before confirmation by the Senate, unless appointed to fill vacancies happening during the recess of the Senate by death, resignation, expiration of term or removal for official misconduct." The passage of this act will prevent the President from turning out any one who might be obnoxious to him except during the session of the Senate & then really only with their consent & that body would have the power of withholding the pay of any one appointed by him to fill such vacancies.

Thus taking from him one means of defense against his political enemies & strengthening the hands of his congressional foes.

Mrs. Davis, in with her husband[78], comfortable quarters have been provided for her & she expresses great satisfaction at the kindness which has been shown to the illustrious prisoner.

---

[78] Jefferson Davis, the captured President of the Confederate States of America was initially imprisoned at Fort Monroe along the Virginia coast. "Irons were riveted to his ankles at the order of General Nelson Miles who was in charge of the fort. Davis was allowed no visitors, and no books except the Bible. His health began to suffer, and the attending physician warned that the prisoner's life was in danger, but this treatment continued for some months until late autumn when he was finally given better quarters. General Miles was transferred in mid-1866, and Davis' treatment continued to improve." – Dodd 1907, pp 366-368; "Varina (Davis' wife) and their young daughter Winnie were

His health seems to have suffered from his confinement.

May 11, 1866

Mr. Thadeus Stevens[79], the republican tyrant of the House, succeeded yesterday, in passing the resolutions of his darling reconstruction committee which have been under consideration for the last two days.

Gen. Banks voted for the resolutions.

Thadeus himself made a violent speech.

In the Senate, the bill for the restriction of the President's right of removal from office was still under discussion.

Father dined yesterday with the Chief Justice. A very pleasant dinner. Several of the foreign ministers were present with some distinguished army officers.

Susie Hodge Maj Penrose & Mr. Beaman were here this afternoon. came with us from church.

March 12, 1866

Dr. Torrey left us this morning, Father accompanying him as far as Baltimore.

The Republicans, it seems, are sighing & groaning over the passage of the Reconstruction resolutions with the third obnoxious section intact is that the Southerners shall be denied representation until 1870, although hey voted for them in a body.

They declare that one more such victory will ruin them.

How men can thus yield their liberty to a party, & be controlled by a single individual I cannot understand.

---

allowed to join Davis, and the family was eventually given an apartment in the officers' quarters. Davis was indicted for treason while imprisoned." -- Blackford, Charles M., ▢he ▢▢▢▢/▢ an▢ ▢▢▢/ ▢▢ ▢e▢▢e▢▢▢n ▢ a▢▢▢. ▢▢/. ▢▢▢▢; On December 25, 1868, President Johnson granted an unconditional pardon to all southern soldiers who fought during the Civil War.

[79] Thaddeus Stevens (1792-1868) a member of the United States House of Representatives from Pennsylvania served as the leader of the "Radical Republicans" who fiercely opposed slavery and discrimination against African-Americans. Stevens views regarding civil rights and punishing the South often fueled bitter battles between he and President Andrew Johnson, who favored fewer civil rights for African Americans and an expedited end to reconstruction.

Thaddeus Stevens, in his closing appeal expressed a wish "That the eight millions of Americans inhabiting the South might be confined by bayonets in the penitentiary of hell.

May 14, 1866

Yesterday had a sermon from Dr. Chester, Dr Gurley having gone to the General Assembly.

No service in the evening.

To day was the anniversary of the Sunday School Union and nearly all the children in the city assembled on the Smithsonian grounds preparatory to proceeding in procession to the Capitol grounds where addresses were delivered & others.

Mrs. Parker and her little son, the Wilkes & Mamy, who has a face that would have charmed Raphael, the little Rodgers, Miss Ramsey, Miss Rucker & Miss Walker & others came over to witness the display.

Carry & I went to the church about two o'clock to give our Sunday school children ice cream & cake.

May 15, 1866

Mrs. Shubrick here this morning with her daughter

Mrs. Climer, Miss Rucker & Miss Ramsey.

Mr. Beaman & Gillis came in the evening to play croquet, Bible study & other things with Father tonight.

Father was asked to address the meeting, but declined, gave me, coming home, a beautiful little speech of things he might have said closing with the remark that we drink in the blessing of the result of the Bible teachings as unconsciously as we breath the air or enjoy the light.

We are so surrounded by them they have to become a part of our daily existence that we are unmindful of them or their source.

Our friend, Mr. Chambers, rather injudiciously brought forward a resolution in the house yesterday, condemnatory of the arbitrary acts of some of the republican members of the house & in approval of the President's course for which he was censured by the House.

Jeremy T.K. Farley

The Henry Family on the Smithsonian grounds after playing a game of croquet. Pictured are Joseph Henry his wife, Harriet Alexander Henry, and their daughters Caroline, Helen Louisa and Mary Anna. Photo courtesy of the Smithsonian Institution.

May 16, 1866

A very cold day for this season of the year, a fire would be comfortable.

The President yesterday, sent into the Senate his veto of the bill to make Colorado a state.

It remained unread, an indignity never before shown to a presidential message.

The body of Preston King has been found after being six months under water.

Dr. & Mrs. Hodge, here also, Mr. Buckingham Smith, also Mr. Foxwith his mother & sister.

200

May 17, 1866

A rainy, disagreeable morning.

May 21, 1866

A stranger preached to us yesterday.

Father & Nell went to the capitol to hear Dr. Hodge.

Read Nature & the Supernatural in the evening.

In the attempt to account for the apparent tendency of Nature to undertake more than she was able to accomplish, Mr. Bushnell said the numerous blossoms that fall to the ground without producing fruit, the innumeral eggs & young of animals that never reach maturity might be a Providential Symbolization of the short comings of the human race, which seemed to me rather an egotistical interpretation of the phenomena in question.

He proceeded in carrying out this system of symbolism to give an account of the wars of the pismires[80] who fight their micro battles with all the ferocity & with much of the military diplomacy of those whom Mr. Bushnell considers their human prototype and were he thinks formed to thus teach man the absurdity of the wars that only desolate & destroy.

To gather such lessons from Nature's processes is well, but that God created the whole race of pismires to teach such a truth to the two or three individuals who may have observed their habits can hardly be.

Father said the numerous surplus blossoms produced was a wise provision of Nature to guard against accidents & how many honey bees did they supply with their sweets. So the surplus in the animal creation might exist for the same reason & also to provide food for other animals.

Mary Felton came tonight.

We received a very surprising peice of news from Oxford.

Yesterday visited the addition of small boy to our little parson's family.

May 22, 1866

Went to play croquet at the Wilkes in the afternoon.

Assisted Father in the morning in sorting pamphlets.

Went from the Wilkes to Mrs. Hooper's to tea. Col & Mrs. Bliss were there also, & in the course of the evening, Mr. Smucker came in.

Mr. Hooper was in the House until a late hour, when he came in, he said we ought to be obliged to him as he had added a clause to some bill exempting dressmakers from a certain tax so that we might hope to appear well at a lower rate of prices if the Senate was refractory.

Mr. Sumner said he would not oppose the bill, certainly as he had been honoured by a call from Madame Demarest herself to induce him to favor

---

[80] Pismires is an archaic term for ants.

it and had commenced his suit by saying she must thank him for his public course in regard to slavery & other things, showing herself as skillful in diplomacy as in dressmaking.

Before we went to the Wilkes, Father had a call from Count Lasteyrie, the grandson of Lafayette who has come to this country to make good his claim to some estates inherited by him through his great progenitor.

May 23, 1866

Mary dined with Mrs. Hooper.

Carry went with her to take tea at the Observatory.

May 24, 1866

Mary Felton went to Mt. Vernon.

Jack Gillis & Dr. Tryon came in the evening.

Mary was particularly pleased with the former.

Father dined with Mr. Hooper in company with Mr. Sumner and the two Lasteyries, Father & son.

May 25, 1866

M. F. went to Arlington.

Gen. Schencks daughter came with Col. Woodhull and another military officer to play croquet.

Mr. Beaman was also here.

At dinner Father showed us a small piece of a basket which had been found in making some excavations in an island near New Orleans, beneath the bones of an elephant of a species now extinct and of which no traces have hitherto been discovered upon this continent.

The specimen of basketwork was exceedingly interesting as indicating the great age of man. In looking at it, it seemed impossible that it could be so old, to have been made prior to when we have supposed our old friend or enemy Adam to have appeared in the world.

I confess I feel somewhat skeptical about it. it was found near a salt spring. It was taken by the gentleman who handed it to Father with his own hands from beneath the elephant.

May 26, 1866

Mary Felton left us this morning we were very sorry to have her go.

May 27, 1866

Sermon on the future state of rewards & punishments.

Dr. Gurley has gone to attend a meeting of the General Assembly.

May 28, 1866

Father & self went to call on Dr. & Mrs. Hodge who are with Gen. Hunter. They were at tea when we entered.

I had the pleasure of being entertained by Gen. & Mrs. Hunter, their nieces & Mrs. Hodge while Dr. Hodge & Father discussed the Gen. Assembly and the question of the union of the new & old schools under consideration by that body.

The Dr. was opposed to it as the radical party in the church now so powerfully opposed to any gentle measures in connexion with the south will then have so great an ascendency.

The Dr. has opposed the actions of the assembly in regard to the state of the country during the war and is denounced by the radicals.

Mr. & Mrs. Chanler passed the evening at home, we did not get back in time to see them.

The reproof received by Mr. C. for advocating the President's policy or rather for what was called his improper manner of speaking of those who did not has made him rather sore.

May 29, 1866

Went to an organ concert with Mr. Torrey in the new baptist church.

Mr. Baber spent the evening here, I was sorry to miss him.

June 1, 1866

Mrs. Bridge's neice came to play croquet.

Mr. Lasleyne was here with his Father. The latter is charming in conversation & the general expression of benevolence which characterizes his features, but he is unfortunately very deaf.

The young man is bright, artless & enthusiastic.

Mr. Bridge came for his neice about ten o'clock

June 3, 1866

Sermon from Dr. Edwards in the evening.

Mother read aloud for our mutual benefit.

The records of the Gen. Assembly from the Presbyterian:

The clergymen do not seem to have exhibited that Christian forgiveness & magnanimity which we have a right to expect from them in regard to Southern matters.

June 4, 1866

Went to Wilkes.

Father dined with Baron Gerold.

June 5, 1866

Festival for the benefit of the News Boys.

Dr. Craig, here, brought a little case of photographs sent to me by Dr., the German physician who was here last summer and took a kind interest in my broken nose. It was pleasant to be remembered.

June 8, 1866

The Wilkes here to play croquet with Mr. Beaman & the French Mr. Lasteyea, Mr. Lastegne, Gen. went with Father to see the Chief Justice.

June 9, 1866

Father went on an excursion down the river with a party composed of the Sec. and some members of Congress.

Alfred Woodhull & others here in the evening.

Nell not well.

June 10, 1866

Mr.. Campbell preached for us

The French man, Mr. Lasteyne, came to say good bye.

He has given to Carrie a picture, a drawing for her album.

A Scotch tourist took tea with us.

Read *Defence of Fundamental Truth* by Dr. McCash.

Nell very sick.

Father is with her now & I here him repeating to her in a low tone, "Sleep balmby, sleep her nightly visit prays" & others.

June 12, 1866

Nell much better today.

Dr. Tyler was very uneasy about her, but is quite happy concerning her now. He pronounced her disease to be varioloid[81].

Mr. T. came with his brother last night.

Father was engaged with a commission of gentlemen in the laboratory & could not see him.

In speaking of Dr. McCosh's book, *The defence of fundamental truth,* he gave me an interesting sketch of the different schools of philosophy of the old world.

He does not think Dr. McCosh quite equal to the task of meeting Mr. Mill.

He asked me how the sculpture was progressing & when I told him I thought I had no talent, said he once said to Father "Prof. do you ever feel yourself to be a fool for I do."

Father said he was glad to hear Mr. T. say so, as he very often had the same experiance.

---

[81] A mild form of smallpox.

It took him a week sometimes to reinstate him in his own good opinion.

Prof. Agassiz, who was present, said that every man of sense felt so at times That only a fool thought himself always wise.

Count Portallis & daughters called to say "good bye."

June 13, 1866

Dr. Craig came in the evening, but stayed not for fear of the varioloid.

Nell continues to improve.

The addition to the constitution recommended by the reconstruction committee has passed the Senate[82].

June 14, 1866

Count de Lasteyrie called to return a book.

He did not leave as expected to do on Sunday owing to the illness of his son.

June 15, 1866

Nell much better but Father not well. His illness probably due to a great change in the weather.

June 16, 1866

The Gillises came last evening to see us.

Both our patients doing well.

June 30, 1866

It is a long time since I have made an entry in my diary.

Mother, Father, Nell have all been sick and Carry & I have thought of little, but nursing and also being nursed having yielded to the general condition of the household.

The Senate & House adjourned on Saturday.

We shall miss Mr. Beaman, Mr. Sumner's secretary as we have seen him almost every day for the last month.

Yesterday, on coming out of church, Gen. Eaton told us of the successful laying of the Atlantic cable.

---

[82] Fourteenth Amendment to the United States Constitution was one of the Reconstruction Amendments. The amendment addresses citizenship rights and equal protection of the laws. The amendment, particularly its first section, is one of the most litigated parts of the Constitution and formed the basis for landmark decisions such as Roe v. Wade, as well as Bush v. Gore (2000).

"It is a great work, a glory to our age and nation, and the men who have achieved it deserve to be honoured among the benefactors of their race." – Article in the "Times of London," which was telegraphed across the cable.

August 1, 1866

Father received a telegram from Valentia today, from the electrician Varly on the other side of the water.

It was dated at Valentia, July 28th, and received at Aspa Bay on the 31st "Saturday."

"Cable laid perfect is not this grand? Give my best wishes to Ex Prest Buchanan. -- Varly."

Have been working on Father's bust all day in the Laboratory.

Father busy at my side with his report. Had rather an amusing visit from two country men who came with some mineral specimens found on the farm of one of them which he supposed to contain gold.

Father told him the story of the man who left a peice of land to his sons telling them a treasure was hidden in. They dug it up diligently found no buried gold, but the working of the soil produced a plentiful harvest and revealed to the brothers the truth of their father's words.

The men laughed and Father told them they had better go on steadily in their agricultural persuits & leave gold speculation to those who had nothing better to do. That gold hunting ruined more fortunes than it made.

August 2, 1866

Worked on Father's bust.

Father still very busy with Report.

Dr. Craig, Mr. Gill & Prof _____ in the evening.

Dr. Craig said the people seemed to have, but little confidence in the working of the cable. More news ought to have been received.

August 3, 1866

Still working on bust.

Gen. Price and Gen. Forsythe here in the evening to play croquet.

August 4, 1866

Father left for Northampton at 2 p.m.

He expected to go in the morning, but was disappointed. I went to the depot with him.

Miss Schenck, Miss Miller, Miss Henley, Gen. Hunter's neice, Gen Price, Mrs. Forsyth & Gen Forsyth here in the evening for croquet

August 6, 1866

Did not go out yesterday, read Mansel's *Limits of Religious Thought*.

Letter from Father this morning.

Slept at the Astor House had a pleasant journey so far.

August 8, 1866

8th Worked on Father's head

Note from Mr. Fillmore containing invitation to stay at his house during meeting of Scientific Association.

Croquet party in the afternoon consisting of Dr. Craig, Mr. Fox & Sallie Kennedy.

Read in the evening.

Discussion in the Senate in regard to the appropriation of $10,000 to Miss Vinnie Ream to make a full length statue of President Lincoln.

The unjust resolution was passed. Sumner opposed it in an interesting speech, but was overruled.

Miss Vinnie is a young lady from the West who has been studying this winter under Clark Mills. She is utterly inexperianced although she seems to have talent.

August 11, 1866

The Marquis here this evening with Judge Otto, also Mrs. Gillis

August 13, 1866

Went to Sunday School yesterday, but not to church. Finished Mansel on "Limits of Religious Thought."

August 14, 1866

Had a letter from Father.

He has enjoyed the meeting of the Academy, although he has not been well. A number of valuable papers were read. He thinks the Academy will prove to be a success.

Mr. Fillmore's invitation he would have accepted if one of us had gone with him.

A visit today from the Queen of the Sandwich Isles[83]. We went down into the museum to be presented to her, that is Nell, Carry and myself.

She was accompanied by Mr. Chilton of the Treasury, who has been deputed by the Government, to looking officers of her suite, also by an English lade Miss Spurgeon, a companion who has been traveling with her.

Her Majesty comes to this country to obtain means for the spread of Christianity in Hawaii.

We found nothing queenly in the dark, but rather comely young woman, to whom we were presented, but were pleased with her modest bearing. There was nothing peculiar in her attire.

The portrait of Queen Emma of Hawaii, wearing the Royal Order and Ribbon of Kamehameha I and her famous tiger's claw necklace.

I forgot the respectful prefix, "your Majesty," one or twice in addressing her, however she did not seem displeased, but gave me a smile at parting, which, quite won my heart.

She did not stay long, it being near her dinner hour.

Mother went to see Mrs. Lindsey, who has lost her son.

He was a classmate in college of our dear Will.

Another letter from Father.

The Academy has adjourned. He does not say when he will be home.

December 3, 1866

Monday. We are a united family once more.

---

[83] Queen Emma of Hawaii. She visited Washington, D.C., on her way back from visiting Queen Victoria of England. On August 14, 1866, President Andrew Johnson hosted a reception for her at the White House. This was the first time anyone with the title "Queen" made an official visit to the U.S. presidential residence.

We left home the 5th of Aug., Father & Nell went to the Bay of Fundy, Mother to Chestnut Hill, I went first with Carry to Rockaway and then to Providence.

Father lectured last week in Baltimore before the Peabody Institute, opening the first course of lectures of that institution.

I have spent the day in unpacking & sewing.

Dr. Craig here in the evening.

Congress opened today.

December 4, 1866

Tuesday 4th.

Mr. Welling passed the evening with us & gave us an interesting explanation of some photographs he brought with him from Europe.

December 5, 1866

Matinee at Gen. Delafield, went at 4 p. m. & returned about 9 a.m.

Sensible party found Mr. Beaman waiting to see us.

Dr. Simpson and his Father and Mr. Gill also came in.

December 6, 1866

Father dined at Mrs. Chandler's, as he entered her parlor, he found her surrounded by her beautiful children whom he soon enticed to his side by the delights of riding upon his foot.

Mr. Stanton was there.

December 7, 1866

Friday. A visit in the morning from Dr. Draper and daughter Dr. Woodhull also here.

In the evening, Miss Draper came to stay with us while Dr. Draper went with Father to the society.

Mr. Taylor & Mr. Foote also came to go with Father.

Mr. Welling was here for a short time and Mr. Beaman came to assist in entertaining Miss Draper.

December 8, 1866

Sat. Sewing all day. Father at the club. Cary gone with Dr. Woodhull.

December 9, 1866

Col. Alexander came to go to church with Nell.

Mr. Beaman took tea with us

December 10, 1866

Monday

Mr. Fox here in the morning went to a meeting for the deaf & dumb with Col. Alexander & Mr. Beaman in the evening.

December 11, 1866

11th Tuesday Miss Draper came to stay with us also Miss Mary Graham.

A small party at Dr. Gurley's

December 12, 1866

Read Bell on Expression.

Father enjoyed the engravings & Miss Mary gave us a history of the burning of Columbia.

She was there at the time & lost all her clothing. She says the distress of the inhabitants suddenly deprived of their homes was extreme.

Gen Sherman promised on the taking of the city that it should be spared, but seemed to have changed his mind.

December 13, 1866

13th Thursday.

Went to the Capitol with Miss G. Col A.

Here in the evening, promised to write a carol and address for our Christmas Sunday School celebration.

December 14, 1866

Went with Mr. Fox and Miss G. to see some fine engravings at Blanchards.

Saw Dore's Bible and Wandering Jew, also a collection of Raphael Madonnas.

Col. Alexander here in the eve, with a piece of poetry in place of the carol he promised, the purport of which was the fairest hand is that which gives also an address, in ryme. "Had a game of Chess with him."

December 15, 1866

Sat. Went to a meeting of the News Boys Home.

The constitution of the society is to be changed and the establishment connected with the Children's Aid Society in Baltimore which will provide homes for the destitute children who take refuge in our Home.

We sent off three boys with the Baltimore agent, happy in the prospect of being well taken care of.

Mrs. Hooper is more than ever interested in the establishment now that there is a prospect that its usefulness will be extended.

December 16, 1866

Sunday. Too stormy to go to church.

Read Bell on the Hand with pleasant interruptions from Father who read aloud extracts from the books he was interested in and repeated scraps of poetry. Miss G. sang Mozart's Twelfth Mass which even Father enjoyed Discussion with Father in the eve about the development theory.

December 17, 1866

Sewed all day. Father interested in the eve, in a book upon the distribution of Mammals over the world with maps which attracted us all.

We were amused to find what a small space was occupied by the negros The same portions being also the home of the ape & the monkey.

December 18, 1866

Tuesday. Mr. Trumbu & Lady here, missionaries from Valverde.

Mr. Beaman came in the eve.

December 19, 1866

Congress has distinguished itself thus far in giving the negros of the District voting privileges.

We shall be inundated by the coloured race and probably soon rejoice in a black Mayor.

It seems very arbitrary to impose such a measure upon us when the pole of the citizens was taken last year upon the subject and found to be by a large majority in its disfavor.

No property qualification is required and only one year's residence in the district or county necessary for securing a vote - a petition was presented to Congress yesterday asking that "the District Suffrage act be amended in such manner as to put all whites of the Caucasian race who are either citizens or have declared their intention to become citizens of the U.S. on an equal footing with the negros.

December 20, 1866

Last evening we had a pleasant little party for Mr. Trumbul. He came with his wife to dinner.

Went to call upon the bride Mrs. Tanner. She was not receiving so we had not the pleasure of seeing her.

Stopped at Mrs. Gen. Delafields. Quite a number of people there among others Mrs. Robert J. Walker.

It was pleasant to see her face again in society. Her daughter and daughter in Law accompanied her.

Mamy looking very prettily in the little cap which has taken the place of a bonnet this winter.

Judge Mason here in the evening. The admission of Nebraska into the Union discussed in the Senate.

December 21, 1866

Friday. Went to the church to dress a tree for the Sunday school.

Mr. Beaman came to assist us, he is going to see the Wilkes in S. Carolina. We shall miss the girls greatly this winter.

December 22, 1866

A stormy day.

Nell & Miss Mary alone ventured out to buy Christmas presents.

Finished Ball on Expression in the evening. Have thoroughly enjoyed the book.

December 23, 1866

Sunday

Church & Sunday School in the morning.

The afternoon passed on the sofa with an attack of termination of blood to the head.

Col. Alexander here in the evening.

Carry went to the Orphan Asylum to see about the children's tree.

They are to sing my carol.

December 24, 1866

Christmas tree at the church for the Sunday School children.

December 25, 1866

Presented our gifts in the morning at the breakfast table

Had time for a poetical inscription for Father's alone, an impromtu which Father told me to keep.

Gen. & Mrs. Vanantwerp passed the day with us. Mrs. Platt and a friend coming in the eve.

January 1, 1867

A stormy day, the snow lying thick upon the ground and sleet & rain falling. Fewer visitors than usual. Father went on his rounds, but returned early. Mrs. Shubrick sent me a piece of cake by him as usual.

January 9, 1867

Small party at Senator Dixons.

January 10, 1867

Mr. Beaman here with a German count also Mr. Alexander.

January 11, 1867

Reception day. Mrs. Foster here had enjoyed her southern trip greatly.

Miss Johnson's call was also agreeable not many calls. Uncle is with us. Carry gone to Opera with Mr. Beaman, Mrs. Dickie, Sen _____ , Mr. Cross here in the evening.

January 12, 1867

Went to Gen. Grant's reception. Carry thanked the Gen. for the letter he wrote to her for her autograph book, but the Gen. had not much to say in reply.

He looked very smiling as if he would like to say something pleasant, but not having something to say said nothing.

Went also to the Mayor's, where dancing was the order of the morning.

January 13, 1867

Sunday. Too stormy to go to church.

Read McCosh on typical forms.

In the evening Father & Uncle amused themselves by reminiscences of their school boy days.

Uncle said those days seemed very far away, like the echo that came to us from the mountain side, clear & distinct as the remembrance might be, there was always a sense of how much lay between.

I'm speaking of some school he attended, Uncle said to Father, "Was that the school where you discovered the India ink was good for the complexion?"

We were all, of course, curious to know the meaning of the question, Elicited from Father the confession that at the school mentioned, he was often teased on account of his pink & white complexion & accused of painting his cheeks.

One evening, a young man much his senior, taking these jokes for earnest came to him & asked him to colour his cheeks for him as he wished to go to a party.

Provoked at the accusation contained in the request & inspired by the spirit of fun, he painted him with India ink & he went off to the party as from being improved by the operation.

January 14, 1867

Miss Miller was married this morning.

The reception was a pleasant one, but the air of the crowded rooms was stifling.

May 11, 1867

Have been busy all day preparing for an excursion into Virginia.

Dr. Denham, a Scotch clergyman & his wife are with us.

Dr. D. is one of a party of clergymen sent from the free churches of Scotland & Ireland as delegates to the churches of America. He is a fine looking specimen of the genus homo.

May 12, 1867

Sunday. Mr. Wells, one of the Foreign delegates, preached for us in the morning.

Mr. Guthree, son of one of the clergymen appointed to accompany the party of free church men, dined with us. His Father had been obliged to turn back after starting on account of sea sickness.

Dr. Fairbairn, another of the delegates, preached for us in the evening.

Dr. Denham went to the negro church & was much schocked by the exebition of animal excitement he witnessed.

May 13, 1867

Dr. & Mrs. Denham left us this morning.

Louis Guthrie here in the evening went with the girls & Father to the hotel to see the Pattersons who came from Phil to day for the excursion.

I join them tomorrow at six o'clock A.M.

May 14, 1867

We are finaly off after waiting about three quarters of an hour on the railroad platform.

The cloudy face of the morning is rapidly brightening under the influence of the sun's rays & soon the vapory reminders of last night's storm will quite disappear.

Our party numbers about fourty, I should think.

We have an entire car to ourselves.

In one end of which., with a seat laid to make a double pew, Ellie & Grace Patterson, Mr. Guthree & myself are seated. A kind, manly face bends over us occasionally to see how we are faring which breaks into a very pleasant smile when we ask the owner a question.

That is Col. Patterson. He occupies the double pew opposite with Mr. & Mrs. Randal & their little girl, the only child of the party.

Mr. R. is a member of the House. In the next seat on that side are Col. Patterson's two daughters, pleasant, intelligent looking girls I know I shall like them.

In the next seat to us Mr. Harrison, a rich capitalist from Phil with his wife & daughter, are ensconced. I cannot see their faces, but a little farther on my eye rests with a great deal of pleasure upon the form of Gen.

Patterson. He is much older than his brother. His pleasant genial face is particularly happy just now, as he is laughing heartily. His every movement betokens the true gentleman & soldier.

I cannot see who is with him, but opposite in the same double seat sits Mrs. Childs, the publisher's wife.

The faces of my other travelling companions have not yet become familiar to me. The modest sweetness of that of a young Quaqueress, a hide attracted my attention while we were waiting on the platform of the station, but I do not see it now.

We are occasionaly visited by rather an odd, but pleasant looking gentleman whose every word is greeted with a smile, it being evidently a settled thing that what he says will be something amusing. Mr. Boothe is his name.

He is a Verginia gentleman married to a Phil. lady.

We move rapidly on.

Mr. Guthrie discourses to us about Scotland, we endeavour to initiate him into the causes of the war.

We all look as if we would be a little sleepy after our early rise if it were not for the immense excitement of the occasion.

A hungry look is also coming into our eyes, but Alexandria & breakfast are near at hand.

So even at the door.

After breakfast --

We are decidedly more comfortable after our meal.

Miss Patterson has come into our pew & Mr. Guthrie is behind us among the shawls & bags. Carry is her name, her face loses nothing by closer inspection

We are all wide awake now.

We are passing over scenes made desolate by the war. The trees have bowed down before the contending armies, like grass & the county is destitute of them, fences & landmarks have entirely disappeared.

Old earth-work, the remains of old encampments, meet us on every side. Chemnies are standing here & there, the sole remnant of former hospitable home.

The land is poor & steril, but deeply interesting, sacred as it is to the memory of the brave dead.

We pass over Bulls Run, a small muddy stream, but not near enough to Mannassas to see any of the fighting ground.

Mr. Patterson has taken me out of my seat & placed me beside Mrs. Childs, opposite Gen. Patterson, I am most delightfully situated & thoroughly enjoy the Gen.'s good stories.

Prof. ____ is also in the seat with us.

He has left his place for a moment & his seat is taken by an individual in such shabby attire we question for a moment his social position, but his courtesy & intelligence soon satisfy us on that point & prove the fallacy of the proverb that a tailor makes the gentleman.

He is Mr. Boling, a southern gentleman who joined us at the last station. Gen. Slaughter & several other southern gentlemen have also joined our party.

A quaker gentleman, the warmest republican among us, stands in the asyle of the car with his arms, about two of them listening & laughing heartily at some stories they are telling. His affectionate attitude, speaking well for the return of Good feeling.

We pass Brandy Station, Culpeper Co House,

Cedar Mt,. where Jackson fought Pope cross the Rapidan.

Look with interest at the old co. house in which Maddison used to address the electors.

This - Orange - is the first settled county. Its very small jails speak well for the morality of its people. Gen. Patterson says the prisoners sometimes run away with the jails.

Am introduced to the President of the Railroad & some more of my travelling companions.

Stop at Gordonsville.

We are passing now the residence of Jefferson. It stands on a high hill, not far from the road & must command a fine view of the surrounding country. We catch only a glimpse of the house.

Pass Ravenna Stop at Charlottesville. The town has about 2,000 inhabitants We see the college buildings.

Onward again, we steam pass Carter's Mt., over very poor land spoiled by tobacco.

Gen. Patterson has gone to the other end of the car.

Miss H___ has come into our seat. She is a quiet lady, with a pair of very fine dark eyes.

We are decidedly growing tired. Mrs. Childs is indulging in a nap & I should like to follow suit, but must listen to the professor at my side, who fortunately requires only a "yes" or "no" from me, occasionally as my voice is quite gone with talking all day in the noisy cars.

Our road lies through a prettier country than that we passed over this morning. It is quite late in the afternoon now, and Lynchburg our resting place for the night, is near at hand.

The whole party have grown quiet, except the Prof, my companion, who discourses steadily.

We are at the landing, bags & shawls are seized with alacrity. There are omnibuses ready for those who wish to ride to the hotel where we are to be accommodated. I prefer to walk.

Mr. Guthrie takes my bag & we mount the steep streets of the queer little town, comparing notes as to the pleasure of the day.

Lynchburg is the principal market for tobacco in Virginia.

We passed some of the warehouses near the depot. The houses we pass are small and badly built & the streets narrow & roughly paved. The place generally has an air of being about fifty years behind the times. The hotel, however, is pleasant & comfortable. As we have come up a steep hill we are not sorry to reach it.

Seven of us ladies are shown into a large airy room which we are told we shall be obliged to share.

We wash off the dust of travel and grow better acquainted under the process.

Mrs. Childs, Miss Harris, the four Pattersons and myself form the party. Supper was ready for us when we came into the parlor again. It was well done & thoroughly enjoyed.

The pretty little Quaker bride was opposite to me and the groom, "John," a merry black eyed little fellow proved to be very entertaining.

We took a walk after the meal. The town is built on the side of a hill which is so steep at the back of the hotel, we had difficulty in mounting it.

We had a pretty view, however, when we reached the top of the town & the surrounding hills bathed in moonlight.

After a little social converse on our return, we retired for the night.

One of the seven inmates of our room, we found was to occupy a cot. It was determined that whoever was destined to sleep in it was to write a poem entitled the Cotter's.

May 15, 1867

Tuesday.

Up early this morning for a walk before breakfast.

Went up the steep hill we mounted last night with the hope of seeing the famous Peaks of Otter.

Could not see them well, but enjoyed the less pretentious hill lying before us very much.

Enjoyed our breakfast thoroughly.

Col. Patterson & his son were my companions at the table. We leave the hotel immediately after breakfast.

I forgot to mention that during our morning walk, we stopped at one of the tobacco markets attracted by a large wagon load of the article which had stopped to unload.

The market was only a large wooden shed in which the tobacco had been stacked into heaps according to its quality, the largest leaves together.

The plant has to be very carefully watched while it is growing and when mature is dried for nearly a year after which it is packed down for nearly a year more, going through a process called sweating.

On our way to the Depot, we saw a negro walking in the middle of the street, blowing upon a horn almost as long as himself which. we were told was the call for purchasers of tobacco.

It is sold at auction in the market sheds to the highest bidder.

The car provided for us this morning is very handsome. The divisions are more like small appartments than ordinary seats.

We are detained some time so I amusee myself in writing some doggerel lines. Keeping occupied the cot.

The Patterson girls, opposite, are entertaining two young officers.

We are off at last, the beautiful Peaks of Otter, how can I describe them?

They eluded our gaze this morning, but now they lie before us all majesty & grace, each change in their outline as we move rapidly on being more beautiful than the last.

They disappear at last, but then reappear at intervals, as if conscious of their beauty & our admiration.

We have an especial train today & stop at various places along the road, some times to wait for other trains, some times for amusement.

The county is most beautiful and the air from the mountains delicious.

Before dinner, this over the Blue Ridge, we stop some times at Big Spring, at the foot of the Alleghany.

A small steam engine is putting wood on the track for the use of the railroad. It does its work rapidly, but puffs as if rather short of breath.

Stop at Christianburg, passing New River, a beautiful stream 2,000 ft above the level of the sea.

Stop at Central Depot, Dublin depot and at various springs, sulpher etc. of which we taste the waters.

The train waiting for us as long as we desire.

It has been day of unmingled pleasure. The car is lighted now and a young officer is claiming cousinship at my side & amuses me with his adventures among the Southern ladies who do not treat our military coats very well.

When the car stops, we move to the end of it to look out upon the moonlit scenes.

As the train moves on again, Mr. Guthrie and the groom, John, come hurrying through the door where we are and the latter and says "don't frighten the ladies." While the former seems desirous of jumping off.

I do not inquire what is the matter, but suppose we are in danger of collision with a train which has not made its appearance at the time & place expected.

"They in the end of the car?" Miss Henry says.

Mr. Guthrie, so wrapped up in his warm woolen "rug" as he calls it.

I sit in the doorway, enjoying the noonlighted landscapes. My companion is on the railing outside. Nothing can be more beautiful than the pictures before us.

We are moving with frightful rapidity over the rails.

We pass through a narrow defile and think with awe how terrible a collision would be there, then out into the noonlight again, with eyes & thought only for the beauty about us.

The car sways from side to side with the rapidity of our motion, we stop occasionally to listen & signal, but reach Wytheville at last in safety.

We are 2,500 ft above the level of the sea.

We enter a large barn like hold, leave our cloaks & bags in an unfurnished appartement, the parlor, I suppose, and we ladies proceed to another room, having for sole furniture a wooden shelf & long table upon which are arising a number of wash bowls & pitchers of white ware and a small looking glass in a cherry wood frame.

We lave ourselves & then proceed to supper which is served in a smoke darkened room on rough board tables, but is delicious in quality.

After supper we are shown to our rooms, seven of us are again together. Our floor is carpetless, our windows without curtains, our beds covered with blue cotton spreads. The smallest of mirrors, a washstand and four chairs constitutes the rest of our furniture, but everything is clean and we are soon asleep with the moonlight streaming in upon us, lending beauty to even the homely objects which surround us.

May 16, 1867

Up early time for a short note to mother before breakfast.

The air is enchanting up here. Breakfast delicious.

We are off again, immediately after our appetites are appeased.

So we go out of the Hotel.

I encounter Mr. Baxster. He has increased alarmingly in rotundity during the war. He made many inquiries about his Washington friends.

We shall have our special train. High bridge over Reed Creek is our first object of interest. Reed Creek is a small stream emptying into New River, as do all the small rivers we encounter upon the broad table land over which we are now moving.

After passing Mt. Airy[84] the streams flow in the opposite direction and empty into the Ohio & other rivers.

Mt. Airy, the highest pt bet. the Gulf of Mexico & the atlantic, over which the railroad passes 2600 ft high.

---

[84] Mount Airy, Virginia, is now named Rural Retreat.

We stop some time so I make a sketch of a few little houses. I see the country is flat here, no view.

I am with my little friends, the Quakers.

The groom grows communicative and tells me all about his court ship and marriage.

The country soon grows picturesque again and we go to the end of the car to enjoy the beautiful mountain views which open out before us.

It is by far the best place to see.

All along the road, we see traces of Gen. Sherman's destructive passage. We stop at various springs along the road & finally reach Salt Ville, our especial destination for the day.

The salt works which have supplied nearly the whole south with salt are situated in a lovely valley surrounded with picturesque hills.

Two large manufacturies of the salt were destroyed during the war. We passed the remains of them.

The large kettles used for drying the salt lying broken by the road side or still in position upon the delapedated furnaces. We left the cars about two o'clock., our party numbered about seventy five as we had been joined by recruits from Wytheville.

We passed through the works with great interest, the water from the hot springs comes up with as much salt in it as it can hold in solution. It is pumped up into reservoirs from wence it is conveyed by wooden pipes into a low wooden building and is then poured by means of short wooden movable pipes, large copper kettles which are imbedded in floor in a double row down the centre of the shed.

Here, the water is boiled away leaving the salt to settle in the bottom of the kettles. As it settles, it is taken up by wooden spades and put into wicker baskets which are hung over the kettles. The water drains off having a pure white mass like white sugar.

My new cousin, the tall officer, showed me everything of interest, his size & strength were advantages. We were very hospitably, entertained by the Mother & son of Gen. Stewart after we had inspected the works.

Mrs. Stewart Sen. is a fine looking lady and very affable & sweet in her manners. We had a very fine collation presided over most gracefully by young Miss Stewart.

The daughter of the Gen., we did not see.

It was five o'clock before we left. A cloud of mist had gradually descended upon the beautiful hills about us and was descending in fine rain as we left our hospitable entertainers.

As we had some distance to walk to the cars, I should have fared badly had not my tall companion given me a military cape which protected me completely coming down to my feet, a rather amusing exhibition of the difference in our size.

We had a rainy afternoon and for want of better entertainment, my poor lines were called for.

I did not think they were worthy or appropriate for such public notice. Gen. added a verse.

The Colliers Tuesday Night:
There's beauty where the moonlight high,
In valley & in fen.,
But Gas light beams upon a sconce,
as bright in No. 10
For seven sylphs are moving there,
Attired in spotless white
With streaming hair unbound to greet
The slumber queen of night
Four of them so united are in mind and will the same
So closely bound in friendships ties
They even have one name
One of them so personifies
The virtues of her race
Baptismal saints were puzzled quite
And simply called her Grace
And one among the happy band
With gentle look and mild
Will ever Father Time defy
And always be a child
One looking glass alone reflects
Those locks of black & brown
It doubles each enticing face
But never shows a frown
Oh jokes however state ye be
Whenever made and when,
A haven ye have found at last
In Merry No. 10.
The lights are out, the forms are fled
To rest the last one goes
For fear to soil her tiny feet
On rites of chubby toes
Sweet sleep the happy seeks
Tis said the wretched doth forsake
But both so close such merry eyes

She keeps these girls awake
But Nature is too strong for her,
The vigil she gives o'er
And some from out those seven throats
Proceeds a gentle snore.
My Pegasus is lame good friends
Excuse any stumbling pen
And view not with a critic's eye
The bard of No. 10

May 17, 1867

Ooccupants of our couches.

Before day we were awakened and taking a cup of coffee, were off at five o'clock with the promise of breakfast at Wytheville.

Our ladies car had been occupied by some of the gentlemen as a sleeping apartment, so we occupied a smaller one for the first hour.

We reached Wytheville in two hours and I almost enjoyed my breakfast under Col. Patterson's care.

Passed the remainder of the day in exquisite enjoyment of the mountain scenery. Sitting in the back of the car.

Stopped at Lynchburg in our old room.

May 18, 1867

Started at nine o'clock, giving up our especial train and car.

The country not very interesting for the first part of the day.

As we approached Richmond, McClellan's earth-works and the embankments of the southern soldiers grew thicker and a small stream with low bushes growing close to its edge was pointed out to us as the Chickahominy and made us thrill with the memory of the sad scenes enacted along its banks.

The clamor of the negro drivers of carriages and hack drivers nearly deafened us when we reached the Richmond station.

We drove immediately to the Exchange Hotel and after dinner & washing off the dust of travel went to view the city.

We visited the capitol, passed through several of the main streets and saw the bank district.

The latter is already built up to a great extent with large handsome stores. Richmond is a very pretty city.

May 19, 1867

Sunday. Went to church & heard an excellent sermon.

The gentlemen have gone to a negro chapel this afternoon. We ladies wished to go, but it was not considered advisable, as the negroes are in a very excited state just now.

Not having obtained the freedom from labor and the great riches they expected with their emancipation, they are ready to visit their disappointment upon the Northerners and Southerners alike.

Saw the statue of Henry Clay in the Capitol grounds as we came home from church this morning, one of the fingers had been shot off by our soldiers.

Church again in the evening.

May 20, 1867

Went on a walking excursion around the city.

The party photographed for Mr. Guthrie's benefit.

Went in the afternoon to visit the oldest church in the place. On the burial ground surrounding it, we were surprised to see upon one tomb stone 331 years as the age of the occupant of the grave.

Farther on, we discovered an inscription to a deceased individual of still greater age.

We began to think Richmond people must have inherited the constitutions of the patriarchs, when the mystery was solved by the discovery of the unfinished work of some rascal who had been interrupted in his sacraligious employment of inserting a number into a monumental inscription. So neatly had he worked in the first two cases it was almost impossible to tell which were the original figures.

May 21, 1867

Went to the cemetery and to Island where our prisoners were confined.

May 22, 1867

A delightful day in Petersburg.

I should rather say a deeply interesting one, as it was not with unmingled pleasure that we viewed the spots where so many of our countrymen have fallen.

We left early in the morning, sailed down the James river, seeing the fortifications of Butler's canal & other objects of interest.

Went to the hotel on our arrival at Petersburg for dinner after which went on carriages to the battleground.

The scene of conflict was upon a farm, the owner of which now exhibits it at twenty five cts a head.

We went over the fortification of the reble & union armies, saw the great hole made by the explosion of the mine prepared by the Northerners.

Saw the underground passage leading to it and the wells sunk by the Southerners, in the attempt to find the passage the Northerners were making

In one instance, the well sunk was so close to the passage the men digging it could here the pick axes of their enemies overhead. Had they continued to dig a few feet they would have accomplished their desire.

I was surprised to find how near the two armies lay to each other.

They were not more than twenty yds apart. The ground was slimy & damp.

We felt as if it might still be wet with human gore.

"Take care" said our guide, as my foot slipped.

"You may uncover a body, a young lady, only yesterday, losing her footing in the same way, disclosed a corpse," He pointed out the spot to us where shreds of blue cloth were still adhering to the clayey soil.

Battered haversacks & canteens still lay scattered about, but the most touching traces of the past conflict were the bright green spots in the neighbouring wheat fields where the grain had grown larger & of a more brilliant tint over the graves of the fallen.

We visited various fortifications, union & reble, and in every case found the latter very rude in comparison with the former.

We were very much pleased in one spot with a beautiful little church made of boughs of trees with the bark on.

The cemetery surrounding it is used for the burial of the soldiers who are removed here.

On our return to Petersburg, we walked through some of the principal streets and saw some fine residents, among others that of Mr. Boling, our southern friend who joined us the first day of our excursion.

Marks of shells were numerous in the lower part of the city, some of the houses had not yet been repaired and were in a terribly battered condition. Others had been neatly mended but still bore plain marks of hard usage. We returned in the evening to Richmond.

May 23, 1867

This morning to my great regret we turned our faces homeward.

We came by boat from Aquia Creek. I bade the party farewell at the south gate, but the Patterson party came over in the evening to see me.

So ends one of the pleasantest episodes of my life.

May 27, 1867

Had a pleasant call from Mr. Seward, a nephew of the Sec. & our consul to China.

A pleasant gentleman about thirty five years of age with manners entirely free from affectation of any kind. Mr. Welling also came & Mr. Beaman.

May 29, 1867

29th Mr. Seward came to play croquet.

June 1867

Beautiful articles brought by Mr. Fox from Russia.

Unpacked in library & brought upstairs to be exhibited in the evening to the club.

Mr. Fox gave a lecture upon them. Father declared to Mr. Fox that the milder climate of the Western part of Russia in comparason with the more eastern portions of the same latitude was due to the influence of the gulf stream.

A statement with which Mr. Fox did not agree, saying that the Mts. of Sweden & Norway intercepted all effects from that quarter.

Father showed that its effects swept over a portion of country lower down, where there are no high Mts.

Mrs. Bache came today. The evening passed pleasantly in listening to Father & herself recall the past.

June 1867 – Saturday

Father went to the club Gave a lecture upon isothermal linesexcited thereto by Mr. Fox's lecture on Russia last Saturday.

June 1867 – Sunday

Sunday.

Father took down incidents of the life of Dr. Bache, given him by Mrs. Bache from memory for a memoir.

Did not go to church.

June 1867 – Monday

Mon.

Mrs. Bache left us this morning.

Bade farewell to the Coast Survey.

She is desolate indeed without her husband, but bears her sorrow with a cheerful patience more touching to one than tears.

Mr. Walling here in the afternoon.

Have been teaching in the News Boy's Home.

Father is overlooking some papers left by Mrs. Bache, says Mr. Hasler the first superintendent, was a very amusing man.

When he was examined for the office, one of the questions addressed to him was "How old are you Mr. H?" His reply was "Why don't you ask me how old is my coat, a coat well worn is old, no matter when it was made & is new if not worn, no matter how old it may be."

June 1867

Dr. from London spent the evening with us, said Charles Sixteenth was king of Norway & Sweden - was very intelligent - & had also a talent for painting - had a prize awarded him for a picture at the National exhibition for the encouragement of arts.

Has only one daughter, will be succeeded by his brother Otto, as no woman is allowed to reign

He is much beloved by his people & very familiar in his intercourse with them.

The Dr. thought both Norway & Sweden in about fifty years would be under the Russian government.

Russia will probably swallow them in order to obtain possession of Port which is open all the year round, the gulf stream making the water warm there.

She is very much in want of a seaport town as her commerce can only be carried on now for a short period of the year. Norway & Sweden would like to belong to a large nation, but would prefer waiting until Russia was more civilized.

He said there was a very large Mormon settlement in Switzerland & many emigrants to this country from there came to join the Mormons. He had been in Paris & was full of admiration of the wise arrangements of the Emperor.

Said the former terrible riots were now hardly possible.

Sement had been substituted in the streets for pavement and paving stones were no longer to be had for barricades?

There were forty commanding the wide streets which could easily be supplied with troops by means of the underground railroads constructed through the sewers.

He thought it probable there would be trouble soon with the laboring classes, as there was no place for them to live the poorer houses having been torn down to make room for palaces.

June 21, 1867

Thursday visit from Col. Alexander

June 22, 1867

Friday. Miss Romero & brother & two daughters of the Mexican president Juarez came to play croquet

June 23, 1867

Mary Lee, Miss Rucker John H. & Sallie & Mr. Abbey for croquet Father left for Princeton.

June 27, 1867

Our first minister from Greece, Mr. Rengade, called with his son.

They were introduced by Mr. Bing.

Mr. H. is a small man with unassuming timid manners, but kind & gentlemanly.

He speaks very little English. He is a literary man & highly esteemed in his own country, has written a book upon Archiology, several romances a work on art & other books.

His son, first Sec. of Legation, wore a short velvet cloak which set off his girlishly fair complexion to advantage. His eyes are blue with white lashes & brows his manners and mode of speaking is English. He has no foreign accent.

June 29, 1867

Sat. Father came from Princeton

July 1, 1867

Monday evening –

The present King of Greece is brother to the Princess of Wales.

King Otho was very unpopular and the people of Greece, while he was on a sailing expedition rose up against him and closed the city so that he could not return.

The United powers who wish to preserve the balance of power, Denmark, Eng. & other nations were then appealed to for a king.

England chose George, son of the king of Denmark, his father consented that he should accept the trust, provided means were supplied to maintain his royalty. England consented to provide 2,000 pounds and gave him the Ionian Isles. He has reigned 4 years.

This information was given Father this afternoon by a former adviser of the king.

Baron Gerdt walked home from the city with Father, he seemed to think he needed to be taken care of his daughter, who is suffering from famine in India.

July 2, 1867

Mr. Rengabe says the new Greek Queen who is only 14 years old, is to be married in Sep.

The king who is 22 years old did not care much about the marriage until he saw the young lady, but is now very much in love.

She is very fascinating, the daughter of the Grand Duke Constantine.

We have a memoir of the Duchess from the library.

Mr. Rengabe came to play Croquet.

Mr. Cushing & C. R. ___ also here.

July 3, 1867

The Papers contain an account of the death of the Emperor Maximilian[85].

The United States, at the request of Austria, interceded but in vain, for the pardon of himself & the two royalists who suffered with him. He was shot in the face, his last word being "Carlotta;" the name of his wife.

July 5, 1867

Mr. Seward here in the afternoon, also Mr. Beaman, Sallie Mrs. Rengabe, Father & son.

July 6, 1867

A visit from Jane Wilkes.

She is in town for a few days, likes High Shoals very much.

Is greatly interested in teaching the poor children near there black & white, & also in building a church for the benighted neighborhood.

Admiral Wilkes came to tea, was much amused with the zucho

Mr. ___ of Sweden called.

---

[85] With the United States on the brink of total collapse, in the midst of a civil war, France invaded Mexico in 1861, to the objection of nearly all of the nations of the world. In an attempt to establish his French influence in North America, Napoleon III set up the younger brother of the Austrian emperor to reign over Mexico in April 1864, Maximilian.

With the Civil War ended in 1865, the Johnson Administration turned much of its attention to aiding rebel democratic forces in Mexico. Not desiring to enter into a war with the United States over Mexico, France withdrew its troops from the territory in 1866, leaving its puppet "emperor" completely defenseless against an angry mob of native citizens. Maximilian was captured and executed in 1867. His wife, Carlota, had by this time, escaped to Europe, where she endured an emotional collapse and was declared insane.

July 7, 1867

Dr. Easter dined with us. He looks bilious & melancholy.

Mr. Dean & Mr. ___ called.

No croquet, too rainy.

July 9, 1867

Mr. Seward, Miss Wilkes, Mr. Dean, Mr. Goodfellow & Mr. Beaman came for croquet.

Mrs. Gerold & daughters came during the game.

Also Prof. Hilgard & his wife, a mexican refugee, a royalist, here in the afternoon to see Father.

Said Maximilian was an exceedingly pleasant, amiable & talented man.

July 17, 1867

Sallie & Miss Ellicott, Mr. Beaman, Alfred Woodhull here for Croquet. Nell looked lovely in a lilac lawn. I arranged her hair in the high style with good effect.

We played late the moon shining almost as bright as day upon us before we ceased.

Read "Good English" by Gould to Father in the evening.

July 18, 1867

Thursday. At work all day on Father's head and very tired in consequence.

Mr. Welling came in while we were at tea. He has been elected President of a college at Annapolis.

Father advised him to supply the college well with what he called "implements of instruction," Maps, pictures, plaster casts & other visible objects for the easiest, most effective way of making an impression upon the mind through the eye & when over such an impression had been made much collateral information might be added thereunto through association of ideas.

Even dull, lazy boys might be interested & improved in this way, he also believed in drilling boys in the practical rudiments of learning.

When he was in the Albany Academy, the senior professors there were of the opinion that the principal object of instruction should be to make the child think.

He contended, however, that the "doing" faculties of the child should first be developed -- precision of memory cultivated & afterward he should be taught to think.

A boy of twelve might find the rules of arithmetic easy to understand, but of what use would his comprehension of them be if he had not be taught facility in the use of them by practice in multiplication, subtraction addition & division

In his opinion, there would be very many bankrupt merchants if boys were taught only to think & not to do. He made an experiment while at the Academy in support of his theory, mathematics was one department of his instruction, including arithmetic.

When the boys came to him, he kept them for the first two years in the simple rules of arithmetic, drilling them day after day.

The school room was surrounded by black boards & those boys who could not be accommodated at the boards were provided with slates. They all became in time exceedingly expert & could add, multiply, subtract & divide with the utmost ease.

Taking five or six boys of about eight years of age who had been thus drilled, he gave them a lecture upon a box of wooden cones & other mathematical instruments, not exceeding three hours.

They were afterwards examined for two hours in presence of Dr. Beck & the other profs, with such eclat that those gentlemen claimed in delight "yes yes this is the "true method of instruction to teach children to think," but said Father "their facility in this instance was due to previous drilling in the practice of simple rules. Their thought had implements with which to work.

After leaving Albany, he met the father of one of his boys & asked him how he was progressing in his studies. "oh" said he, "after you left he did admirably." "You could not pay me a higher complement," replyed Father, "his success was due to the drilling I gave him."

But while he thus strongly advocated the doing faculties in the instruction of youth, he would not have the thinking faculties neglected.

The Professors in England went to the opposite extreme & only a few days ago he had been surprised by the ignorance of a fellow Oxford who asked him simple questions in science which a school girl in this country could answer.

He closed by saying, "I have always, Mr. Welling, merged self in the question of the cause in which I have been engaged. It is the only way to succeed."

Laughed at Mother and her protégé, Mary, the guardian angel who has lost her sight & having no home, Mother has taken her on.

Father got her a permit to sell matches on the avenue & one of the servants takes her to the stand and brings her home every day for which she blesses Mother with true Irish highperbole "May her blessings reach you Madame," said Mr. Welling "as he rose to go. May the Blessing of the Holy virgin & all the saints follow your honour."

The Diary of Mary Henry: The Civil War Out My Window

Said an Irish beggar to a gentleman who took out his purse to give him an alms, "but never reach ye," he added, as the purse disappeared unopened in the gentleman's pocket. Good night.

August 10, 1867

Father amused us this evening by undertaking to comb Mother's hair. The gravity with which the unusual favor was given & received was comical in the extreme.

October 23, 1867

We came home last evening, that is Father & I.

We have been away over two months.

We went first to the Catskill Mts., where Father spent a week with us enjoying entire rest & freedom from care

We separated on coming down from the Mts, Mother & I going to Albany, Nell & Carry to Princeton & met again in Phil. at the wedding of Stewart Patterson.

Father was engaged in high business at Sandy Hook & did not reach P. in time for the wedding. I came away with him on Tuesday.

We find the house in great confusion.

It is being repainted. We eat in the kitchen & use the Laboratory as a parlour.

We are very cosy among the chemicals, to night we have been interrupted by a son of Judge Dunlop, an individual of somewhat peculiar appearance. Not being satisfied with the amount of fore head granted him by nature, he has shaved his hair off, partly in front, which gives a very odd look.

Mr. Reese also came in.

He discussed the Canal question with Father. Said, his proposition to make a Sewer of it was objected too on the ground that it might bust in case of unusual rise in the water.

Father said that difficulty would be easily remidied by making large gates in it which would rise with certain amount of pressure & let the water out. It would only be occasionally thus overflowed.

October 24, 1867

Have been writing letters & have just returned from a visit to the cook to see about dinner. The cook is making oyster soup.

Recipe:

Strain the liquid in two, a pot with celery & parsly. powder two or three crackers & put them in, also peper & salt. Put the oysters in. Let boil.

Eve.

Henry Elliot showed me some of his sketches. We are not interrupted by visitors.

October 25, 1867

Another visit from the individual with the artificially high forehead.

He stayed some time discoursing upon historical subjects. Came to inquire about a book he wanted.

October 26, 1867

Went for a walk with father this afternoon, we stopped to look at some specimens of photosculpture. Recognized Gen Grant & our old friend Admiral Farragut among them.

Went to Mrs. Peals to take tea. She was very glad to see us. Entertained us with stories & photographs.

On our return home met Dr. Craig, on the grounds. He went back with us.

Mr. Dunlap called again about his book.

October 27, 1867

Sunday Went to church & received a warm greeting from all our friends after our long absence.

The President was in church.

Went to Mrs. Peals to dinner & remained also to tea.

Dr. ___ & his wife & child were there also.

October 28, 1867

Busy moddeling a Meerschaum pipe.

Induced Father to retire early & read him to sleep with extracts from Channing

October 29, 1867

Read Jane Eyre at night while Father was busy on the Eulogy of Prof Backe.

Dreadfully jealous of Henry Ellet who is his assistant instead of myself.

October 30, 1867

Went to Mrs. Peals to see about flowers for Nell. Had a pleasant morning digging & planting. The painters proceed very slowly in their work.

November 1, 1867

Mother & Carry came home. Nell stayed to take care of Mrs. Bache.

The Diary of Mary Henry: The Civil War Out My Window

November 2, 1867

Saturday. Spent the morning in looking for wall paper, the eve. in the laboratory with Father.

November 15, 1867

Thursday. Have been very busy all of us in house cleaning & in making a walking dress for Nell who is still in Phil.

Were very much disappointed in not seeing the meteoric shower on Tuesday night.

We gave direction to the Watchman to wake us if he saw any falling stars, but did not do so - said he did not see any drop. Saw a few wavering up above, but nothing more.

The display was very fine, it is said more than fifty stars were seen to fall a minute.

Last night, we charged the delinquent to call us if he saw one star shoot & explained to him that they would not fall at his feet, as seemed to have expected.

It was supposed that the display might be even finer than the night be before, but we were doomed to disappointment.

At two o'clock, we arose in the light of the moon, attired ourselves in some what fantastic garb and descended with Father to the office & thence out into the dampness of night.

A very bright moon, we saw, & some isolated stars, which shone down upon our upturned faces, their steady rays testifying to their determination to keep in their places, but the erratic visitors we expected were no where visible.

With strained vision & stiffened necks we soon returned to the office where Father gave us a lecture upon meteors in general & the meteors in particular which we desired to see. The latter he informed us probably a comet which we in our orbit around the sun has come in contact.

Fortunately for us, that its solidity were no greater or we might have had practical proof of how small a part our little world plays in the drama of the universe.

How little the harmony of the spheres would be disturbed were it eliminated somewhat perhaps to the astonishment of such our philosophers & theologians who labor under the slight delusion that the whole of God's creation was intended for the edification of Man.

Father said the meteoric shower in thirty three he witnessed with great delight. He had just gone to Princeton then & was awakened by one of the students.

The sky was brilliant with them shooting, apparently in every direction, but he soon perceived that they all came from one point in the sky, near the constellation Leo. & the apparent divergent lines they pursued was the effect of perspective.

After looking at the globe & determining how high Leo ought to be, we again proceeded to look "for stars."

This time our viligence was rewarded by the sight of one. A farewell wish of the tail of our fiery neighbor. We retired discomforted to our couches & were awaked all too soon by a call to breakfast.

November 20, 1867

Wed. Went to hear Mr. Gough, but could not get into the Hall where he was to lecture on account of the crowd, so went to call on Mrs. Johnson. Found Mr. Ashley, there the great impeacher, also Mr. Sen. Elliott, Mr. Baumgrass the artist came in the latter part of the evening.

November 22, 1867

Went to hear Dr. Hall of London. His lecture was an explanation of some of the actions of the English people during the war and a declaration of the amicable feeling existing in the mother isle for the Americans.

He managed the subject skillfully at the close of his address, he spoke of the common memory of England & America, the battles which were alike sacred to them, the dead that lay in Westminster Abbey & the many quiet graves under the yew trees.

Hand in hand ought they ever to advance, Mother & daughter no, rather two sisters, the elder & the younger, their only rivalry, that of love.

Dr. Hall is very English in appearance. He was amazed at the size of his audience, and so not pleasing to us in appearance at first, but his face when speaking was much more agreeable.

We had a good seat in one of the boxes which overlooked the stage.

November 23, 1867

Saturday.

At work at Father's bust and very tired in consequence.

November 24, 1867

Sunday. Dr. Hall preached in the House of Rep in the morning. Father & Mother went, but could not obtain a seat.

In the afternoon, he addressed the colored people.

Carry heard him, "said his address was interesting, but not remarkable."

We heard him in the evening in our own church. Long before the usual hour for service, the building was thronged. We could, with difficulty, obtain seats.

A more thrilling sermon I never listened to. He took for his theme the simple, but sublime plan of Salvation, its completeness & fullness & held his listeners entranced to the end.

Saw Dr. Climer after church, also the Chief Justice & his daughter who has just returned from Europe, both were delighted with the sermon.

November 25, 1867

Went to hear Dr. Hall again. His sermon, not so fine as that of last evening. Dr. Climer there.

Saw Sec. Browning & daughter after lecture.

November 27, 1867

Gave Henry a French lesson.

Read Buchanan Reed's poem, *The Wagoner of the Aleganies*.

Stewart Patterson here.

Dr. Climer here in the morning read aloud to Father all this eve.

November 29, 1867

Thanksgiving Day.

Dined with Prof & Mrs. Baird.

Speaking of Dickens, Mrs. B. told us she had passed a day with him & was very anxious to hear him lecture.

Father told us a somewhat amusing anecdote about himself.

I like Thanksgiving day. I always feel then like God's pet-child, as if I had more than anyone else.

November 30, 1867

Busy today with Carry in making some fern hills for the conservatory out of stones moss & other things. I think they will be very pretty. It is raining fast.

December 1, 1867

Monday. A very great change in the weather, the pleasant warm days of Indian summer have been replaced by a cold as keen as any we experianced last winter.

Mrs. Stall, a strong minded lady from Boston, and her daughter, came today.

She has written several books & rumour says has delivered political speeches.

We expected to see quite a masculine person, but were agreeably disappointed in her.

She is ladylike in appearance and very agreeable in conversation. Her daughter is a pleasant, healthy little thing. She seems to have taken her Mother's personal appearance into her especial charge.

They have gone to take tea with Mrs. Baird, where Father & Carry will join them after a call on Miss Chase.

December 2, 1867

The strong minded lady we still find very pleasant. She went to visit the colored schools this morning & was much pleased with their appearance.

She asked Father after dinner how the Inst. was supported. Father told her the old story. That Smithson was an illegitimate child of the Duke of Northumberland, ashamed of his birth, but declared that his name should yet live when the titles of the Percy's & Northumberland's were forgotten.

The original bequest was 515,000 pounds.

The Hon. Richard Rush was sent to England to obtain it.

Father dined with him in London in company with Prof. Bache, while he was attending to the Smithson money, but Father had no idea then that he would have anything to do with the dispensing of it.

While Father was talking about the conduct of the Inst., the increase of Funds & other things, Mr. Bartlett came in. He was just from Providence, Had been abroad during the summer & had greatly enjoyed his trip.

Mr. B. asked Father why the Library of the Inst. has been given to Congress and regreted it. Father said he considered that an exceedingly good transaction.

The library was an exceedingly fine one, but the cost of binding was great and the room required for its accommodation inadequate.

Congress assumed the expense of the binding in the present arrangement which cost this three thousand dollars. The books were equally at their disposal of the Smithsonian for reference and loan.

Anyone pursuing a particular branch of study and requiring books for such a purpose could apply as before to the Inst. & be furnished with not only the books belonging to the Inst., but the whole Congressional library which it was stipulated should be kept open during the entire year instead of a few months as formerly.

After the Smithsonian contribution to the Congressional library, Congress was induced to purchase that of Peter Force & now we have in the capitol, the largest library in the country & worthy to be what Father wishes it to be called a National Library.

Father said his next desire was to induce Congress to take the building and make a grand museum, leaving the Smithsonian fund entirely untrammeled for the encouragement of original research & additions to knowledge.

A museum on a grand sale could be collected as most of the museums of the world were indebted to the Smithsonian upon condition that they should supply specimens if they should ever be required.

Lord & Lady Amberly the son & daughter in law of Lord John Russel called today with a letter of introduction to Father.

She is said to be the most cultivated lady of her age in England. Mrs. Dall says she has seen them. That they are agreeable and would be pleasing in appearance, but she is traveling without a maid & the gentleman without his valet & they neither of them know how to attire themselves.

December 4, 1867

To day, the great question of the impeachment of the President was to be brought up, but was deffered.

Cary & guest went to the Capitol, heard nothing of interest.

All the family except Moth & myself have gone to a small party given to Miss Frelinghuysen, daughter of the N.J. senator.

The Sunday School conventioneer has come in and retired for the night. He has been on a whaling voyage and spent several years in the Sandwich.

Father discovered, last night, In the absence of the rest of the party, Mother & I have been entertained by a visit from Mr. & Mrs. Peale & Alfred Woodhul.

The former greatly admired the fern baskets.

Mother's addition to the conservatory and the shells of plant she arranged as well as the grottoes of rocks & moss Carry & I made to catch the water from the hanging basket.

The plants are growing well and the conservatory really looks very prettily.

I have been in bed all day with headache so have not been able to work on Father's bust.

December 5, 1867

Thursday. Busy all day at Father's bust.

Mrs. Dale & daughter left this morning.

Father & Carry went to call on Lady Amberly. She is the daughter of Lord Stanley. They found her very agreeable. She has married a widower with a small child of two years old. She told Carry she was very anxious to get back to England in order to see the little boy.

Carry told her we had an acquaintance of hers with us. "Mrs. Dale," She tiresome said she. "She is strong minded" said Cary. "Oh I don't object to her principles, but to her voice," said Lady A. Mrs. Delafield & Mary

Sorring were calling upon her also. She was very much pleased with Father & said she had enjoyed her visit at the Smithsonian very much.

She wants to go to the church of the colored people on Sunday and Father promised to let her know when it was to be found. "We shall have to call up all our little negro boys and ask them where they go to church," said Miss Sorring, "for your benefit Lady Amberly."

She goes to Richmond on Monday.

We were invited to meet them at Adm. Shubrick's last evening & wanted to invite them here on Sat., but Father has an engagement.

The conventioneer left us this evening for his Sunday School meeting & on his return bade us "good bye" as he intended to go home early in the morning.

Read the President's message to Father after dinner.

He objects to the military government of the southern states to the enfranchisement of the negro, to the bill passed near the close of last session, preventing him from appointing government officers or rather making such appointments invalid unless ratified by congress.

Recommends a return to specie payment in part and shows the evil of our present inflated paper currency. Father says to return to specie payment in part would be still worse than to remain as we are.

Now Gold is a commodity and, but a small portion comparatively goes out of the country, but if currency much more of it would be spent for foreign goods. It would go to foreign lands and leave us our worthless paper.

The more foreign commerce we have where we have to give out gold and receive paper at home will be worse for us.

We have been quite pleased this evening by the arrival of six numbers of *the Bazaar*, a magazine of fashion for which we have subscribed and all of them including the S.S. conventioneer dived into them hoop skirts & head gear.

Train dress & short ones, how to arrange one's back hair & how to crisp front locks, stories to fill up spaces such are the contents of the valuable paper.

If we are not attired well now, it will certainly not be the fault of Mr. Harper.

Mr. Gill brought in Mrs. Dale's' book, "The court, the market & the college," but it was quite cut out by the fashions. Father looked through it, but laid it down soon.

December 6, 1867

Another day with Father's bust

Father had a call from Hon. Mr. Shutt, Fellow of Trinity College Cam., a pleasant intelligent individual.

Carry went this morning to ask Mrs. Baird to come with some friends staying with her to tea with Miss Sullivan. A young lady from England who has brought us a letter of introduction from Dr. Grey, who says he sends her in return for Miss Frere, whom we sent to him last winter.

He says she is superior to the latter lady, but I doubt it.

I have made my toilette and am writing in the dining room to employ the interval of time before they arrive.

Father had just come, in comfortable consciousness of company, coat & smooth hair.

Mother is appearing & disappearing into the pantry, somewhat excitedly, hair in order, dress not in accord.

Carry appears in brown silk & turns on lights. "Guests are here,"

They come, Mother where art thou?

December 7, 1867

I hope our guests last evening enjoyed themselves as much as I did.

Miss Sullivan came first, attired in white muslin & the ribbons, evidently prepared for a much larger entertainment than we had provided for her.

She is about fourty years old with dark eyes & hair and rather heavy features. Very pleasant, but not nearly as attractive in manner & appearance as Miss Frere.

She is the neice of Lord Palmerston & came to America in the same vessel with Lord & Lady Amberly.

Prof. & Mrs. Baird & Lucy were the next arrival & Mr. Post, a missionary from Syria, completed our small tea party.

Mrs. Baird told us that in the _____, women are obliged to wear all the hair cut from their husbands heads in rolls at the back of their heads like our water falls?

The gentleman from Syria told me some interesting things about the antiquities of the country. Told me he had traced for miles the remains of a roman road, to be seen on the promontories jutting into the sea. The ruts of carriage wheels & the horses hoof tracks worn deep into the rock.

Went this morning to look for a carriage with Mother.

Father went with Miss Sulivan to see the President, the Patent Office and other places. He is going to the club to night which meets at Judge Chase's and is preparing to give an account of his experiments on sound made at Sandy Hook this Fall.

Mrs. Baird said last night that Mrs. Dall tried to obtain the pulpit of the Unitarian church for tomorrow, but it was otherwise engaged.

She preaches in Wilmington instead. I should like to have heard her.

December 8, 1867

Sunday. A sermon from Dr. Nevins from China, a missionary who gave us a great deal of interesting information in a short time.

Said that China was in many respects like the United States. In extent, it was equal to the whole United States from ocean to ocean, rather the addition of a line of states in width that like them, it extended north & south giving great diversity of climate.

It was divided into eighteen provinces, corresponding with our states, with divisions & subdivisions similar to our counties & townships.

One remarkable feature was the walled cities. Each province & each division & subdivision of a province has its capitol, which is a walled town, like walls consisting of solid masonry without, lined with embankments of earth--could these enclosing walls be extended in a straight line, they would extend a distance equal to half the circumference of the globe.

The towns have in every instance overgrown the walls and a third of the population are sheltered without them.

In speaking of the cities of the Dead, he said one grave yard extended ten miles, a mile in width, and had been abandoned as too full to use.

He spoke in the afternoon to the Sunday School children and in the evening we had a sermon from Dr. Brown from Japan.

He spoke of the early history of Japan of the early attempt of the Romanists to Christianize the Islands and the jealousy of the natives in what they supposed was a political effort to bring them into subjection to the Pope.

A political intrigue they supposed which caused them to issue an edict banishing them from the country.

He said the Tycoon was not the emperor, but one, the greatest of a member of Lords, who had their retainers as in the ancient feudal system.

He spoke of a military class to which belonged most of the young men of good birth who in time of peace had nothing to do, it being considered derogatory to them to engage in any useful employment. They are retainers of the Feudal lords before mentioned, One of these he told us became very much interested in the Christian religion from some references made to it in the books brought into the country by the Dutch traders.

His desire at last to know more of the God of the Christians became so great that that he sold his property and embarked secretly & at the risk of his life for America. On arriving at Boston he went to the owner of the vessel and told him his purpose in coming. The merchant told him what he wished to know. He was sent to a seminary at Andover where is now making rapid progress in his studies.

Miss Sulivan was here just before dinner. Father went with her to see the Chief Justice and afterwards to see whether Lady Amberly wished to go to the colored church. Came to our church during the sermon. The Chief Justice was there also was much interested.

240

December 9, 1867

A cold windy day.

Have been out looking for a carriages & furniture.

Mr. Franklin is here to dinner. He thinks Chase's chances for the Presidency are nothing, seems to think Sherman will be elected.

The Impeachment affair has entirely fallen through.

A delightful little party this evening.

Mrs. Brown, the wife of the missionary, came with Mrs. Parker to tea and was joined later in the evening by Dr. & Mrs. Gurley who brought with them Dr. Brown from Japan.

Dr. Norris from China, Dr. Morrison from China with his wife & another gentleman whose name I have forgotten.

Gen & Mrs. Harwood and Mrs. Smith were also here, the latter came in search of Mrs. Brown. We all enjoyed the evening very much.

Miss Brown had an album with her with Japanese photographs in it.

December 11, 1867

Wed. A party a Gen. Humpry's. Father gone to Princeton.

December 12, 1867

Thurs. A cold stormy day. An invitation to breakfast for Father from Mr. Paugn to meet Mr. Morley.

Tried to work on Father's bust, but not well enough.

Henry Ellet in to see about S. school children's tableaux.

Letter writing in the eve. The house very desolate without Father.

December 13, 1867

Friday. A letter from Father. He has been urgently entreated to accept the Presidency of the college made vacant by the resignation of Prof. MacClean.

A call from Dr. Nevins, went through the building with him. The ground is white with snow and sleigh bells are jingling merrily.

December 21, 1867

I commence my journal for 1868 with the meeting of the Academy or rather with the arrival of some of its members.

The evening train brought us first Dr. Lorrey & Hensfort & Dr. Barnard, who were speedily followed by Dr. Gould & Miss Hensfort.

All merry & well. Prof. Davies came in after tea. I looked at him with interest as the author of the Algebra whose equation delighted my young brain in days gone by. His broad fine face is genial & kind. While Father & himself were going over in imaginations various circumstances of their pastlives. We, that is Dr. Lorrey, Carry, Mr. Post of Syria & Mr. ___ who had come in just before Prof. Davies & myself were amusing ourselves with Mr. Bacon's new book on the Nile. Dr. Lorrey reading aloud from it an account of a Rhanoserous hunt with various comments by his auditers.

The Academy opens tomorrow.

December 22, 1867

Wed. At the breakfast table in speaking of personal identity, mentioned an amusing mistake he had made in claiming a most cordial acquaintance with Gen. Sherman, thinking he was the Rev. F. Vinson of New York.

He gave an amusing description of the question answered & asked until, completely puzzled, Gen. Sherman exclaimed, "Who in the world do you take me for!"

The Dr., discovering his mistake, went home & took Dr. V. for Gen. Sherman.

December 23, 1867

Thursday. A rainy day.

Prof called after breakfast.

Prof Guyot left us to our great regret. He has to lecture in Baltimore. Prof Agassiz called, while he was here Dr. Gould came in & told us Father had been elected President of the Academy. The election was unanimous.

Later, Father has come home tired. He has accepted the Presidency as the vote was so unanimous.

Soirees at Senator Morgans & Secretary Randall, Nell went with Miss H. & some of the gentlemen.

December 25, 1867

Sat. Went to the capitol this morning, but did not stay long. Have lost Dr. Barnard. Dr. Hall, Prof Newton, Dr. Gower, Dr. Lorrey & Miss H. will remain on a few days longer.

Father has gone to Nice with Baron Gerolt.

We are all tired out with the excitement of the week.

February 1, 1868

Sat. A week of parties & on and on. I have not gone out as much as the rest, but have done duty as general decorator & dressing maid.

The contest between the President & Stanton continues.

February 4, 1868

Went to hear Dickens read.

Was much interested in seeing the great novelist, but was not especially delighted with his performance. His delivery of Mr. Pegotty's lament over Emily was well done & greatly affected the feelings of a dog near us who unable to control his emotion gave vent to a loud howl.

February 8, 1868

Sat. Another gay week, low necked & high necked parties, matinees receptions & other things. We have no guests with us for a wonder.

Stanton has been turned out & reinstated and the contest between him & the President & Gen. Grant continues.

February 15, 1868

Sat. This week's programme very much the same as lasts. The pleasantest party to me this season was one at Mrs. Hooper's.

February 16, 1868

Sun. Prof Pratt preached for us. Dr. Gurley has left us for six months on account on his health.

February 17, 1868

Mon. Judge Otto called with _____. After they left Prof Lane came & read a book on optics to Father & himself.

February 18, 1868

18th Party at Pomeroy's

February 19, 1868

Wed. Mr. Varley[86], an Englishman here to dinner also Mr. Franklin Mr. Varley assisted in laying the Atlantic cable, gave us much interesting information concerning it. John Young here in the evening. Prof. Lane also here. He came for more French optics but had Atlantic cable instead.

February 20, 1868

Thursday. Jack Gillis here also Mr. Pierce of Cambridge.

Mr. Varley has taken up his abode with us and we have also Dr. ___ as perennial guest. He has a small Indian boy with us whom he has adopted.

---

[86] C.F. Varley, (1828 – 1883) was an English engineer who assisted in developing the transatlantic telegraph cable. From this time forward, Varley became interested in Spiritualism, the notion of being capable of communicating with the dead. Spiritualism experienced explosive growth immediately following the Civil War.

February 21, 1868

Fri. Reception day. Cloudy, only seventeen here.

Jack Gillis came to dinner. Showed us sketches he made while at work on the Pacific R.R.

A discussion with Mr. Varly after he left. Father not very well.

February 22, 1868

The city in a great state of excitement on account of the impeachment of the President.

Yesterday, the President sent up a message to the Senate announcing that he had by virtue of the power vested in him, removed Mr. Stanton from the position of Sec. of War & appointed Gen. Thomas Sec. adinterim.

This morning the Reconstruction Committee held a long session at the house of Thaddeus Stevens, and concluded to report a resolution impeaching the President of high crimes and misdemeanors for turning out an officer of the government in face of the tenure of office law.

At 20 min. past 2 o'clock, this resolution was presented to the House by Mr. Stevens amid profound silence.

Nell & Carry went to a matinee at Mrs. Prague's. Nothing talked of but the impeachment.

The House is in session. Carry has gone up with Mr. Franklin, Dr. & boy left us at dinner time.

Mr. Varley is still here.

10 h. P.M. Carry has returned, she was fortunate in obtaining admission to the floor of the House

. Speechs were made by Bingham, Farnsworth, Butler & other prominent members spoke in the morning.

In the evening Farnsworth, Kelley, Beck, Lorgan, Phelps, Holman, Peters, Nublack and Ingersol continued the debate. The House journed or rather took a recess until ten o'clock on Monday morning.

The vote upon the resolution will be taken at 5 P.M. The members allowed a half hour each to speak upon it

February 23, 1868

Sun. The excitements is still great. Numbers of people have visited the White House & War Department, Sec. Stanton has possession of the latter and the building is protected by a guard.

Gen. Thomas was arrested yesterday, but was released on parole.

Prof Hansford here in the afternoon.

G coming to go with us to the Capitol tomorrow morning.

Read Ecce Homo in the evening.

About nine o'clock, Mr. Hall came in with *Evening Express Extra*.

Gen. Grant said to be arrested & a rumor that Hon. Thomas Ewing has been appointed Sec. of War.

It is said that a hundred thousand armed men are preparing to come to Washington at a moment's notice to sustain Congress.

February 25, 1868

Tuesday. The paper this morning contains the President's Message. He takes the ground that the turning out of Stanton is not a violation either of the Constitution or the Laws of the U.S. including the tenure of office law.

It was not in violation of the Constitution as the right of the President to appoint & remove his own officers was distinctly recognized in that & had been excised by his predecessors from Washington down.

As to the demise of Office law, the first section of that act is as follows:

"That every person holding any civil office to which he has been appointed by and with the consent of the Senate and every person who shall hereafter be appointed to any such office and shall become duly qualified to act therein is & shall be entitled to hold such office until a successor shall have been in like manner appointed and duly qualified except as herein otherwise provided. Provided , that the Secretaries of State of War of the Treasury of the Navy and of the Interior the Postmaster General & the Attorney Gen. shall hold their offices respectively for and during the term of the President by whom they have been appointed , and for one month thereafter subject to removal & by the advice of the Senate."

The President contended that he had not violated this act because Stanton had not been appointed by him and was Secretary only by sufferance.

He had always obeyed the laws that had been passed over his vetoes. He considered the Tenure of Office Law unconstitutional & action in the present case was for the purpose of making a judicial decision necessary & proper.

He was willing to suffer in his own person if necessary rather than be unfaithful to important trust confided to him, the guarding of the rights of the Presidential office.

Jack Gillis has just been here.

Thinks the impeachment will be hurried up. We may, next week, have Ben Wade[87] in the White House.

---

[87] Benjamin Franklin Wade (1800 –1878), U.S. Senator from Ohio. A leading "Radical Republican." Should President Andrew Johnson was a United States Senator during Civil War reconstruction known for his leading role

February 27, 1868

The excitement about impeachment continues unabated.

This is our reception day, a number of calls, among others, D. J. G. de Magalhaens, the new Brazilian minister & his wife.

They do not speak English, but understand much, so it was easy to manage with them.

Mr. Thornton, the new English minister was also here.

Mrs. Trumbul told Carry to come to her house on Monday & take lunch & then go to the capitol, which would be crowded as the impeachment resolutions were to be brought into the senate & she was going on the floor.

February 29, 1868

The debate commenced this morning by Mr. Ashley, Mr. Cook followed in favor of the resolution of impeachment. Mr. Boyer in opposition.

Mr. Washburn's speech in opposition to the President was the most severe.

The vote was taken at five o'clock 124 to 42. The galleries were crowded and a detachment of policemen was placed at the various entrances and passages of the capitol to preserve order. The President sent to the Capitol his appointment of Hon. Mr. Ewing as Sec. of War. & also a message protesting against the action of congress in impeaching him.

He has received messages from democratic citizens of New York & other places offering to sustain him with money and men.

About eleven o'clock today, Gen. Thomas went to the War Department where Stanton is still in voluntary confinement, remaining in the building night as well as day & said he had come to take possession of the Office in obedience to the repeated order of the President.

Stanton ordered him from the room.

Gen. Thomas went to the principal employee & ordered them to bring him the papers & packages passing through their hands as head of the office.

The position of these underlings is decidedly disagreeable not knowing whom they must obey.

March 1, 1868

Sunday.

---

among the Radical Republicans. Had Andrew Johnson been removed from office, Wade would have become the 18th President of the United States.

Mr. Ried preached for us, a candidate for the pastorale ad interim. We did not find him very interesting.

Went to Susie Hodge's to dinner.

Read *Ecce Homo* at night until Mr. Gill came in with a paper & impeachment news.

The author of *Ecce Homo* is certainly a very interesting & clear thinker, He brings out in a new light the wonderful adaptability of the Christian plan of salvation & moral restoration to man & his needs.

How he can show as he does the wonderful wisdom of that plan, the wonderful power it has exerted and not consider the originator divine. I cannot understand. Truly that one admission is needed to make his book an exceedingly beautiful tribute to the Lord of Glory. Like a beautiful gilded temple in the dark.

The gold is there, but it needs the light of the sun to show its beauty. I am sometimes half inclined to think he is a true Christian in disguise, not fully avowing his sentiments in order to catch the infidels unawares & bring them unwillingly to a contemplation of that wonderful combination of wisdom power & purity displayed in the character of our Lord so that while saying ecce homo they must in spite of themselves explain Ecce Deus.

March 2, 1868

A stormy day at work on Father's head. The impeachment resolutions will not be presented until tomorrow

March 3, 1868

Nell & Carry went to Mrs. Trumbal's this morning & from thence to the capitol.

The impeachment resolutions did not come up.

Read French for Father & articles upon electricity. He is going to talk upon the latter subject at the club on Saturday evening.

His unpublished researches in that department of knowledge made in Princeton are still in advance of the knowledge of the times.

March 4, 1868

The resolutions were brought up to-day. Nell & Carry went to the capitol, I stayed at home to work, not caring to lose a day on an uncertainty.

A letter from the Chief Justice in to night's paper remonstrated upon the reception of these resolutions by the Senate until it is formed into a court.

March 5, 1868

This morning, the galleries of the senate chamber were crowded to the utmost.

At one o'clock the Chief Justice entered the chamber & Mr. Wade formally surrendered the chair.

The oath of office was then administered by Judge Nelson. After which the Senators were sworn in. It was an impressive scene.

When Johnson of Maryland came forward, he asked for the Bible, the others had sworn by simply raising the hand. He laid his hand upon the holy book when it was brought and reverently kissed it when the oath had be taken.

When Wade came forward, Sen. Hendrich arose & objected to his voting, & with propriety it seems to me as he will take the place of the President if the trial goes against him. After some debate, it was concluded to swear in the other senators & discuss Wade's claims afterward

Meeting of Sunday School Teachers in the evening Mr. Shanklin here to dinner. He was not well, so mother asked him to stay all night.

March 6, 1868

It was decided that Mr. Wade should take the oath and thus become a part of the impeachment court.

A small party this evening, Mr. & Mrs. Gurley, Mrs. Lambert sister & two sons. The Peales.

I had a headache & could not appear. Mr. Franklin here all night again.

March 7, 1868

Father has gone to the club to night, at the Chief Justice's & to deliver a lecture on electricity. We have been warming an apparatus at the fire and have sent off the delicate creature, wrapped up in warm shawls.

Mr. Gurley and two other gentlemen came to go with them.

March 8, 1868

Sunday. Mr. Ried preached for us in the morning. Semi Centenarian anniversary of the Sunday School.

My scholars were in high glee considering the occasion a highly festive affair.

I am afraid the Superintendent thinks me rather lax in discipline, but I dislike to check the laugh of a child, I would as soon crush a flower.

My youngest darling soon went to sleep in my arm, under the nose of Dr. Chester, who was delivering a discourse interesting enough to the older part of the community, but decidedly above the heads of the little one before him.

The church was crowded and the children presented a very sight as they came up the centre aisyle two by two. The singing was spirited & sweet, & entered into with great enjoyment by my frolicsome little colts.

Went to dine at the Kennedy's. Had a long talk with Annie who is to be married next month to Gen. Bidwell. They will be very happy I hope. He is a good man & one of the richest in California.

March 9, 1868
9th Monday. The papers to day are down upon the Chief Justice for his letter criticizing the senate for receiving the resolutions of impeachment before it was formed into a court &c. The family have all gone to tea to was formed into a court.

Father went first to the President's soiree, with an officer of the British Navy. I was not feeling quite well enough to join the party, so Mr. Franklin & I are spending the evening alone.

March 10, 1868
Tuesday. The Senate to day concluded to have tickets of admission to the galleries during the Impeachment trial.

When Mother read aloud at the dinner table the names of the fortunate individuals to whom these were awarded, Father's was down, but we found out afterwards that at the suggestion of Mr. Fessenden, we had been cut off with the admirals of the Navy & the heads of departments.

Only the Senators & Members, the Secretaries & the Judges now have the right of admission.

A number of tickets will be given to the Sargent of Arms every day for distribution.

We are too proud to ask for what ought to have been given to us, so I suppose will not be present at all.

March 11, 1868
Mr. Stansbury has resigned in order to become part of the President's council.

Mr. & Mrs. Gurley called after tea, then Prof. Doesker & lady came, then Mr. Patterson & Mr. Drexel.

Mr. P. thinks the country will be much quieter after the impeachment. Said he had lost any ambition he might have had to be in the cabinet since the war.

To be in congress yesterday, to be President he would despise tomorrow, there was nothing left but the church.

Hand over the collection plate suggested Mr. Drexel.

"Yes," said Mr. P., an office which in the days of my worldliness, I despised.

Mr. D. said it was rumoured that the President intended to resign. The radicals would be delighted at that, as they would get rid of him without the decision of the trial.

Mr. Patterson said he believed the President to be a conscientious man with a remarkable faculty of doing the right thing at the wrong time.

Father said he had been to the White House a few evenings ago to introduce an English Officer to the President.

Mr. Johnson took his hand in both of his & seemed much pleased & touched at a call from him. As they went away, the Englishman said, "He does not look like a bad man."

"No," said Father. "I believe him to be honest & well meaning."

"I was told" said the Englishman, "he had committed very great crimes."

The President feels every little attention paid him at the reception last Monday.

A little boy said, "I love the President who loves the constitution," "God bless you boy," said. Mr. Johnson, took him up in his arms & kissed him.

Nell & Carry went to the Browning's this morning.

Mrs. B. hope the trial will be over soon, as she wishes to get home soon to make her garden.

"Of course we'll have to go you know," said she.

Mr. Wade will have a new cabinet, either Mr. Washburne or Fred Douglass will be Sec. of Interior I hope the latter that the radicals may have their heart's desire for once.

March 12, 1868

Thursday. Teacher's meeting this evening. The new clergyman not very entertaining.

Lottie Alexander came last night.

Father went to call on Mr. Fessenden with Mr. Patterson & Mr. Drexel.

Mr. F. said that when he had cut us off from the ticket list, he had said on the floor of the senate that he was sorry to cut off his friend, Prof. Henry, but that he would see that he was provided with tickets, so call on me Prof. if you want them.

The apology was very well, but I wish he had let us alone.

March 13, 1868

Friday We did not receive today, as the girls wanted to go to the capitol & Mother was not well.

The Fessenden tickets took Carry & Lottie in.

Nell was going with Mr. S____, but came home as she had to wait some time in the Library. The indignation about the tickets is great.

To day the court opened.

The President's council appeared and asked for more time fourty days.

The Senate went out for one hour & half to discuss the expediency of granting this request & then returned to continue the debate in the senate chamber.

The girls did not know how the question was decided.

Read Phaedo with Father before tea. Father says he has 1,500 gallons of wiskey to sell, distilled during his experiments with meteors at a Government distillery in Georgetown.

The tax on the article is two dollars, & it sells for only $1.40 showing how great must be the frauds to make any profit.

The cost of experiments of the commission have amounted to 2,000 dollars.

Father went to the senate to day to know what was to be done with the wiskey as Government is not authorized to sell it.

It is difficult to know how to dispose of it.

I am glad the meetings of the commission are over, they have tired Father out & he has been besieged by numbers of people wanting him to favor certain members.

He says the business makes him feel uncomfortable, of the 100 men presenting members, he can only make one happy & must make 99 uncomfortable.

March 14, 1868

Saturday. The impeachment is put off for ten days. Mr. Franklin said at dinner, that the President it is supposed will resign.

Sec. Browning takes Mr. Stansbury' place.

Father has gone to the club. It meets to night at Sec. McColloch's. Lottie is low spirited to night about badly.

We have had a misty damp day, I am afraid it will rain tomorrow.

March 17, 1868

Tuesday. Last Saturday at the club Sec. McColloch & others told Father of a wonderful spiritualist who had effected them powerfully.

He had told the Sec. & Mrs.. McCulloch some very strange things and they were very anxious to have Father see him.

He was sent for them, but had a headache, so a meeting was appointed for him this evening in the Regents Room.

We ladies had no suspicion of what was going on, we should have joined the party as it was we were in bed when Father came in, but we were too impatient to hear about the affair to wait until morning, so Father at our urgent request came into our room & told us about it.

Sec. McCulloch, Dr. Craig, Mr. ___ & some other gentlemen were present.

The Spiritualist was a dreamy sympathetic, very interesting in appearance.

Mrs. Eames had told him that Father's will was so strong he would not be able to do anything with him.

He made the raps openly with his hand upon the table, He began very adroitly by messages to those he had already contacted in order to enlist Father's sympathies before trying any experiments with him.

He had a printed alphabet and the person who had someone in his mind with whom he wished to communicate passed his finger down this alphabet—

The spirits rapping when the letters of the name of the person thought of were touched.

When Father's turn came he thought of a certain Bill Johnson whom he had known as a young man & who had promised to come back from the world of the dead if he could & tell him about it.

He hesitated a little at the letter W, thinking he could call him William Johnson by which the spirits were deceived & rapped out William Henry.

It is not the name I was thinking of said Father.

The spirits do not always succeed said the medium. Father was interested in the man & would like to have got under this hat. He thought He did not want to come in as he thought it a dangerous matter to meddle with as when once the imagination was affected, the judgement was not as he depended upon.

I wish I had been there.

The interest would have been to me in the questions Father asked and the great ingenuity displayed by the man.

It would take a great deal to make me believe that spirits from beyond the grave are coming back for such trivial child's play as picking out names and telling what is in folded papers.

If they told us something worthwhile we might be more credulous. The medium evaded all direct questioning as when Father asked him if he could say that he knew what was passing in the mind of another.

"I cannot say," he replied. "I only know I am impressed by something & the spirits rap with my hands."

The tricks thes media do, do not seem to me at all wonderful. The wonder to me is that people are impressed by them, they can read what is folded papers thrown down upon the table & apparently untouched by them which any good juggler could do with skill of slight of hand. They of course manage to get a sight of the inside of the papers. As to the knowledge they evince of the private history of affluent strangers that is not remarkable.

They of course make it their business to find out about every thing they can about every body. Studying registers of all kinds. To be a good medium would require an excellent memory for dates names small events, a great facility in reading faces, a sympathetic nature, sensitive to changes in others, which we find more often in woman than in men, combined with great tact.

This man seems to possess all these qualities in a high degree and to be quite a genius in his line.

The thing that excited the Sec. most in the seance was the asserted presence of his first wife.

That the medium knew of the existence of that individual was not strange. He would of course know all about the prominent men of Washington before he came here. If the information had been about a more private individual it would have been more remarkable.

March 18, 1868

Wed. Father came upstairs today for a while & sat for me while I was working. He has had another séance with the spiritualist.

He tried him today with magnetism, but he did not do much in that line. Father asked him if he could make the spirits rap as other media did. He said he could and produced some raps so well executed that if Father had not made as many experiments as he has in sound he would have sworn that they came from a certain part of the room.

As it was, he was convinced that they came from the man himself. After certain experiments, he told the medium so.

"I do not know," said the man, "perhaps they do, I will not say."

He said he could produce raps upon the glass of a case in the room which he did by means of a long stick.

Father asked him if he could produce the raps if a non-conductor were introduced between the stick and the glass.

Thinking Father meant a piece of glass which is a nonelectrical conductor, but Father put a piece of fur around the end of the sticks. There were no raps.

"The spirits are not always in a humor for rapping, said the man & tried it again with the fur, there were no raps of course, that was all balderdash.

Father says the man is a most consumate actor.

Took up *Ecce Homo* this afternoon to finish it.

Am shocked at the author to day. He takes those beautiful words of our dying Lord, "Father forgive them for they know not what to do" & interprets it to mean forgiveness alone of the ignorant soldiers about him who executed the sentence of the Law while his heart was full of bitterness and resentment towards the rulers who brought him to such an ignominious death.

He was speaking of the law of resentment and showing that there were some men whom Christ never forgave & against whom his anger was always great, but how different is the prose & wildest indignation against injustice & wrong from anger the personal anger of fallen human nature.

Perhaps how ever the author may mean to ascribe the former feeling to Christ and not anger in the ordinary acceptation of the term.

I have dropped the book just now, It seems sacriledge almost only to read such an assertion. I shall take it up in a day or two if I get over my disgust.

At present, I do not feel as if I wanted ever to see it again.

Alfred Woodhull here to night to see if the Carry & Lottie will go to Mt. Vernon tomorrow. He asked us all, but Nell & I concluded two were enough of a draw upon his purse.

March 19, 1868

Thursday. A beautiful day for the Mt. Vernon excursionists. He started them with a fine lunch.

Alfred brought a young medical student, Mr. Curtis, as an addition to the party.

I worked hard all day until four, then wrote some notes of invitation for a small party for Minnie Hunter & Lottie.

Sallie H. here to dinner.

Went to Bible class in the evening.

In the prayer meeting preceding, a young man read "This old old story," a poem simple sweet & touching. It almost made me cry.

The new clergyman answers questions very well.

Went home with Sallie H. after the lesson was over.

Annie is very busy with marriage preparations.

March 20, 1868

Friday. A most dismal day for our small party.

The snow falling fast, we did not expect any body would brave the storm but Marion Hussey & Minnie Fowler came and some time after, Alfred and Mr. Curtis followed by Dr. Otis.

Mr. Curtis entertained us with a song.

A decidedly new version of the story of Washington & the apple tree. In which it was asserted, "It is better to tell ten thousand lies than cut one apple tree."

Carry & Minnie gave us a charade.

We finished up the evening with Count Papolini.

Gen. Hunter came early for the girls & seemed to enjoy them.

March 22, 1868

Sunday. Carry & I off for school before the rest of the family were up.

A very pleasant hour with my dear little girls. If I thought I did them as much good as they do me, I should be satisfied.

May the great Teacher of All teach me how to teach them.

I made a mistake about *Ecce Homo*. I took the book up again this afternoon.

The bitterness of feeling ascribed to our Lord in his dying hours is the just & proper indignation of a pure & holy nature against wrong. The author is rather unfortunate & misleading just there, no words of shame or resentment.

Read some of it to Father who was pleased with the ingenuity of the author in explaining the temptation.

March 23, 1868

Monday. The Impeachment has commenced again, the President asks for a longer time for preparation for the trial.

March 24, 1868

Mr. Trumbull sent two tickets for the trial. Nell & Carry.

The court still discussing the proposed postponement of the trial. Have given the Pres. until next Monday.

March 26, 1868

Thursday. S.S. Teacher's meeting.

Went afterwards to the K___'s & had a jolly time. Mr. ___ there also.

Dr. Woodhull, Gen. Bidwell having lost in a bet, promised to treat us to candy all around whereat we children rejoice.

A. W. called in our absence with a pound of sugar plumbs. Oh how we regretted the loss of his visit.

Father & mother in their own room having a cosy time together over a novel.

Before we left the H___s we went up to see the front head of the house. He has had a hard time. Looked ill & weak but very comfortable propped up in his easy chair. We told him he deserved a great deal of credit for looking so cheerful under difficulties. He made us eat raisins & laugh & talk with him for half an hour. He said the President had been to see him and that he looked sad.

Mr. K___ offered him sympathy in his troubles. He said this was a world of trial & he did not expect to be exempt, he asked to do his duty. That he is sincere in that, I firmly believe.

The veto of the Supreme Court Bill which he sent in this week in face of the Impeachment is a proof of his determination to do what he thinks right at whatever cost. But he is not always judicious.

March 27, 1868

So tired to night that I passed the evening in the bed. Read "Old Curiosity Shop." half crying over poor little Nell.

How inimitable in pathos and humour is Dickens.

March 28, 1868

Saturday. Mr. Shanklin thinks the Pres. will resort to face in his resistance to Congress, leaves tomorrow for the mountains of Penn.

He is glad to be away until the Impeachment is over.

The girls have gone to the H____s to tea.

Father at the club.

Cut out Nell's dress. She wants to go to Phil. when Lottie goes to be with Mrs. Bache. Had a pleasant little note from Miss Hooper. She could not come to small party on account of illness produced by cutting her Wisdom teeth.

March 29, 1868

Sunday. Ecce Deus after tea.

I enjoy the latter very much.

Mr. Shranklin off at six for the mountains.

Henry Ellet to tea. He said that Thad Stevens who has been carried to the Senate lately on a chair by two young men, stopped them a day or two ago & exclaimed, "What shall I do when you young men are dead?"

Mr. S. feels he is very kind hearted, said a few days ago he met a poor market woman in great distress, having lost her market money.

"You are fortunate, good woman" said he, "I have found it" & gave her five dollars. He is anything, but charitable in his expressions. I am glad he is in his deeds.

It is said he is an _____ and opens his house every Sunday evening when at home to instruct young men in his notions upon religious matters.

Poor man, the mysteries hidden beyond the grave will soon be known

Thaddeus Stevens, "Radical Republican" member of the House of Representatives. Stevens died on August 11, 1868, at the age of 76.

to him he is very feeble.

March 31, 1868

The last day of March. Chilly & damp.

Went out shopping with Mother.

Father lectured to night before the medical association without letting us know anything about it. Did not want us there I suppose.

Came home very tired.

The impeachment trial commenced again to day.

Long speech from Gen. Butler.

The lectures of which Father gave, the opening one this evening are a course of 24, to be delivered under the auspices of the Columbian College, on the plan proposed many years ago by Mr. Corcoran & in the building erected by him for this purpose & now the National Medical College.

Have been enjoying Gen. Bidwell's candy. He sent me a pound on Saturday by the girls. I have been in high favor since its sweet arrival. My popularity is rapidly decreasing.

April 4, 1868

Sat. Lottie left us this morning.

The club met here this evening. H. Ellet & I made some drawings to illustrate Father's discourse. Sec. McCollock said he was in his happiest mood.

Father gave me a slight sketch of it after the gentlemen left. His subject was the importance & place of theory or hypothesis in science, illustrated by the theories & speculations in regard to light.

Theory is at first a simple explanation of certain phenomena, but in studying these phenomena in the light of the hypothesis advanced for their explanation in their various relations new facts are discovered, additions must be made to the hypothesis to meet these facts and in time the theory wh. was at first simple becomes so complex that it is abandoned and another substituted in its place, but it has not been useless. By its means intelligent questions have been asked of Nature & many interesting facts added to the sum of human knowledge.

The next theory in time may be likewise abandoned, but not until like its predecessor, it has added new facts to those already known.

His illustration of the subject as I said before, was light.

It was known that the reflection of light from a mirror and the rebound of a ball were governed by the same laws. The angle of incidence being equal to that angle of reflection in one corresponding to the angles of approach & rebound in the other.

The theory was advanced that light consisted of atoms proceeding from the sun, rebounding from polished surfaces in reflection as the ball rebounds. So far, the theory was simple enough. But it was objected that if light consisted of atoms, rays proceeding in all directions from the different luminous bodies would interfere with each other. It is known that the impression of light upon the retina of the eye remains the eighth of a second & if a burning stick were whirled rapidly around eight times in a second so that a new impression were produced upon the eye at the cessation of the first, the appearance of a continuous ring of light would be produced.

Light travels at the rate of miles the eighth of a second so that the atoms of light coming from the sun might be that far apart and still seem like a continuous ray in which case different beams of light could pass each other without difficulty,

Addition no. 1 to the Theory.

In passing through a prism, a ray of light is divided into colours. To explain this, it was supposed that the atoms from the sun were compound consisting of several colored bodies bound together into one which were separate in their passage through the glass.

Addition No 2.

Again it is discovered that at certain equidistant places in a prism the rays of light go through at others are reflected. To explain this it is sugested that the atoms are polerized that they revolve in space and that the distance at wh. they go through & are reflected from the prism is equal to half a revolution. But it is also discovered that the atoms must have different sides as well as different ends. They will go through prism in certain directions & not in others. The theory has become more and more complex and is at last abandoned but very many interesting and valuable phenomena have been discovered by its means. It is known that sound is produced by undulations of the ethereal medium it is now suggested that light may be attributed to the same phenomenon. Two waves of sound may be made so to interfere with each other that intervals of silence are produced. The crest of one wave meeting the hollow of another if we may so speak - as in the beats of an organ pipe. If light consists of waves intervals of darkness ought to be produced in the same way.

This by experiment is found to be the case.

The great thing in testing a theory is to devise experiments that will give the information desired with accuracy. We were here interrupted much to my regret. The diagram made were showing the equality of the showing refraction.

The Diary of Mary Henry: The Civil War Out My Window

And so ends the diary of Mary Henry, just as abruptly as it began.

The girl who came of age in the midst of the American Civil War, residing inside the Smithsonian Castle, a true Washington insider in every since of the word, closes her letter to future generations with an in depth discourse on theories regarding light.

Nearly a decade had passed since she first began to pen in the sacred book of her diary.

Her words reveal a forgone time, gripped with troubles, injustices and sufferings on a scale that simply cannot be fathomed by modern-day Americans.

Through her simple entries, we have been provided with a first-hand view of a world in motion – moving toward both justice and imprisonment at the same time, at a pace which simply seemed far too fast for some, while not fast enough for others.

The great lesson we can take from her words is this: no matter how hard we fight, time will inevitably change our words.

In the early pages of this book, we find a young girl critiquing the uniforms of soldiers going off to war, toward the latter end, however, we see an aged woman nursing the wounds of captured enemy causalities.

In September 1864, Mary was calling President Abraham Lincoln "a totally incompetent bear," while on April 15, 1865, seven months later, Mary described the slain President as being "true hearted, magnanimous and kind."

Like all of us, she was human, full of faults and prejudices, yet at the same time, full of life, full of love and ever changing… just as we should be.

What happened to many of the other individuals mentioned in this diary?

President Andrew Johnson

Despite being the object of scorn for the "Radical Republicans" in Congress, who criticized him for being "too lenient with the Southern traitors" and for his fierce opposition to civil rights, the nation's seventeenth president successfully gained an acquittal and was not removed from office.

Generations later, most constitutional experts agree that the charges brought against him were baseless.

At a time when America was rife with internal problems and questions, Johnson's brilliance in foreign policy has often been overlooked. It was during his administration that France's hostile takeover of the North American nation of Mexico was ended, as well as the Alaska Purchase secured – both of which sent an undeniable message to the powers around the globe that this hemisphere intended to act as the master of its own house.

Johnson did not seek reelection in 1868 and was succeeded by Civil War hero, General Ulysses S. Grant.

After leaving the presidency, Johnson returned to his home state of Tennessee, a place he had not visited since the war.

To his astonishment, large public celebrations were held along the way in his honor.

Sadly, that same year, Johnson's son, Robert, committed suicide.

In the years that followed, the former President would attempt in vain to reenter public service, failing to secure seats as both a U.S. Senator and member of the House of Representatives.

At last, in 1875, Johnson was successful in his quest to return to Washington, being selected to serve as a U.S. Senator from Tennessee.

Tragically, however, Johnson's tenure in the Senate was short lived, as he died roughly three months into his service, following two stroke.

In his typical "tough as nails" demeanor, Johnson refused medical attention and suffered a second stroke two days later, and died hours later on July 31, 1875.

A copy of the U.S. Constitution was placed under his head, at his burial, according to his wishes.

Dr. Gurley

On February 16, 1868, Mary briefly mentions that her church, the New York Avenue Presbyterian Church, in Washington, D.C., had a fill-in preacher, as their beloved pastor, Dr. Phineas D. Gurley was taking a six month leave on account of his health.

Dr. Gurley would not return to his pulpit, as the former Chaplain of the United States Senate and friend of Abraham Lincoln died on September 30, 1868.

His loss was felt throughout the nation and especially in Washington, where he touched the lives of so many and acted as pastor to a nation at war with itself.

Father

A renowned scientist and member of Washington, D.C.'s elite, Joseph Henry served as the most important man in his daughter Mary's life. His affectionate title of "Father" adorns nearly every page and the wholesomeness of their deep relationship is felt throughout her life's most enduring work.

On January 13, 1877, Joseph was privileged to test out a new invention, made possible by a Scotsman named Alexander Graham Bell and was thoroughly impressed and amused.

The Diary of Mary Henry: The Civil War Out My Window

Bragging on Bell's work, Joseph praised "the value and astonishing character of Mr. Bell's discovery and invention."

Throughout this book, we read that "Father," as he is most affectionately known to the readers of this diary, was met by many callers, ranging from influential Senators to distinguished Scientists, yet none of those visitors could compete with the finality which accompanied one such visitor who arrived on the morning of May 13, 1878, the chilly hand of death.

Father's passing was exceedingly difficult for every member of the Henry family, but most exceedingly for Mary, who was 43-years-old at the time.

He is buried in Oak Hill Cemetery in the Georgetown section of northwest Washington, D.C.

Mary Henry

Author of this, the story of a nation at war with itself, Mary Henry, continued to serve as an active member in her Washington community, even after the pages of her diary elapsed.

In the days following these entries, she dedicated much of her attention and resources to the News Boys Association, a home for orphaned children, as well as her church and its Sunday School ministry for children.

An artist, Mary continued to expand her artwork, including paintings and sculptures in her studio in the East Range of the Smithsonian Institution Building.

Remarking on her work, she humbly stated, "I had no talent."

In 1878, following her father's death, Mary and her family were forced to vacate the Castle that had been her home for decades.

Though no longer a resident of the sacred building which housed so many of our nation's memories, Mary remained in the city for the balance of her life.

Near the end of her life, she dedicated herself to preserving the memory and legacy of her father's work as a scientist and American hero.

Successful, the United States Coast Guard named a cutter after him, the *Joseph Henry*, which was launched in 1880 and was active until 1904.

In 1915, Mary's father was inducted into the Hall of Fame for Great Americans in the Bronx, New York.

Bronze statutes of Henry and Isaac Newton represent science on the balustrade of the galleries of the Main Reading Room in the Thomas Jefferson Building of the Library of Congress on Capitol Hill in Washington, D.C. They are two of only 16 historical figures depicted in the reading room; each pair representing one of the 8 pillars of civilization.

At Princeton, the Joseph Henry Laboratories and the Joseph Henry House are named for him.

On April 10, 1903, at the age of 69, Mary, powered by an unwavering faith in Christ, joined her dear father, unassuming mother and brother Will in eternity, dying while on an annual trip with her sister to Europe, in Seville, Spain.

Though her views on civil rights fell far short of 21st century standards, we must judge Mary within the context of her times and to that she was a revolutionary; an unmarried woman who debated politics with Presidents, cabinet secretaries and Senators.

With a view of both the Confederate States of America out one side of her castle and the Northerm capitol building out her other, Mary Henry's diary, commentating on the Civil War outside her window is a true American masterpiece.

Made in the USA
Middletown, DE
03 October 2020